GOOD
BUSINESS

Exercising Effective and Ethical Leadership

James O'Toole and Don Mayer, editors

Routledge
Taylor & Francis Group

NEW YORK AND LONDON

A PUBLICATION OF THE INSTITUTE FOR ENTERPRISE ETHICS
Daniels College of Business, University of Denver

First published 2010
by Routledge
270 Madison Ave, New York, NY 10016

Simultaneously published in the UK
by Routledge
2 Park Square, Milton Park, Abingdon, Oxon OX14 4RN

Routledge is an imprint of the Taylor & Francis Group, an informa business

© 2010 Routledge

Typeset in Times New Roman by
Brandon Russell

Printed and bound in the United States of America on acid-free paper by Walsworth Publishing Company,
Marceline, MO

Library of Congress Cataloging in Publication Data

O'Toole, James.
Good business : exercising effective and ethical leadership / James O'Toole and Don Mayer.—
1st ed.
p. cm.
1. Corporate culture. 2. Leadership. I. Mayer, Don. II. Title.
HD58.7.O86 2010
658.4'092—dc22
2009049757

ISBN 10: 0-415-87997-3 (hbk)
ISBN 10: 0-415-87998-1 (pbk)
ISBN 10: 0-203-85062-9 (ebk)

ISBN 13: 978-0-415-87997-2 (hbk)
ISBN 13: 978-0-415-87998-9 (pbk)
ISBN 13: 978-0-203-85062-6 (ebk)

Table of Contents

Dedication

To Daniel L. Ritchie and Carl M. Williams with gratitude.

Foreword

One of the most significant advances in organizational studies since the 1980s has been new insight about how organizations create and sustain an ethical and responsible corporate culture. Born in studies of how things could go so wrong—illegal corporate political contributions, overseas bribery, illegal dumping of wastes, financial fraud, and more—academics and practitioners have increasingly focused on how to make things right.

This collection of essays advances that knowledge. The essays—practical inquiries into how ethics and responsibility can be made integral to the lives of individuals, to organizations, and to public policy—add significantly to our understanding of how to create ethical and effective cultures.

This collection demonstrates the reality that ethical failures are not solely caused by a few "bad apples" in an organization, although the moral education of employees and their leaders is important. Ethical failures more often are the fault of organizations—their ideology, ways of doing things, formal systems, and reward structures. These characteristics, along with the leadership provided by executives and supervisors at all levels, constitute the ethical culture and tone of an organization.

Most of the essays in this collection explore the provocative issue of how that culture and tone can be shaped. The Daniels College of Business at the University of Denver has assembled a team of faculty members who take this question seriously and have dedicated their academic careers to answering it. These essays are clear evidence of that commitment.

The most interesting aspect of this particular collection of essays is their focus on how corporate ethics, social responsibility, and sustainability can be integrated into corporate strategy, in particular, *global* corporate strategy. Only in the past five years have corporations become truly open to the possibility that a core business strategy can and must have ethical dimensions, and that ethics and responsibility can be key factors in the execution of such a strategy. Companies and executives willing to take on the challenge of creating such strategies will find these essays extremely helpful.

—Kirk O. Hanson
Executive Director,
Markkula Center for Applied Ethics
Santa Clara University

Prologue

by Bruce Hutton

The Daniels College of Business, the eighth-oldest business school in the United States, celebrated its 100 year anniversary in 2008. We were in good company, as Harvard's business school was founded that same year. The founding of several of the new schools being established at the time, including what is now called the Daniels College, had been at the urging of the Society of Certified Public Accountants who were seeking higher standards of performance and conduct for their profession. Indeed, the Colorado Society of CPAs supported the establishment of The School of Commerce, Accounts, and Finance at the University of Denver with a $100.00 commitment towards initial startup expenses. Since that time, our College of Business has been on a journey to provide an educational experience that provides students with the technical skills to be successful in their chosen careers, while maintaining the highest standards of personal and professional conduct.

To be sure, the College's long journey didn't start by offering students the kinds of classes we find in the Daniels curriculum today, courses in Ethics, Values-Based Leadership, Corporate Social Responsibility, and Sustainable Development. In 1946, for example, the College created a Department of Comportment to provide student counseling on such matters as etiquette, professional conduct, interpersonal relations in the office, and dress! In 1950, one of the educational objectives of the College was to develop a student's "personal attitudes and such an understanding of…today's dynamic world as will enable him to live happily with himself and to work cooperatively with others." Today, we have a Department of Ethics and Legal Studies, but issues of "comportment" are still relevant. But now comportment is all about nurturing appropriate values and attitudes in a globalized world where stakeholder relationships are keys to success in multinational ventures.

I believe the chapters in this book accurately reflect where the Daniels College has arrived today on its continuous journey to educate tomorrow's leaders and practitioners. In all that we teach, we stress the importance of "good business"—by which we mean creating value for an enterprise through actions that respect, maintain, and enhance the physical, social, and personal environments in which a company operates. In creating a curriculum that makes ethics fundamental and integral to both enterprise and personal success, our goal is not simply to teach but, rather, to *inspire* our students to live the values of "good business."

We believe education should be about finding, and expressing, meaning in the *context* of our work and in all that we do. Psychologist Howard Gardner suggests it is not enough to simply espouse high standards; one must live up to them and help others to do the same. This requires what he calls an "ethical mind." A person with an ethical mind asks, "If all workers in my profession did what I do, what would the world be like?" Then, depending on one's answer to that question, the ethical person behaves according to what is right for the world in the long run. Hence, teaching business ethics entails not only giving students the tools they need to recognize and evaluate an ethical dilemma, it also involves encouraging them to *act* ethically. For example, many employees may recognize an unethical or illegal act in the workplace, but few are willing to take steps to stop, or to change, such behavior. The goal of the Daniels College is to turn out graduates both with the ability to discern what is right, and the requisite moral courage to take positive action when faced with wrong doing.

This brings us to the issue of *context* that I alluded to above. There is strong evidence that it is particularly difficult for business people to exercise "an ethical mind" because business is not a profession with an established and enforceable code of conduct. A quick etymological review helps us to understand why "business ethics" presents special challenges, both in workplace settings and in the classroom. The word "ethics" comes from ancient Greek word, "ethos" which meant "an habitual gathering place." The Greeks thus understood that the setting, or *context,* within which humans are nurtured is critical to the development of the values that are characteristic of a virtuous life. The city of Athens had an ethos of civility—it was a place where justice, respectful discourse, moral courage, and charity were habitually practiced (at least, toward ethnic-Greek men). The ancient Greeks understood that ethics is fundamentally about *community*—that is, the context in which history, relationships, stories, laws, rituals, and "habits of the heart" form an environment conducive to meaningful and purposeful human development. We at the Daniels College work to provide just such a context for our students, because we believe the modern notion that ethics is merely a study of rules and norms is as far off the mark as it is possible to get. Instead, we believe ethics is about context: the relationship of people in communities.

The chapters in this book highlight the wide range and interdependent dimensions of ethical issues typically found in a business context. The first set of chapters addresses ethics in the personal, or professional, context; the second examines ethics within an organizational context; and the final group explores ethical issues from a global perspective and across sectors (public, private, and civil). While most of these chapters do not have the word ethics in their titles, they all have their roots in ethics. The topics covered—stakeholder theories, corporate social responsibility, sustainable development, global corporate citizenship, and leadership—all focus on moral conduct, duty, virtue, and the expression of values. Thus, in one way or another, all the chapters deal with making ethical decisions in the context of the four communities in which all our students are members: the enterprise, the local community, the nation, and the world.

In recent years, the Daniels College faculty has faced the daunting challenge of creating a practical curriculum to deal with the ethical issues found in those four communities, and to weave those issues into our students' entire educational experience. For example, we have had to search for ways to effectively deal with the expanding social role of business in a global economy. Harvard professor Lynn Sharp Paine argues that this recent "moralization" of the corporation represents a revolutionary change from its historically amoral and mechanistic role. As a consequence of this change, she argues that it is now necessary to integrate ethical considerations into the fundamental decision-making processes of a global enterprise. Paralleling those new ethical requirements has been the increasing demand for businesses to accept more responsibility for their actions that affect communities in terms of the environment, employment, and other social issues. For example, the creation of the Dow Jones Sustainability Index exemplifies a growing number of measures recently designed to link a corporation's financial performance to its record in terms of social responsibility and sustainability. At the College we have attempted to respond to such changes by creating a variety of new courses and programs dealing with corporate citizenship and social innovation.

The title of a recent book by Harvard's Rakesh Khurana, *From Higher Aims to Hired Hands: The Social Transformation of American Business Schools and the Unfulfilled Promise of Management as a Profession*, captures the essence of another challenge we at the Daniels College are facing. Khurana argues that business schools originally were formed to educate a professional class of managers in the same spirit as medical and legal education. Unfortunately, he says that most business schools lost that focus along the way; instead, they evolved in the direction of technical training, thus leaving a moral gap in the education of business leaders. In the *Harvard Business Review*, professors Warren Bennis and James O'Toole (a member of the Daniels faculty) suggest that business schools have further lost their way by becoming over-focused on theoretical research and, thus, neglecting the value of practical business experience. The result is that graduating MBA students are not prepared to deal with the complex, real-world problems that often lack the black and white clarity of academic solutions. That is why our curriculum is designed to link theory with practice (as Cynthia Fukami explains in Chapter 4). Finally, we have sought to deliver a curriculum that stays relevant in a complex, perpetually changing, and increasingly interconnected world.

The importance of meeting all these challenges was recently underscored in a report by the 4,000 member international trade association, Business for Social Responsibility, which cited the absence of attention to environmental, social, and governance concerns in the *curriculum* of most b-schools as a contributing cause of the lack of attention to those same concerns in business *practice*. The report concludes that business schools are failing to provide relevant leadership skills for managing in complex operating environments, arguing that MBA graduates lack familiarity, let alone expertise, in ethical decision making, and that most cannot effectively factor political risk into investment decisions, or grapple with trade-offs when business theories conflict. Hence, the authors of the report offer five "how-to" strategies for training future business leaders more effectively. They say the curriculum of b-schools should incorporate: more practice in decision making skills with reference to complex, often unquantifiable, matters; more experiential learning; broader understanding of the interdependent nature of business functions; more integrated and multidisciplinary teaching; and a more consistent cross-cutting emphasis on ethical leadership.

It pleases me greatly to report that the Daniels faculty has been actively engaged in addressing those issues for the better part of the past two decades. This book is a reflection of those efforts, which started in earnest in 1988, and continue today. The late 1980s found the University of Denver facing declining enrollments and great financial difficulties at the end what the media called the "Decade of Greed" (highlighted by the great savings and loan "meltdown"). It was in that context that two DU business professors were called to their dean's office and asked to write a proposal to redesign the College's MBA program for consideration by a potential donor who, for the time being, preferred to remain anonymous. The proposal they wrote focused on introducing ethics, creativity, entrepreneurship, interpersonal skills, leadership, and a global perspective into the curriculum. The program was accepted by the donor who funded it with an $11 million matching gift (at the time, the largest single contribution in the university's history).

The College immediately went to work on program design. Heavy faculty involvement was matched by the parallel efforts of a committee of professionals from business, government, and civil society who provided the faculty with perspective, issues identification, and critical reality checks. The faculty endeavored to translate the needs identified by the outsiders into a teachable curriculum and, when the new MBA program was launched, all the courses were totally integrated around interdisciplinary themes, team taught, and grounded in experiential learning—including a week long "boot camp" to develop leadership, team building, and ethical decision-making skills. The importance of community was reinforced through G.I.V.E. (Graduates Involved in Voluntary Efforts), a student-driven, mandatory program of community service.

Significantly, this MBA program (introduced in 1990) anticipated many of the reforms that are being widely called for today in the curriculum of the nation's b-schools.

The "anonymous" donor in 1989 was, of course, Bill Daniels, a pioneer of cable television who said his gift was prompted by two factors: the College's commitment to the importance of ethics in the curriculum, and the recent appointment of Daniel Ritchie as Chancellor of the University. Ritchie was the retired CEO of Westinghouse Broadcasting, and Bill Daniels knew his reputation as a business leader of unmatched integrity. Thus, for Bill Daniels, it was *all* about ethics.

Daniels' contribution to the MBA program went beyond his financial gift: his behavior as a business leader influenced the development of our approach to ethics education. His reputation for ethics was legendary, an example of which was his ownership of the Utah Stars in the now-defunct American Basketball Association. When the league folded in 1975, and many of its teams declared bankruptcy, creditors and season ticket holders were left holding the bag. Unlike other team owners, Bill Daniels made a promise to himself to pay back all those who were owed money, a debt of some $5 million, in all. Five years later, he returned to Utah and paid off all of his creditors and ticket holders, giving them full value, plus eight percent interest per year. He wasn't legally obligated to do so, but that wasn't what mattered to Bill Daniels. He felt *morally* obligated.

In addition to his integrity, Daniels also was well known for being innovative, community minded, a calculated risk taker, and committed to excellence (in his own words, "The best is good enough for me."). Over the past twenty years, those characteristics have become imbedded in our MBA program. Daniels is the first b-school to have a totally integrated, interdisciplinary, team-taught curriculum. It is the only b-school to attain AACSB re-accreditation using criteria that place greater emphasis on teaching and applied research than on narrow academic scholarship. Community participation continues as a requirement for all MBA students, and all participate in an intensive "boot camp" experience in the Rocky Mountains focused on team building, leadership, self-awareness, and problem solving under pressure (based on the experience of the legendary 10th Mountain Division, the World War II volunteers who developed innovative ways to engage in combat in mountain and snow environments).

We are honored by the fact that, increasingly, we are recognized for these accomplishments: Daniels has been ranked as high as third in the world by the *Wall Street Journal* for having "ethically sensitive" graduates and, in 2009, the Aspen Institute's Business and Society Program ranked our college 20th in the world in terms of its ethics, CSR, and sustainability curriculum (in its bi-annual "Grey Pinstripes" review of some 150 MBA programs).

We are now turning our efforts outward, to work in ever-closer collaboration with companies in the Rocky Mountain area who share our concerns about ethics, the environment, and the expanded social role global corporations are expected to play. To this end, we recently launched the Institute for Enterprise Ethics dedicated to providing a public forum for sharing knowledge and research in those areas where Daniels has the competence and expertise to be of practical assistance to business leaders. Funded by a start up grant from Carl M. Williams, the Institute is affiliated with the prestigious Markkula Center for Applied Ethics at Santa Clara University which, for over two decades, has served corporations in the Silicon Valley. Indeed, this book is the first product of the Institute, and represents the culmination of all that we on the Daniels College faculty have come to learn, and to teach, about the essence of "Good Business." We trust that you will find it a useful guide through that dense and thorny thicket of social, political, ethical, environmental, and regulatory issues in which business is increasingly enmeshed.

PART I

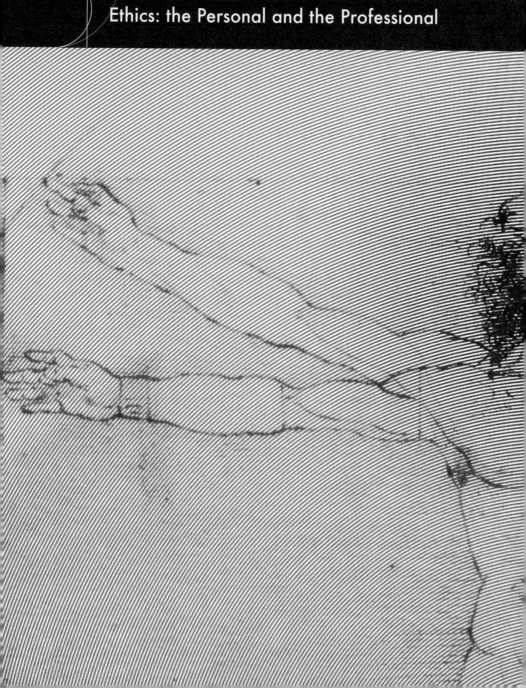

Ethics: the Personal and the Professional

CHAPTER 1

The Content and Practice of Business Ethics

by Buie Seawell

Framing the structure and content of business ethics is a presumptuous undertaking; yet, it is one I believe to have real merit. Over more than twenty years of teaching ethics to undergraduate business majors and graduate business students at the Daniels College, a significant consensus has developed among the school's faculty as to "what it's all about." This chapter is an attempt to put into summary form the consensus on the content and practice of business ethics that a faculty from diverse fields of business education—marketing, management, finance, legal studies—have developed over years of teaching and working together.

What is Ethics?

Ethics is the branch of philosophy concerned with the meaning of all aspects of human behavior. Theoretical Ethics, sometimes called Normative Ethics, is about discovering and delineating right from wrong; it is the consideration of how we develop the rules and principles (norms) by which to judge and guide meaningful decision-making. Theoretical Ethics is supremely intellectual in character and, being a branch of philosophy, is also rational in nature. It is rational reflection on what is right, wrong, just, unjust, good, and bad in terms of human behavior.

Although business ethics is in part reflective and rational, its theoretical character is only a prelude to its essential task. Business ethics is best understood as a branch of Applied Ethics, which is the discipline of applying value to human behavior, relationships, and constructs. Business ethics is simply the practice of applying value within the context of the enterprise of creating wealth (the fundamental role of business).

There are three parts to the discipline of business ethics: personal ethics, professional ethics, and corporate ethics. All three are intricately related, and it is helpful to distinguish between them because each rests on slightly different assumptions and requires a unique focus in order to be understood. In a sense, we need to look at business ethics through a trifocal lens: close up and personal, intermediate and professional, and on the grand scale (utilizing both farsighted and peripheral vision) of the corporation.

Personal Ethics: Four Ethical Approaches

In spite of some recent bad press, business executives are first and foremost human beings. Like all persons, they seek meaning for their lives through relationships and enterprise, and they want their lives to amount to something. Since ethics is chiefly the discipline of meaning, the business executive, like all other human beings, is engaged in this discipline all the time, whether cognizant of it or not. We should therefore begin by looking at how humans have historically approached the process of making meaningful decisions.

From the earliest moments of recorded human consciousness, the ethical discipline has entailed four fundamental approaches, often called ethical decision-making frameworks: **Utilitarian Ethics** (outcome based), **Deontological Ethics** (duty based), **Virtue Ethics** (virtue based) and **Communitarian Ethics** (community based). Each has a distinctive point of departure as well as distinctive ways of doing the fundamental ethical task of raising and answering questions of value. It is important to understand that all four approaches overlap and have common elements:

- **Impartiality**: weighting interests equally

- **Rationality**: offering reasons a rational person would accept

- **Consistency**: applying standards similarly to similar cases

- **Reversibility**: using standards that apply no matter who makes the rules

These are, in a sense, the rules of the ethics game, no matter which of the following four schools or approaches to ethics one uses.

Utilitarian Ethics

The Utilitarian approach is perhaps the most familiar and easiest to understand of all approaches to ethics. Whether we think about it or not, most of us are doing Utilitarian Ethics much of the time, especially those of us in business. Utilitarians ask a very important question: "How will my actions affect others?" They then attempt to quantify the impact of their actions based on a least common denominator, such as happiness, pleasure, or wealth. Therefore,

Utilitarians are called *consequentialists* because they look to the consequences of their actions to determine whether they are justified or not.

"The greatest good for the greatest number" is the Utilitarian motto. Of course, defining *good* is no easy task because what some people think of as good, others think of as worthless. When business people do cost-benefit analyses, they are practicing Utilitarian ethics. In these cases, the least common denominator is typically money. Everything in a cost-benefit analysis from the cost of steel to the worth of a human life is assigned a dollar value, and then some business people *just do the math.*

The Ford Pinto automobile was a product of just such reasoning. Thirty years ago, executives at the Ford Motor Company reasoned that the cost of fixing a gas-tank problem with their Pinto cars was larger than the benefit of saving a few human lives. Several tanks subsequently exploded, people died, and ultimately the company lost lawsuits when judges and juries refused to accept the Ford executives' moral reasoning.

One of the most common uses of such outcome-based reasoning occurs in legislative committees in representative democracies: how many constituents will benefit from a tax credit, and how many will be marginalized? Indeed, representative democracies make most decisions based on the Utilitarian principle of the greatest good for the greatest number. While democratic governments are naturally majoritarian, there are some things in constitutional democracies that cannot be decided by just doing the math (adding up the votes). Some questions should never be voted on. The founders of our nation expressed this fundamental concept with three words in the Declaration of Independence: *certain unalienable rights.* Even if the majority wishes to do so, it cannot vote to take away the freedom of speech of an unpopular minority. There are issues where the Utilitarian approach clearly is not applicable.

Deontological Ethics

Enter the **Deontological Ethicists**. Immanuel Kant is the quintessential deontological (duty based) ethical theorist. Kant, who lived in 18th century Prussia, was one of the most amazing intellects of all time, writing books on astronomy, philosophy, politics, and ethics. He once said, "Two things fill the mind with ever new and increasing admiration and awe...the starry heavens above and the moral law within." For Kant there were some ethical verities as eternal as the stars.

Deontological means the study (or science) of duty. Kant rejected Utilitarianism because he did not believe humans could predict future consequences of their actions with any substantial degree of certainty. Any ethical theory based on a guess about future consequences appalled him. He believed if we use our facility for reason, we can determine with certainty our ethical duty. As to whether or not doing our duty would make things better or worse (and for whom), Kant was agnostic!

Duty-based ethics is enormously important for (and consistently ignored by) at least two kinds of folks: politicians and business people. It is also the key to a better understanding of the responsibilities of team members. Teams (like work groups or political campaign committees) are narrowly focused on achieving clearly defined goals: winning an election, successfully introducing a new product, or winning a sailboat race. Sometimes the coach (or boss) of a team will say, "Look, just do whatever it takes." Ethically, "whatever it takes" means the ends justify the means, the very Utilitarian rationale Kant rejected.

For Kant, there were some values (duties) that could never be sacrificed to the greater good. He wrote, "So act as to treat humanity, whether in thine own person or in that of any other, in every case as an end withal, never as a means only." To some extent, one's team members, employees, customers, and partners are our means to various goals (ends), but they are also persons. Persons, Kant believed, cannot be merely used. They must be respected in their own right, whether or not our goals are achieved. He called this absolute respect for persons the Categorical Imperative.

In any team the goal is critical, but treating team members with respect is imperative. Teams fall apart when a member feels used or abused (treated as less important than the goal). Leaders thus carry the ethical burden of achieving a worthwhile end without treating those who sacrifice to achieve it as expendable means. Persons are never merely a means to an end, they are ends in themselves!

Virtue Ethics

It is one thing to understand there are duties that are not conditional (that is, we must perform them regardless of consequences); it is quite another to develop the character to act on those duties. Aristotle (384-322 B.C.) wrote the first systematic treatment of ethics in Western civilization: *Nicomachean Ethics*. Today we call his approach **Virtue Ethics**. For Aristotle and other Greek thinkers, virtue meant the "excellence" of a thing: the virtue of a knife is to cut, the virtue of a physician is to heal, the virtue of a lawyer is to seek justice. In this sense, ethics becomes the discipline of discovering and practicing virtue. Aristotle begins his thinking about ethics by asking, "What do people desire?" He discovers the usual things—wealth, honor, physical and psychological security—but realizes these things are not ends in themselves; they are means to ends.

Within virtue ethics, the ultimate end for a person must be an end that is self-sufficient, that which is always desirable in itself and never for the sake of something else. This end of ends Aristotle designates with the Greek word *eudemonia*, usually translated by the English word *happiness*. While *eudemonia* does mean happiness, its signification is of a higher-order than the modern signification of happiness. The problem is not with the Greek word *eudemonia*; the problem is in our English word happiness. *Happiness* comes from the ancient word *hap*, meaning chance, as in happenstance. "Why are you smiling," we ask, "did you win the lottery?" But to Aristotle, happiness was not something one acquired by chance. Happiness was the grand work of living, the very practice of being all that you can be. Self-fulfillment and flourishing are far better words to translate the concept contained in the Greek word *eudemonia*. For Aristotle, this state of virtue is achieved through intent, reason, and practice. To us, happiness is a feeling; to Aristotle, happiness is something you do.

Aristotle thought that one becomes virtuous by exercising the unique gift of human reasoning—that is, through study and rational contemplation. "The unexamined life is not worth living," Socrates said almost 100 years before Aristotle. Like Aristotle and Plato (Aristotle's teacher), Socrates knew humans must first engage our brains before we open our mouths or spring into some decisive action. For Aristotle, the focus of the brainwork was to find a proper balance between extremes to which the human condition tempts us. Between our fears (deficits) and exuberances (excesses) lies a sweet spot, or *golden mean* he called virtue.

At times of physical peril, say in a big storm on a small sailboat, a crew member may be immobilized by fear and unable to function, placing the lives of everyone on the sailboat in danger. Or, the opposite could happen. A sailor with a devil-may-care attitude in the face of real danger can as easily lead a boat to disaster. Aristotle says courage is the virtue located at the mean between cowardliness and rashness. Yet, identifying that virtue, and making that virtue part of one's character, are two quiet different things. Aristotle thus distinguishes between *intellectual virtue* and *practical virtue*. Practical virtues are those developed by practice and become part of a person's character, while intellectual virtue is simply the identification and understanding of a virtue.

Practice is how one learns to deal with fear, how one learns to tell the truth, and how one learns to face both personal and professional conflicts. Practice is the genius of Aristotle's contribution to the development of ethics. He showed that virtues do not become a part of our moral muscle fiber simply because we believe in them, or advocate for them. Instead, virtues become part of our character by our exercising them. How does one learn to be brave in a storm at sea? Aristotle says, "Just do it."

The ultimate goal of developing virtue is *eudemonia*, the full flourishing of our best selves, which Aristotle calls true happiness. While practitioners of the Judaic-Christian tradition tend to think of ethics (or morality) as the business of figuring out how to be good rather than bad, it is not the true end of ethics so far as Aristotle was concerned. To Aristotle, the highest good is a state of fulfillment: becoming who you truly are, realizing the potential you were born with, and being at your best in every sense.

Just as the virtue of the knife is to cut well, and the virtue of the boat is to sail well, the virtue of the self is to become the best human he or she can be. That is, to most fully utilize our capacity to reason, to apply reason to difficult moral and ethical questions, and then to put our ethical decisions into practice. Thus in joining reflection with action, the virtuous person fashions an excellent life. After years of such practice, excellence becomes habitual. Just as a perfectly trimmed sailboat cuts through the water effortlessly in synch with the waves and the wind, the man or woman in a state of *eudemonia* has achieved excellence and fulfillment.

Professional and Communitarian Ethics

All three approaches to ethics described above are principally focused on the individual: the singular conscience, rationally reflecting on the meaning of duty or responsibility, and in the case of Virtue Ethics, the ethical athlete practicing and inculcating the capacity to achieve the state of *eudemonia*. **Communitarian Ethics** has quite a different point of departure. The critical context for Communitarian ethical decision-making is the community (or team, or group, or company, or culture) within which the individual engages him/herself.

The Communitarian asks the important question, "What demands (duties) are made of me by the community(ies) of which I am a part?" The Scottish ethicist W. D. Ross (himself a student of Aristotle) focused on the question, "Where do ethical duties come from?" His answer, they come from relationships. We know our duties toward fellow human beings by the nature and quality of our relationships with them. In a sense we define ourselves, and our responsibilities, by the company we keep. Duties we owe our colleagues in the workplace are different from duties we owe a spouse; different from the duties we owe our country. The Communitarian asks us to look outward, and to face up to the duties of being social creatures.

Communitarians today are quite critical of the attitude of so many in our society who, while adamant about their individual rights, are negligent about their social duties. The "me generation" has created the need for a new breed of ethicists who insist the communities in which we live, from family and neighborhood to nation and global ecosystem, require us to accept substantial responsibilities. Environmentalists, neighborhood activists, feminists and globalists are some of the groups loosely identified today with the Communitarian Movement.

Amitai Etzioni's *Spirit of Community: Rights, Responsibilities and the Communitarian Agenda* describes the principles of this (somewhat disorganized) movement. His thesis is that we must pay more attention to common duties as opposed to individual rights. Our neighborhoods can again be safe from crime without turning our country into a police state; our families can once again flourish without forcing women to stay home and not enter the workforce; our schools can provide "essential moral education" without indoctrinating young people or violating the First Amendment's prohibition of establishing religion.

The key to this social transformation is the Communitarian belief in balancing the direct relationship between rights and responsibilities. Etzioni states:

> Correcting the current imbalance between rights and responsibilities requires a four-point agenda: a moratorium on the minting of most, if not all, new rights; reestablishing the link between rights and responsibilities; recognizing that some responsibilities do not entail rights; and, most carefully, adjusting some rights to the changed circumstances.

Here, if nothing else, is a frontal attack on both the Libertarian mind-set of our age as well as the culture's deep-set entitlement mentality.

Communitarianism is not new. Most of the world's great religions are communitarian. It is from a community of common belief that the faithful develop a sense of self and responsibility (or, in Confucian thought, the extended family which nurtures this development). Ethics cannot be separated from the ethos of the religious or familial community. The modern Communitarian movement may or may not be religiously inclined, yet communitarianism is clearly a part of a tradition as old as human association.

In the context of teams, the Communitarian approach to ethics has much to commend itself: How much of one's personal agenda is one willing to sacrifice to the overall goal of winning? Under what conditions is one willing to let the values or culture of the team alter personal ethical inclinations? To what extent do the relationships one has with team members give rise to duties that one is willing to honor? How willing is one to share credit when the team succeeds? How willing is one to accept blame when the team loses? Under what conditions would one break with the team? If Ross is correct that duties come from relationships, paying attention to such questions about the company we keep may be more than a social obligation; perhaps it is our ethical duty.

Ethical Egoism and The Divine Imperative

There are two pervasive ethical approaches not yet treated here: Ethical Egoism and The Divine Imperative. Each has a broad and dedicated following, and each is deeply problematic to the ethical maturing of any society. Briefly (and with pejorative intent), here is what these extreme, yet interestingly similar, approaches assert.

Ethical Egoists say ethics is a matter of doing what feels right to the individual conscience. If one asks, "Why did you do that?" the answer is, "Because I felt like it." This approach is often dressed up with statements about being true to yourself: "Let your conscience be your guide," or "Do the right thing." How does one know what is true for the self? How does one develop a conscience? How is one to know that doing what is right (what feels right to you) is the right thing to do?

If nothing else, Ethical Egoism is a conversation stopper! How does one communicate to colleagues, friends, children, or any other human being when the reference point of behavior or ethical judgment is how one feels inside? How does a civil society emerge if the civilians cannot deliberate in common, understandable language about their motives, intents, values, and duties? In essence, Ethical Egoism is the ethics of teenagers rebelling against being answerable to outside authority. To enter an ethical dialogue is to take the radical risk of having one's values and actions challenged. Apparently, there are many adults who still have not grown up enough to risk being challenged. Better to repeat the mantra, "I did what my conscience dictated."

Just as there is no possible meaningful ethical dialogue with the Ethical Egoist, neither is there much hope of effective engagement with Divine Imperialists. For this growing community, ethics is the simple business of doing what God tells one to do. There is therefore no reason or need for discussion. The issue is conversion, not conversation. In a constitutional democracy like ours, with a fundamental commitment to "the non-establishment of religion," the Divine Imperialist is stuck on the horns of a dilemma: either make all ethical inquiry personal (no social or political value deliberation), or take the "ayatollah approach" and bring the state into conformity with the revealed will of God. Divine Imperialists do not deliberate. They dictate, because they believe there is nothing to deliberate about. God has spoken. It is in The Book.

Religion, at its best, understands that faith confers no special status of political insight. Believers, agnostics and non-believers can, and do, contribute to the culture's continuing struggle to understand what is good, what is just, and what is true; that is why democracies (as opposed to states founded upon some Divine Right of Kings) survive.

A Note on Narrative Ethics

Narrative Ethics is diagnosis through the use of story. Among the professions, particularly medicine, law and counseling, narrative has become a powerful tool in developing ethical insight and perspective. To tell a story is to invite participation from the hearer, and also a means of communicating the richness and complexity of human dilemmas. The benefit of Narrative Ethics over the four traditional ethical approaches is that a story invites both ethical engagement and ethical creativity.

Oliver Wendell Holmes, an American jurist who wrote stunningly comprehensible decisions even in some of the most complex cases imaginable, has a famous quote: "I would not give a fig for the simplicity this side of complexity, but I would give my life for the simplicity on the other side of complexity." It is the role of narrative to lead us through the thickets of overwhelming complexity to the clarity of enriched simplicity.

In business, as in law, a great deal of teaching is done through the use of cases. This is nothing more or less than using the pedagogy of Narrative

Ethics. The narrative invites the student into the complexity of issues involved in personal, professional, and organizational dilemmas; and the narrative provides a road through the complexity to the simplicity on the other side.

Of course, there are some people who congenitally cannot stop to ask for directions when lost in life's thickets. For them, storytelling is a waste of time. The "male" mantra *just cut to the chase* comes to mind. This may shed light on why some women (ethical feminist Margaret Wheatley, for example) have a fondness for narrative. At all stages of the ethical decision-making process, narrative is a useful tool of analysis for exposing the facts, conflicts, feelings, and values that are the stuff of the human predicament.

Management: The Meta Profession

In 1912, Louis D. Brandeis addressed the graduating students of Brown University.[1] Tradition dictated the graduating class was divided between those receiving *learned degrees* in the professions of law, medicine, and ministry, from those in the *skill-based disciplines*, such as business management. The future Supreme Court justice did an interesting thing that graduation day: he turned away from the professional degree candidates toward the business degree candidates, and said:

> Each commencement season we are told by the college reports the number of graduates who have selected the professions as their occupations and the number of those who will enter business. The time has come for abandoning such a classification. Business should be, and to some extent already is, one of the professions.

Brandeis minced no words in defining what professionalism was all about:

> A profession is an occupation for which the necessary preliminary training is intellectual in character, involving knowledge and to some extent learning, as distinguished from mere skill...It is an occupation which is pursued largely for others and not merely for one's self...It is an occupation in which the amount of financial return is not the accepted measure of success.

Spoken to clergy, physicians, and lawyers in 1912 these words would have had a familiar—if unheeded—ring. But spoken to businessmen? Brandeis' intuition about the decisive character of business management, and its importance for human welfare, has been borne out across the tortured years of this past century. However, his argument that business management was essentially professional in character is debated still.

Three characteristics of professionalism cited in Brandeis' address detail the nature of both the need to, and the controversy about, calling business management a profession:

> First. A profession is an occupation for which the necessary preliminary training is intellectual in character, involving knowledge and to some extent learning, as distinguished from mere skill.

> Second. It is an occupation which is pursued largely for others and not merely for one's self.

> Third. It is an occupation in which the amount of financial return is not the accepted measure of success.

Within Brandeis' three paradoxical pronouncements lies the answer to what it means to be a professional in business.

The Paradox of Skill

All professions require unique skills. While demonstrated proficiency in particular skills is necessary for admission into a profession, skill mastery alone is not sufficient to define the professional. If it were, a surgeon would be simply a plumber employed to mend human pipes and valves; a lawyer, a carpenter crafting together legal words and phrases into motions, wills, or contracts; a teacher, an actor skilled at presentation or lecturing. While the surgeon must be extraordinarily skilled in the crafts of incision and suturing, the lawyer adept at the craft of legal word-smithing, and the teacher a master of the practical arts of communication, such skills are not the essence of who they are as professionals, nor are they the be-and-end-all of their practices. Understanding this difference is key to the classic distinction between a trade and a profession.

Both trades and professions require practice and perfection of significant skills, but a trade is completely defined by its accumulated skill, while a profession is not. As Brandeis explains, "A profession is an occupation for which the necessary preliminary training is intellectual in character involving knowledge and to some extent learning, as distinguished from mere skill." I would add that it is not just in preliminary training that intelligence and learning are required, but in all aspects of the practice of the continuing professional life.

In a time when everyone wants to be called professional, a real danger lurks in Brandeis' distinction: a form of elitism ("mere skill"), a snobbery, or a class bias that is inappropriate, both to the tradesperson and the professional. The trades were once a source of enormous pride and distinction. Through

Medieval guilds, a revolution in human worth and work was set in motion, laying the foundation of the industrial and technological revolutions. Through the guild structure, trade skills were passed from generation to generation, and the pride of association with quality and integrity was maintained.

The professions were something else entirely. As the Middle Ages yielded to the Renaissance, "The Learned Professions" (priesthood, law, and medicine) required rigorous training in particular skills, but the application of those skills required a dimension of commitment and integrity not necessary in a trade. The wisdom to counsel human beings in the midst of spiritual, emotional, physical, or legal crisis necessarily requires more than technique. It requires a learned and practiced wisdom: an ethic. It is one thing to entrust your bathroom to a plumber; it is another thing entirely to entrust your life to a heart surgeon. Those willing to assume the unique burden of the spiritual, physical, and legal care for humans in existential need were designated, or set apart, as learned professionals.

As I write this chapter, I am in the process of recovering from open-heart surgery. The experience of putting my life in the hands of a physician is vivid. I also am sitting in my home which is being extensively remodeled. On both scores, I am fortunate to have a relationship with two excellent people: Dick, my heart surgeon, and Craig, the skilled construction craftsman (carpenter, plumber and electrician) restoring our home. Both are highly skilled and wise men. Dick, however, is integral to the care and counseling that guided my family and me through my decision to go under the knife. Craig is full of sage wisdom about public and foreign affairs of our times, but in no sense is my life vulnerable to insights we share while he restores my kitchen and replaces the bedroom window.

Exactly three weeks ago, Dick sat on the side of my bed in a Denver hospital surrounded by twelve members of my family and talked to me about the alternatives for dealing with a most unexpected heart problem. He showed me very worrisome pictures of several partially blocked arteries, and told me, in his opinion, I had no choice but to have quadruple bypass surgery. He said he would send my file to anyone I wished for a second opinion, but felt I should reach a decision soon. My kids asked all sorts of nervous and caring questions and he responded openly and fully. Never have I been with someone as comfortably open and trustworthy at a time when so much was at stake for me.

As I made my decision to move forward with this personal ordeal, I would learn from friends that Dick was one of the most skilled surgeons in the country. Reassuring me, but I already knew he was a professional: that is, a person wise and caring enough for me to trust with my life.

The Paradox of the Public Pledge

A profession is literally so-called because the aspirant to the office is sworn to specific public commitments—he/she publicly professes legal and ethical obligations unique to the vocation of lawyer, physician, counselor, or priest. The public pledge is the portal into the unique relationships afforded the vocation.

To be clear, it is not primarily a privilege that the professional assumes with the pledge, rather it is a fundamentally self-imposed burden. No one is forced to swear they will put another's interest above their own, yet this is the common condition of all professionals.

Quite a great deal is made of the special relationship between professionals and their parishioners, patients, or clients—the sanctity of the confessional, the doctor-patient relationship, or the lawyer-client relationship—each special, private, and protected both in law and ethics. In thinking of the confessional booth, the examination room, and the lawyer's office, the idea of a uniquely protected privacy—of an almost sacred space—emerges. The priest, doctor, and lawyer are sworn to hold sacred the disclosures within this zone of professionally-protected communication. Thus, being a professional means nothing less than willingly and publicly affirming that the client's, patient's, or parishioner's interest shall come before one's own interests.

For many professionals, the matter stops with the pledge: "I swear the patient's interests come first, end of discussion." This commitment to the vulnerable client is only half the issue, as the business and professional crises of our times illustrate. Not only are priests sworn to care for particular souls, they are sworn to see to the care of "the people of God," the moral welfare of the parish, the salvation of the world. There is a tension between a professional's public responsibility and commitment to the private, vulnerable client. Louis Brandeis includes both in stating, "A profession is an occupation which is pursued largely for others and not merely for oneself."[1] The paradox of "the other" is the paradox of the public pledge.

Not only are doctors sworn to put the interest of the patient above their own, the health of the patient's family, neighborhood, and the public is also their professional obligation. The lawyer is not simply employed to represent a particular client, but also sworn to be an "officer of the court." While accountants may be employed by Arthur Andersen to do the books for the Enron Corporation, they also are sworn to keep the interests of the public uncompromised (after all, we call the profession Certified *Public* Accountants).

I know of no professional comfortable with the tension inherent in this public pledge. No one likes hard choices; no one likes moral ambiguity; each of us wishes to live in a world where things can be reduced to some least common ethical denominator (a single duty, for example). When teaching business students, the mantra of Milton Friedman is the droning undertone of almost every class discussion: *the business of business is business*, implying the sole responsibility of the business executive is to increase shareholder return.

Yet, the very essence of professional responsibility is to address the difficult and unavoidable ethical tensions between public and private interest—the priest who hears the confession of a disturbed and homicidal parishioner intent on killing yet again; the lawyer who discovers a client has misrepresented the facts of his case, and is asking for a plea to the court based on lies and distortions; the doctor who is asked to prescribe extraordinarily expensive treatments to a patient too ill, or too old, to have reasonable chance of curative benefit; or the engineer bound by a confidentiality agreement, in spite of a conviction that a plane, bridge, or space shuttle is likely to fail and potentially cause extensive loss of life. These are not plot summaries for Hollywood films; in an infinite variety, they are the stuff of professional life in the complex world of the 21st century.

It is by design that professionals are thrust continually into such ethical predicaments. The professional's public pledge is an acceptance of ethical burdens not incumbent on the rest of society—an acknowledgement of the reality of human existence where things do not come out even, where real ethical insight must be exercised, and where benign outcomes are far from assured. Someone must live in the land between the rock and the hard place, and those who do so are designated professionals.

I think of professionals as the value bearers of society, those particularly burdened and practiced to address the most difficult and sensitive human dilemmas. I do not mean to imply that a businessperson, lawyer, doctor, psychiatrist, or teacher is better in some moral sense than anyone else. Instead, that they have agreed to assume a unique ethical burden to work at the transaction-point where issues of significant human value are on the line. The professional is sworn not to desert this post—to be there to counsel, reflect, and bear with the human condition in the midst of transition and crisis. This is, to me, the essence of professional practice—the practice of raising the value content of human decisions and choices. This is precisely the professional's sworn burden, and it is the very nature of the ethic that defines who the professional is.

It astounds me that anyone would want the title of professional. To make sure this point is underlined, let us consider the Paradox of Pay, perhaps the most confounding issue of all to the business professional.

The Paradox of Pay

A local sportscaster interviews a member of the Harlem Globetrotters, in town for a game, on the evening news. The interview goes something like this:

> Sports Guy: Al, I was surprised you never turned pro.
>
> Al: What do you mean? I'm a pro. I get paid pretty good for playing ball.

Almost everyone assumes that being professional means getting paid (and paid well) for one's work. People assume there are professionals and there are amateurs; the former get paid, while the amateurs do it for the love of it. Well, no. Originally, the professions were too important to receive wages in the usual sense. Professionals were not paid for their work; they received an honorarium, a gratuity from the community intended both to honor and disassociate the vocation from the necessities of the market, to thus free the vocation for the selfless task of caring for others.

Three days before my heart surgery, I happened to watch a *60 Minutes* piece on a cardiology group in California, which was prescribing and performing, unnecessary bypass surgery in order to increase revenues for their practice. It was chilling. I thought of a case we use in business school about the Sears Company, some years ago, pressuring employees in their auto servicing division to increase revenues by pushing unneeded work on air filters, mufflers, brake relining, and the like. But, heart surgeons realigning ethical responsibility for market considerations? The medieval notion of honoraria for professionals may make a lot of sense in this time of triumphant capitalism. There are some values the market is not designed to dictate.

I love to tease business students about the matter of pay and the power of money. I ask, "Considering the 'oldest profession,' what would you rather be known for: doing it for money, or doing it for love?" In the realm of lovemaking, most us prefer to have non-market forces determine the dimensions of our intimate lives. Let's hear it for true amateurs!

In a real sense, professionals do it for love. It is difficult to imagine bearing the burden of a physician, lawyer, counselor, or a professor without having a deep and effusive passion for what one does. Professionals cannot leave their work at the office, because what they do is who they are. As I have discovered, teaching is the most rewarding thing I can think of doing. I do not just teach; I *am* a teacher. I am glad I am paid for my work but, truth be known, I would do it for free. I walk away from a class where the students and I have really "connected," and I do not have words to say how good it feels. I can describe historically and intellectually what a professional should be, but even better, I know what it *feels* like. No amount of money can compensate for that feeling.

Considering the ethical burdens of true professionalism—the fact that skill alone is not a sufficient qualification, that a professional is publicly pledged to work on the unrelenting tension between the welfare of the client and the good of the society, and that financial reward is not the fundamental criteria by which success will be judged—why would anyone, especially a business student, choose to "go pro?" I have only one answer: professions are in essence vocations, literally, callings. Men and women become priests, lawyers, physicians, professors, and business executives because they cannot do anything else; they cannot be who they are outside the realm of what they are impelled to do. With the rising challenges of the 21st century, business in particular needs such driven and principled practitioners. The responsibility for managing some of the largest and most powerful organizations on earth necessitates unique moral and ethical commitments. That was the Brandeis brief at the beginning of the last century, and it is the categorical imperative of our time.

The true challenge of business is that it encompasses not just personal and professional dimensions, but also the responsibilities of managing the corporation—that unique creation of law and enterprise.

Corporate Social Responsibility

The legal and historic roots of the modern corporation reach well back into the 18th century, but it was during the 19th century Industrial Revolution that this truly extraordinary form of human organization came into its own and, in the 20th century, when the corporation became the dominant economic force on earth. Consider the Corporation's amazing characteristics—concentration of management, accumulation of capital, shielding of ownership from liability, and being granted a legal existence not necessarily bounded by either space or time—both ubiquitous and eternal! As well, consider its fearsome prospects vis-à-vis its lack of accountability, its deficit of democratic governance, its often-uncivilized competitive engagement with all other sectors of society (not to mention its transcendence of both national sovereignty and legal jurisdiction). Is the transnational corporation the answer to the fundamental questions of human survival, or the fundamental threat to life itself? In short, will the corporation of the 21st century be a corrupt Robin Hood, or a virtuous Sheriff of Nottingham?

Corporations are not natural persons, they are juridical persons created by law. Consequently, the ethical considerations one might use when dealing with natural persons (a friend, associate, or stranger) are significantly different when the subject is a corporation. Getting this straight is critically important to an adequate understanding of business ethics. Natural persons are judged ethically and legally based chiefly on their intentions. Ethical analysis of the behavior of natural persons begins with consideration of what a person meant by what he or she did, said, or produced. In contrast, ethical analysis involving the corporation must forever begin and end in law and public policy, with reference to the political economy that brought forth the beast. The legal entity of the corporation was created to shield investors from liabilities beyond the limit of their investment (a result that neither sole proprietorships nor partnerships could accomplish), with the legislative intent of facilitating the aggregation of private capital. This legal experiment, which began in the 19th century, has succeeded spectacularly.

For people to survive, they need physical and emotional nourishment and familial and social support. In contrast, corporations survive solely by their ability to return value to their shareholders. Hence, corporations are consequential persons, Utilitarian to the core. A friend may forget a lunch date and hurt your feelings, but when he says, "I'm really sorry, I can't believe I forgot," you say, "Hey I missed you, but it's OK. Let's try again next week." When a company tanks a $100 million new product launch, shareholders do not want to hear about how sorry management is that things did not work out, or that management meant well. It will do the CEO no good to say, "My heart was in the right place."

When we talk about the ethical criteria for judging the behavior of corporations, we speak not of intent but responsibility (which means, quite literally, the capacity to respond). Corporate ethics is the ethics of corporate social responsibility (CSR), not corporate personal responsibility.

The responsibility of a corporation is shaped by two realities: (1) obligations created by society through law and public policy (legal responsibilities), and (2) obligations created by corporate culture, that is, obligations to stakeholders (customers, employees, neighborhoods, natural environments). The two overlap and reinforce each other, but their limits lie within the boundaries of a company's tangible capacities.

Corporate ethics is about gaining understanding of mixed motives. When natural persons have mixed motives (giving a hundred bucks to the opera because you want your boss, who supports the opera, to think well of you) we somehow know the act is not unambiguously laudable. When a company that makes computers gives 100 laptops to the public school system with the hope that exposing children to their brand of computers will lead to increased sales—this "doing good to do well" is not only laudable, it is responsible both to shareholders and stakeholders.

Corporations, as a matter of fact, can only act with mixed motives. By law they are created to serve the bottom line of returning wealth to investors. Corporations have a fiduciary responsibility—the highest standard of loyalty and trust owed by agents to principals—to their shareholders, as legal owners of the corporation. To do good, a corporation must do well. But as a business ethicist, I argue the reverse: to do well, a corporation must do good. People have consciences, and some would say souls; corporations have neither. Corporations are creatures of law and public policy; they are cultural creations. As such, they have unique cultures of their own. Corporate ethics is therefore about the creation of a culture of responsibility within the corporation.

Lynn Paine, a professor at Harvard University, has made a major contribution to the understanding of how corporate responsibility is achieved through her distinction between compliance-based organizations and integrity-based organizations. In reality, CSR is a product of both compliance (legal and regulatory constraints) and integrity (the internal culture and self-regulatory environment).

This is underscored by such new laws as the Sarbanes-Oxley Act as well as the Federal Sentencing Guidelines (policy guidelines established in part to determine corporate criminal punishment in U.S. federal courts). Sarbanes-Oxley is particularly interesting given Paine's compliance/integrity construct, in that it requires both integrity structures (such as a corporate board of ethics and internal protections for whistle-blowers) and increases fines for violations of antitrust and other federal statutes regulating interstate corporate behavior. Corporations are creatures of law and policy and are regulated externally. Corporations have no conscience, per se, but like any social system, can develop a guiding culture, maintained through education and reinforced by the habits and interactions of the people within the corporation.

In a world of over six billion people, there is little alternative to having large and complex organizations designed to feed, house, heal, and help meet basic human needs. The multinational corporation is here to stay; the issues of how these behemoths are guided and controlled is far from settled. And how the humans who work and manage these—business professionals—maintain their own integrity within the Utilitarian cultures of multinational corporations is a chapter of history we are only beginning to write.

The Social Contract between society and the multinational corporation today is being radically renegotiated. Cascading collapses of the dot-coms, followed by the Enron, WorldCom, and Adelphia Communications scandals and, most recently, the meltdown of capital markets across the globe portend a turbulent future indeed for both the corporation and the business professional. At the Daniels College of Business we believe ethical education and practice is not an elective. For those who dare to ride these currents of extraordinary change, personal, professional, and corporate ethics is a required course of practice—not merely for graduation, but for a lifetime. This is why the Daniels College of Business is so passionate about the challenge of teaching business ethics to future business leaders.

---

[1]"Professionalism," Louis D. Brandeis, an address to Brown University, 1912.

How to do the Right Thing: a Primer on Ethics and Moral Vision

by Stephen L. Pepper

"The right thing"—that's what most of us want to do, but we don't have a guide, and we don't think about it much. And when we do think about it, we don't have much in the way of an explicit or articulated method to follow. Not long ago I participated in a panel presentation where the lead advice on how to be an ethical executive was to exercise "courage, candor and conscience."[1] Sounded good to me, but it seemed too vague, abstract and elevated to provide much practical assistance in actual decision making. What follows is a translation of "courage, candor and conscience" into simple and usable guidance for doing the right thing as a business executive. My intention is to be helpful in understanding the ethics of one's day-to-day working life.

A Working Definition of "Ethics"

To begin, I want to clarify what I mean by ethics, and to distinguish compliance from ethics. Complying with the law is, of course, usually the right thing to do. But merely being in compliance—avoiding violation of the law—does not mean that one is doing the morally right thing in any particular situation. "Ethics" refers to rational deliberation about questions of right and wrong (that is, moral questions) and to the results of that deliberation. In other words, ethics is simply serious thinking about moral questions and the results of that thinking. "Ethics" in this sense is moral philosophy (one of the three main branches of philosophy). It has a long secular tradition in Western culture and universities and—in the form of professional ethics—is commonly studied in university law, business, and medical schools. From this perspective it is clear that conduct in compliance with law may well be morally wrongful. For example, a fair and genuine debt might be blocked from legal enforcement by a statute of limitations or by the statute of frauds. In other words, a legal technicality might prevent enforcement of a debt justly owed and due. Although it would not be a violation of law to refuse to pay the debt, most of us would say—all other things being equal—that refusal to repay what you justly owe is a moral wrong. Similarly, some years ago it might not have been unlawful to use "off-the-books" entities to create a misleading accounting representation of a corporation. Yet, again, most of us would say that misrepresenting the financial situation of an entity to one who will rely on that misrepresentation is a moral wrong, even if the technique by which it is accomplished is not legally prohibited. Thus, if one is interested in doing the right thing (that is, if one is serious about business or professional ethics), compliance with the law is only a first step.

For the purposes of this discussion, we will assume the conduct being discussed is lawful. The question then becomes: is it the right thing to do?

Moral Vision

The first insight I would suggest is that *ethics is problematic not so much in the deciding what to do, but in being aware that our conduct involves an ethical problem to begin with.* I have defined ethics as rational deliberation about questions of right and wrong. But you can't deliberate unless you notice there is a question facing you. Most of us who run into ethical difficulty do not have bad character or wrongful intentions. Our problem is failing to notice that there is a moral question to begin with. Seeing (observing and perceiving) is thus the first and crucial step in morality. And this step—always difficult—is more difficult in organizations because of the dilution of responsibility: there are others to notice, others one can rely on. A classic psychology experiment demonstrates this phenomenon. Participants were placed in a room and asked to fill out a form. Smoke was then sent into the room through a wall vent. If the subjects were alone, 75 percent reported the smoke to the experimenters. If two other seemingly unconcerned subjects were also in the room, only 10 percent reported. Thus, almost all subjects would follow the passive lead of the others, continuing to fill out the form and ignore the smoke (and the danger possibly indicated by that smoke).[2] This now well known—but usually ignored—fact about human nature can have severe consequences. In the winter of 2005, a remote mountain lodge in southwest Colorado was destroyed by a propane gas explosion; three children died. In the hours before the explosion many guests and employees smelled the odd odor of the gas. One guest mentioned it to an employee, who suggested the odor was just "sewer gas." No one acted to find the leak, identify the odor, or evacuate the lodge.

The lesson is that moral vision is a prerequisite to thinking about an ethical question. You have to notice the smell of the gas, you have to register that you are seeing and smelling smoke, before you can think about it. If seeing (perceiving) is perhaps the key moral art, then courage, candor and conscience—as elaborated below—serve as the foundations of the moral vision required for ethical deliberation and conduct.

First, let me translate "conscience" into something a little more tangible and close to home. By conscience I would suggest we understand simple everyday "intuition" about right and wrong. Each of us has a sense of right and wrong. It is near at hand, part of us. Yet often the further we go in life, the more we tend to find ourselves in situations where we suppress that intuition. We think:

a. we're grown-ups now, out in the big "real" world; or

b. we're in a "hardball" business or litigation situation with large stakes for our company and our own advancement; or

c. we're part of a smart, savvy, mature organization (or team)— and these people know what they're doing.

Here lies the danger for suppression of moral intuition, for distancing ourselves from ourselves and undermining our own integrity. Here lies the very real risk of suppressing our perception of that propane gas smell, or of that smoke coming into the room as we do our job and fill out that form. To avoid that risk we need to cultivate our intuition about right and wrong, not ignore it.

Ask yourself, how would I feel about telling my spouse (or child, or parent) about this situation in ordinary language? Would I want to have it reported in the newspapers? Notice when thinking about a situation if it causes a little queasiness in your stomach (and don't, one or two layers down in your consciousness, blame it on lunch). For example, if your organization or client is, for some arguable reason, resisting paying a just debt: notice the queasiness; pay attention when the thought drifts by that you're contemplating "stiffing" a creditor who is really owed the money (or material, or machinery, or whatever).

There is no overemphasizing the importance of this initial step. It is the gateway to ethical behavior. Imagine an example from your actual work. Let's call it "D." D is attractive from a business or professional perspective; it is not prohibited by law. Nobody else seems bothered by D. To cultivate your intuition (or conscience) you need to go further:

- Is D the right thing to do?

- Is there some perspective from which D is the wrong thing to do?

- Will it harm people who don't deserve to be harmed?

- Is it dishonest (although not unlawful)?

To be ethical it is essential that you go beyond your business or professional identity as executive, accountant, lawyer, or board member. It is essential to pay attention to what you as an ordinary moral person would think about the proposed conduct. The somewhat lofty and elusive concept of "conscience" can be understood in this way as simply your intuition about right and wrong. But to make it accessible and useful you have to cultivate it, pay attention to it, listen to it.

As exemplified by the smoke experiment (among many others), there is a great deal of empirical evidence that our moral perceptions are worse when we are in groups or when authority figures may be participating. (Imagine: a board of directors, a business project team, a working group with the supervisor present.) In such contexts most of us tend to assume that if there were really an ethical problem, somebody else would notice it and point it out. "I'm here with a lot of smart, talented, experienced people. If they aren't bothered, there must not be anything bothersome" is the natural assumption. This is reinforced or heightened if the group has a leader or hierarchy. We naturally tend to defer to the leader: "If George doesn't see a problem with this, there must not be a problem."

Resisting that common reaction is the second step in moral vision, and the second translation. I suggest a very modest and close at hand understanding of courage: self-confidence. The first and most crucial step is noticing that something may be wrong (conscience); the second is not burying that perception, not pushing it aside (courage). Moral vision and ethical analysis require bringing a vague perception to the surface, looking at it squarely, thinking about it directly. That requires confidence that your individual, lonely sense that something may be amiss might just be right. (And you have to be willing to follow this perception despite the fact that no one else in the group—including the leader—seems to have noticed.) It is so easy to defer in groups, or to leaders, particularly when that deference is implicit, when the issue hasn't been raised for discussion, isn't on the agenda, hasn't been perceived. In fact, it is very difficult not to defer. Having the self-confidence to take your perception (hazy and ill-formed as it may be) seriously requires courage. There may well be several others in that room, or in that working group, who have a similar vague sense that something is not quite right, but who are also deferring, remaining silent on the issue.

But there are many pressures and incentives not to notice a moral difficulty. Even within one's own thoughts, those incentives and pressures commonly remain unconscious and unarticulated—we don't notice the problem because it's uncomfortable to notice it. When that moral queasiness nudges, when there is a little something pushing at the edges of our thoughts, there is usually a tendency to push it back, to keep it out of focus, to half-think the queasiness is just something from lunch. And if the perception becomes a little clearer or more articulated—if, that is, we do notice—it is easy to decide that we are probably mistaken, or overcautious, or idiosyncratic. Most of us don't want to be the squeaky wheel. We want to move the project forward, not slow it up with imagined difficulties.

Moral vision thus requires (1) focusing on and developing that vague sense of uneasiness, and (2) having the courage to believe that you—alone—may well be on to something that should be dealt with. When no one involved has a developed moral intuition (conscience) and the self-confidence to trust that intuition (courage), your group or organization may be on its way to trouble. For the ethical life of the organization and for your own personal integrity, it is essential that you not defer to the silence, that you not push that ill-formed perception somewhere out of sight, out of mind.

The third element of moral vision is candor, which I would translate to mean simply honesty with oneself. You have to be able to bring your intuitions into focus and face them directly. You have to be honest with yourself about what you are seeing or feeling, and you have to be able to articulate your insights before you can think them through. You have to know what you are thinking, or seeing, or feeling before you can exercise self-confidence in regard to that perception. In this sense, candor is tightly connected with our definitions of conscience and courage. Candor and courage reinforce each other. Honesty with yourself may well be a necessary precondition to self-confidence about your intuition. This is much more difficult to accomplish than it sounds. As we have seen, all the incentives often pull in the opposite direction: it is so much easier to just let that possibly troubling thought drift on by, or find some quick (and usually superficial) reason for dismissing it.

Courage, candor, and conscience are the essential ingredients of moral vision. They need not be lofty abstractions, but can be close at hand and familiar: (1) everyday moral intuition, (2) honesty with oneself about that intuition, and (3) self-confidence about one's moral vision.

Ethical Deliberation

At this point let's assume you have a moral intuition. You've been honest enough with yourself to have a fairly clear idea about a problem, and you have the self-confidence to conclude that the problem may be sufficiently serious to merit concern. This is the beginning, not the end. You now know there *may* be a problem, not that there is a problem. What now?

I'd suggest two further steps. First, think through the problem carefully and analytically. *Why* do I think this may be a problem? Will innocent or undeserving people be harmed? Will someone be cheated? Will the market be deceived? Who will gain from the conduct, and will that gain be earned or deserved? What values are at issue: Honesty? Fair value? Shareholder value? Transparency? Generosity? Equity? From what perspective can the conduct be criticized? From what perspective can it be justified? Which is the more truthful, accurate, or generous perspective? This is ethics in a nutshell: rational deliberation about right and wrong. You may already have accomplished much of it in the process of clarifying and being honest about the initial intuition.

Deliberation, as most effectively practiced, involves a second step: including someone else. Seek additional input and the benefit of a different point of view. Discuss the situation with at least one—and preferably several—people whose judgment or perspective you trust or value. This two-step process provides a check on your intuition and your analysis, and will help you decide whether you are seeing clearly. You may be mistaken, idiosyncratic, or over-cautious—these steps help you measure that possibility. Often the two steps can be combined: thinking the situation through analytically may be most effectively accomplished through conversation with a friend or colleague.

An Example

Picking the role closest to your own, imagine you are either (1) a corporate executive, (2) a member of the board of directors, or (3) a professional advisor—perhaps a lawyer, accountant, or consultant. A major product line—several similar electronic toys—are assembled in China by young women workers, approximately 18 to 23 years old. Each is required to work 110 to 120 hours a week. Ordinarily, working fewer hours would reduce the pay for these young women, which is already very low. But your company can clearly afford to lower the hours significantly and still pay each worker the amount she now earns for the 110 to 120 hour week. Even with the higher labor costs, the product could still be sold competitively and at a worthwhile profit. Chinese government officials, however, prefer that the hours not be changed because your company's workers would then be treated more favorably than comparable workers at state-owned factories. The disparity would create pressure on the state-owned enterprises. Finally, workers are selected by the government. This complicates matters because of the very real possibility that many of your workers are in fact younger than 18, despite assurances to the contrary by government officials.[3]

Take a little time and effort here: pause, and try to *imagine* yourself into this situation. What would you feel? What would you think? Don't go on to the next paragraph without spending a few minutes trying to put yourself into this situation.

. . . .

For most of us, some sense or intuition suggests that something is wrong here. One hundred and ten to 120 hours of intricate physical work every week, week after week—what kind of life is that? To the extent we can identify with these young women as fellow human beings, something in this situation does not feel right. What time is left for the things we value in life aside from work? How do those hours of work, week after week, wear on the body, the mind, the spirit? Would you want this life for your daughter? What would your spouse or child or parent think about this? About you participating in this situation? How would the newspapers or magazines react to it? Aside from what you think about it, how do you *feel* about this situation?

That feeling—that moral intuition—is unfortunately easy to brush aside. And in the real world of business such feelings and intuitions are frequently suppressed. For example, the following quick reactions are easily available brushes: (1) This is China we're considering, with vast differences from our own culture and economy. Any queasiness we might have isn't applicable to a situation so far away geographically, culturally and socially. (2) If these young women had a better option they'd take it. From the perspective of basic economics, if they choose this work we have to assume it's better than the alternatives, and we'd be doing them no favor by taking it away. That's the beauty and comfort of the market. (3) Paying wages above the market is dangerous. It invites our competitors to come in and produce similar products at a lower price. (4) This situation may be a problem, but it is not *my* problem. It's not in my division, not my job, not my responsibility. I am not the officer in charge of this operation; it's her problem, not mine. (Or, it's management's responsibility, not the board's. Or, local management's responsibility, not the executive officers'. Or, this is for senior management to worry about, not us on the line.)[4]

One or all of these justifications may be correct, or at least partly correct. But it is not time for that yet. Conscience—cultivating your moral intuition—simply means not being so quick to dismiss: first you have to bring to the surface, refine, and clarify the intuition that there may be something wrong here. Following that is the time for those modest translations of courage and candor. The fact that nobody else in the organization is bothered by these long hours of labor is not crucial at this stage. (In fact, many others may share your concern, and just not be saying so. Or, they may not have thought about it. Or thought briefly and dismissed too summarily.) The fact that the leader is not bothered (or not saying so) is also not crucial at this stage. What is crucial is whether *you* are bothered, whether *you* think there may be something troubling here. It takes courage (self-confidence) to think that you may have noticed something of moral significance that no one else has noticed, or is willing to mention. And it requires honesty with yourself (candor) to look squarely at the situation and clarify your perception that something about this situation seems wrong.

Thus the right answer is: this situation is ethically problematic. There is at least a *possible* problem of right and wrong. But that only begins the ethical analysis; it doesn't end it. The question then becomes: is this conduct ethically justifiable? That moves into the more complicated questions of ethical deliberation mentioned earlier. It seems wrong, but in context and analyzed, is it in fact wrong, and if so, why? This chapter is not the place to create a business school ethics "case" from the Chinese workers scenario, thoroughly examining the many relevant and arguable factors. But we can briefly canvas some of the questions raised.

First, it does seem that innocent people undeserving of harm may well be harmed by this conduct. Second, market deception does not seem to be involved (except to the extent customers assume that the products they purchase were produced under humane working conditions). Third, the company and its customers both gain. Whether that gain is earned or deserved seems to circle back to the root question: is this unjustifiable exploitation of the vulnerable? Fourth, of the values listed above, "generosity" and "equity" seem to suggest that finding a route to lowering the hours without lowering the pay at least merits serious consideration.

Now, switching to the other side, from what perspective can the conduct be justified? *This* is the point at which to consider seriously each of the four "brush offs" listed above, and each has some weight and persuasive power. The fact that the women apparently have no better option (the basic economics argument) seems particularly weak because the company can afford to provide them with a more attractive option: significantly lower hours for the same pay. The fact that taking that course of action would displease the Chinese authorities due to the pressure it would put on other factories with similar excessive hours is significant, but requires more information. What are the likely, or possible, consequences of causing that displeasure? How likely? How much would those consequences harm the company or the workers? Might the pressure and its consequences help those workers employed in the government factories and possibly have a small positive effect on the conditions of employees in the area in general?

We can combine, refine, and to some extent summarize these questions: our corporation didn't create this general economic and social situation, but is it acceptable to profit from it? What alternatives do we have? How, if at all, would those alternatives improve the situation for these young women? And, finally, what of the arguable fact that this is someone else's responsibility? At this stage, that last factor seems to be primarily a means of avoiding ethical responsibility and analysis. It is premature. At this point the task is to engage in sufficient analysis to decide whether the issue ought to be raised and brought to the attention of, or forced on, those who are more immediately in charge of, or responsible for, the situation. As noted above, this kind of deliberation can often be best accomplished through conversation with others who can help think through the issue. Discussing the matter with someone whose judgment and discretion you trust can be crucial in reaching reasoned conclusions.

Assuming you conclude there is a significant ethical problem, what do you do about it? With whom do you raise the issue? This is where we come to the question of "whose problem is this?" The answer will depend on the organization, your position in the organization, and the specific nature of the problem. You should consider who you are comfortable approaching, lines of communication, and who is trustworthy. Where does the responsibility and authority for this matter rest? What responsible person is most likely to be open to considering the situation as ethically problematic? These are the kind of practical questions that must be addressed in order to turn your ethical perception into possible positive action.

Conclusion

Two final observations. First, if your group or organization is relatively informal, and if you are sufficiently comfortable and confident of your position in it, the final two steps of analysis and reflection with others might be accomplished within the group itself. If raising a half-baked idea is acceptable in this group, this more spontaneous and direct route may well be the better way to go. The more comfortable your group is with raising and considering moral questions, the less likely it is to have ethical problems. Second, modesty and tentativeness are often appropriate in raising ethical issues. The self-confidence I suggested earlier is something quite different from arrogance or self-righteousness. Being tentative about assertion and conclusions, speaking in terms of "possibilities" or "perhaps," and moderation in tone and substance, all may be helpful in being heard and understood.

With these questions of how and where to raise ethical issues we are moving toward another topic. Some observers think business executives have lost the ability to deliberate together about questions of right and wrong. Organizations should be concerned about that possibility, and should carefully consider how to address it. In this chapter, however, I have been primarily concerned with the moral vision which precedes that deliberation.

What I have tried to provide here is a little low-key advice about the day to day practice of ethics. Conscience we can understand as ordinary intuition about right and wrong. Pay attention to those intuitions; focus, don't dismiss. Courage can and should mean a lot more, of course, but for this process to work it calls for no more than self-confidence about what you see and feel. Finally, think straight and be clear. Don't fool yourself by finding some easy way to dismiss what may really be a problem. The candor required is simply the self-discipline to be honest with oneself. Conscience, candor and courage—moral intuition, honesty with yourself about that intuition, and self-confidence in regard to what you're seeing—are all close at hand and not so difficult, but they can make a big difference.

---

[1] The panel's topic was "Board Leadership: Courage, Candor, and Conscience," the title of a paper by the lead speaker, Roger Raber, then president of the National Association of Corporate Directors. See Stephen Pepper, "A Short Primer on Ethics and Moral Vision," 30 *Directors Monthly* 19 (July 2006), for an early and less developed version of the advice suggested in this chapter.

² John M. Doris, *Lack of Character* 32 (Cambridge University Press 2002), discussing the 1969 experiment by Latane and Darley.

³ This "hypothetical" was suggested by my colleague at the Daniels College of Business, James O'Toole, Daniels Distinguished Professor of Business Ethics.

⁴ All of these responses were evoked when this scenario was presented to a monthly meeting of a local chapter of the National Association of Corporate Directors in a state I won't identify. The assembled directors, asked to imagine themselves as members of the board, were extremely reluctant to characterize the situation as a moral or ethical problem. And, if it was an ethical problem, many were quite firm that it was not the board's problem.

CHAPTER 3

The Psychology of Ethics Education

by Sam Cassidy

*Morals excite passions, and produce or prevent actions. Reason of itself
is utterly impotent in this particular. The rules of morality, therefore, are
not conclusions of our reason.*

—David Hume

Too often we teach ethics to business students, law students, accountants, and other professionals as if it were a rational thought process. We give them a set of rules and then teach them how to apply those rules to different scenarios they are likely to encounter in their professional lives. It is my purpose here to highlight two critical shortcomings in this aspect of ethics education. Both require attention to extra-rational mental processes now largely ignored.

In business ethics education we are beginning to move beyond the rulebook approach. Instead, we are teaching students how to understand, critique, and even create ethical rules and standards of conduct through an independent, rational thought process. This is a step forward, because it equips tomorrow's professionals to create standards of conduct where none exist, or where the existing rules are inadequate, and teaches them to question the rules others make when such rules are unethical. It encourages them to set personal standards of conduct higher than the minimum required by laws or rules. Most importantly, it embraces the duty of independent judgment, which is the cornerstone of professionalism. Unfortunately, the world these students will enter does not always encourage independent responsibility for ethical conduct, and few will find the emotional resources required to persist in their independent ethical development and resolve. This is the first shortcoming with the current approach to teaching ethical conduct.

Second, it is difficult for professionals to act on rules, regardless of who makes them. When professionals try to practice ethical conduct, their failure rate is high. For example, businesspeople know it is wrong to trade on insider information, yet they may do it anyway. They also know it is wrong not to report it when their colleagues are acting dishonestly, yet they let it go.

In short, the rational mind knows what to do, but knowing and doing are two different things. The transition from knowing the ethical course of action to acting on that knowledge is not simply a rational process. It is also an emotional one, with subconscious roots that ethics teachers have yet to master and integrate into our discipline.

I will use the ancient debate (Heraclitus 540-480 BC) between the Positive Law and the Natural Law schools to illustrate how ethical decision-making is composed of a peculiar mixture of rational and emotional elements. The debate is essential to independent moral agency—a cornerstone of ethical training in which people are responsible for making their own moral judgments and acting in a moral manner. The issue is not limited to law, and applies just as well to business people, accountants, and other professionals exercising authority. This age-old conflict is rich with emotional content that is usually discussed in rational language, that is, as if emotion played no role.

Examples of Decision-Making

Below are three examples that illustrate the conflict between Positive Law and Natural Law. They are also examples of ethical dilemmas—that is, problems containing a conflict between two or more positive values, and successfully resolving such conflicts is the essence of both professionalism and making ethical decisions.

Example One: In 1879, the Connecticut legislature passed a law prohibiting the possession, distribution, or use of "any drug, medicinal article or instrument for the purpose of preventing conception."[1] The law was still on the books in the early 1960s when Estelle Griswold and Dr. C. Lee Buxtom of Yale Medical School opened a birth control clinic in New Haven, Connecticut. They were arrested, tried, and convicted of violating the statute. Their conviction was sustained on appeal, both in the Appellate Division of the Circuit Court and the Connecticut Supreme Court. They were clearly guilty of violating the law, but were their convictions "just" in terms of Natural Law? To answer this we must first decide whether a legislative body, elected by a majority, can act as the final arbitrator on moral conduct—for example, in this case, without accounting for the independent judgment of a married woman, her husband, and their physician concerning whether or not they want to conceive a child. The Positive Law, represented by the Connecticut statute, is clear. But is there more to consider?

Example Two: Consider an employer who adopts a wage policy that discriminates against older workers. The Age Discrimination in Employment Act, as created by Congress and interpreted by the courts, says the employer is perfectly within its rights to do that.[2] The employer's action follows all the *rules*—it is in accordance with Positive Law. But, is it *just*?

Example Three: Consider a chemical company that relocates its plant to a country with no emission standards. That is, there is no Positive Law restricting the company's discharge of poisonous emissions. The local residents are poor, have a short life expectancy, and the plant's emissions are a serious health hazard. Thus, without local regulation, the only factor restricting the company's conduct is its own sense of fairness.[3] Without a high sensitivity to Natural Law, or justice, the company will likely discharge waste directly into the community. Here, two values conflict: the company's duty to stockholders to maximize profit, and its duty to not harm neighbors.

These examples are all manifestations of the conflict between justice and order—or, what philosophers and jurists have debated for thousands of years, Natural Law vs. Positive Law. In practice, lawyers and jurists are professionally trained to focus on Positive Law.[4] MBA programs teach future business leaders that compliance with such law is essential. Beyond complying with the law, the core value which typically controls business decision-making when values conflict is *maximizing stockholder profit*, not *justice*. We train professionals to look to rules created not by themselves but by Congress, the boss, the necessities of a competitive marketplace, or some other authority, and to apply those rules to their professional practice for ethical guidance when they must decide right from wrong action.[5] Occasionally, we teach students how to abstract new rules of conduct or to question existing rules. However, we teach this only as a *rational* exercise.

But what if, unknown to our conscious mind, we actually make these decisions based on emotional instinct and then develop a rational argument to support that decision? Indeed, because people, in fact, make decisions before the rational process of justification, there is need for ethics education to search beyond the rational mind and to focus on the roles emotion and instinct play.

What Is Positive Law?

Positive Law offers an easy way to solve our dilemmas about ethical conduct. It contends that designated authorities should make all the rules so we don't need to exercise our own judgment: We can just follow theirs. Within a political community, elected representatives create the codes, statutes and regulations that make up Positive Law. In the United States, we give governmental entities such as Congress and state legislatures the sole authority to make such rules. Everyone in society, other than empowered governmental officials, must then obey. Thus, citizens give up their right to independently judge the ethical rules authorities create. The two advantages of having a few authority figures make the rules are order and efficiency: we know clearly what the law is at all times, regulate our conduct accordingly, and predict how others will act.

Similarly, the authority to develop rules is institutionalized in a business. A small business owner, or leader of a large corporation, has the power to make rules governing its employees, the quality and price of its products and, to a large extent, how the company interacts with the surrounding community. While government retains some authority in this area, business leaders have a great deal of discretion to make rules of conduct within their organizations. In large corporations, the authority to make rules is distributed among stockholders, boards of directors, officers, managers, and other designated employees. Power hierarchies define the rule-making function of each member of the organization, and while most business cultures encourage employees to use their own judgment rather than follow a detailed list of policies, ultimately, the power to make rules is reserved for those at the top. This is how companies address the tension between Positive Law and their employees' independent judgment when they attempt to make an ethical decision.

Advocates of Positive Law contend that order and predictability are the most important values in all situations; order requires a set of rules everyone must follow. Rules create predictability in human behavior, which is more important than justice. Advocates of Positive Law fear there would be no common standard of conduct if every individual were responsible for judging which rules are fair and which are not. Humans would do whatever they felt they could justify using their own subjective standards of conduct. Positive Law advocates do not trust people's personal sense of justice, because they generally view humans as competitive and self-interested by nature. Some exalt those instincts, reasoning that self-interest colors the average person's sense of fairness in any situation. Without rules, positive law advocates see only chaos—with human behavior rising barely above that of wild animals. For them, strict adherence to authority, without questioning the rules, creates the fabric of civilization and controls the beast within.

Seventeenth century English social philosopher Thomas Hobbes' *The Leviathan* portrays life as a nightmare in the absence of a central authority. He viewed human nature as self-serving: Without rules, individuals are the sole judge of their own standards of conduct, unconcerned about the good of society or others. In such a world, neither one's property nor one's life is safe. There are no restraints to stop one from acting on innate tendencies to rob and murder out of self-interest. Life under such circumstances is, "solitary, poor, nasty, brutish and short."[6]

Like Hobbes, advocates of Positive Law contend that laws—and an all-powerful enforcer of those laws—are necessary to control people, given their self-serving, egocentric nature. Advocates of Positive Law also argue any authority, just or unjust, is better than leaving people free to follow their conscience. Since individuals are incapable of controlling themselves, strict rules of conduct must come from an outside authority, such as a government, that enforces those rules. Adam Smith's theory of economics is built, in part, on this view of human nature:

> It is not from the benevolence of the butcher, the brewer, or the baker that we expect our dinner, but from their regard to their own interest.

We address ourselves, not to their humanity but to their self-love, and
never talk to them of our own necessities but of their advantages.[7]

Much of the debate over economic policy in this country today can be viewed
as a debate over whether business leaders can regulate themselves—or whether a government, or "Leviathan," is needed to stop them from violating rules of
conduct intended to benefit everybody in the marketplace. Many experts contend the Great Depression, and America's current economic meltdown, were
the result of unregulated self-interest at work in the marketplace. This view
is the cornerstone of the perceived need for some authority to develop and
enforce rules literally and uniformly to avoid chaos and ensure that groups act
efficiently. Such a view of human nature has a large psychological component.
Self-interest, I will argue, is more emotional than rational.

The rigid lines of authority once found in the European feudal system is an
extreme example of a Positive Law system. Three percent of the population—
the monarch, aristocracy, and church officials—wielded all decision-making
authority. The rules created by those in power were not to be questioned by
the people. Enforcement was brutal, and a person's conscience was useless
and subject to the atrophy of non-use. Today, political authority, specifically
the power to make rules within a business, is more widely dispersed than in
feudal times. Those in a position of authority use the underlying core value
of order to justify the uniform enforcement of their rules. Philosopher John
Locke's "majority rule" has replaced divine authority of the nobility and
clergy, but the authority of Positive Law is still sacred in some circles. Good
and bad laws alike must be enforced. If a law is bad, or unjust, it must still
be enforced until it is changed. If Congress enacts an unjust law, the courts
must strictly enforce it. A judge thus must leave personal conscience at home
and do injustice until Congress sees fit to change the law. If a judge wants to
produce justice in a particular case, and follows personal conscience by inter-
preting a statute narrowly or the Constitution differently, that judge will likely
be accused of "legislating from the bench," implying the judge is wielding
inappropriate power.

In some businesses, if the CEO creates a policy that harms customers, employees will follow it. Employees are not free to interject their own conscience
or judgment, regardless of the damage their obedience causes. As customers,
we experience this when an employee tells us, "I'm sorry. That's our policy
and I don't make the rules." Among managers, responsibility for a bad policy
is often passed up the corporate ladder to the CEO or board of directors. That
way, managers can wash their hands of any responsibility for the unfair, or un-
foreseen, results that a bad policy or rule produce. Nonetheless, there is order,
predictability, and submission to authority; for many, a little injustice here or
there is a small price to pay for such efficiency.

In sum, Positive Law—be it laws enacted by a government, rules created
within a corporation, or codes of professional conduct—promises order and

efficiency by withdrawing decision making discretion from lower levels. But is a society's preference for order, or a corporation's adherence to efficiency, a rationally based preference, or does it have an emotional component?

What Is Natural Law?

Natural Law advocates are willing to question authority and rules. They believe all individuals are capable of, responsible for, and required to participate in, the making of important decisions about their own actions. In other words, people are able to decide right from wrong. Enlightenment thinkers believed the right to make law flows from the people, or the governed, not the governors. They believed all individuals have an equal capacity to know justice. The American Declaration of Independence and French Declaration of the Rights of Man are predicated on a view of human nature that is incompatible with blind allegiance to authority. This view of humans as independent moral agents requires individuals to use their own judgment—even after elected authorities make the rules—because majorities can be guilty of tyranny.

Historian Bernard Bailyn's *The Ideological Origins of the American Revolution* says of the central philosophy of the American Revolution: "faith ran high that a better world than any that had ever been known could be built where authority was distrusted and held in constant scrutiny." Thus, our democracy was conceived on the belief that individuals could rise above self-interest to act justly with the welfare of society as their guiding principle.

Natural Law advocates generally are more optimistic about human potential than Positive Law thinkers, believing human nature can be developed to overcome self-interest, and people can act in the interest of the collective good. Each of us can recognize justice in a particular situation, and can act on it in ways that are much more likely to produce just outcomes, as opposed to when we obey stagnant, inflexible laws or rules created by a remote authority.

It is important to note this human ability is a *potential*, not a reality. Natural Law advocates recognize self-interested passions may control how humans make decisions. They also recognize this untrained, misdirected instinct can be changed through contemplation, education, and a culture of individual responsibility—to the point when it becomes a habit on which society can rely. Natural Law dictates humans are independent moral agents given the right *and* the responsibility to question authority when necessary to assure that injustice is not perpetrated against others. Such individuals are capable of controlling themselves and making ethical judgments without constant micromanagement from an outside authority.

All this suggests six basic principles of Natural Law:

> *1. A higher law exists above man-made law.* Kings, legislators,
> and bosses often make unjust laws that do not take into ac-
> count all the potential circumstances in which the rules will

be enforced. We must acknowledge there is a higher law more deeply rooted in the human psyche, more farsighted than man-made law, universally recognized as proven and unchangeable.[8]

2. *People can discover such a higher law.* Each one of us can discover this law inside ourselves through effort, study, and thought. It is in all people as a self-evident truth of the human condition. The moral precept requiring all to do unto others as we would have them do unto us is an example of such a basic human truth.

3. *This higher law is universal and reversible.* Natural principles of justice and standards of conduct are universally recognized and applied. They provide a consistent guide for our actions no matter the situation, the geography, or the culture. These principles are reversible. If we change places with another person we find the same principle applies equally—regardless of our standing.

4. *Humans can be relied upon to act on principles of Natural Law, without being forced.* People learn what justice is, regardless of whether it is innate or learned through education. These principles become habitual through practice.

5. *All people must act in accordance with Natural Law.* It is not enough to know what justice is, individuals are bound to act in accordance with those higher principles. Each of us is held personally accountable for our own violations of Natural Law when we act, or do not act, in a particular situation.

6. *Humans are emotionally compelled to act on their own instincts about Natural Law.* This principle is discussed below.

The Emotional Aspects of Human Decision-Making

When teaching ethics, we often try to apply logic when looking at the way people make decisions. In doing so, we miss something because human thought is not always entirely rational. People are also emotional decision makers, as Daniel Goleman observes:

> A view of human nature that ignores the power of emotions is sadly shortsighted. The very name *Homo sapiens*, the thinking species, is

misleading in light of the new appreciation and vision of the place of emotions in our lives that science now offers. As we all know from experience, when it comes to shaping our decisions and our actions, feeling counts every bit as much, and often more, than thought.[9]

Proponents of both Positive and Natural Law point to powerful emotional factors that drive how people make decisions. For Positive Law advocates, self-interest is the emotional driver (it is in one's self-interest to obey the law rather than suffer the consequences). For Natural Law proponents, the emotional driver is empathy (an injustice inflicted on a fellow citizen is intolerable because we can identify with that citizen). Aristotle recognized the ongoing struggle between emotion and reason in all of us, arguing that we thus need to develop moral character so we can control and direct our most powerful emotions. Advocates of Positive Law view self-interest as central to human nature; advocates of Natural Law view people as interested in the welfare of all members of their community and able to control egotistical tendencies. Human nature is central to the disagreement between the Positive Law and Natural Law factions. Is self-interest logical, or is it emotional? Once we accept a theory as fact (self-interest generally is accepted as a fact of life), we tend to assume its rationality. But just how rational is self-interest? I posit that the idea that my own self-interest is more important than the self-interest of anyone else is illogical. I am just one person out of more than 6.5 billion others on the planet. My very survival depends on the health and well being of countless others. Hence, there is little logic or rational basis for my self-interest. Still, I am very likely to choose self-interest over community benefit when deciding between the two despite the fact tragedy often results for the community as a whole when everyone chooses self-interest. Ironically, communal tragedy goes against my own self-interest in the long run. In sum, choosing to act self-interestedly often is not a product of the rational mind, but likely emotional and rooted in the subconscious.

Scottish philosopher Thomas Reid describes this strong emotional instinct as, "a natural impulse to certain actions, without deliberation and without any conception of what we do."[10] Carl Jung added to this characterization by noting:

> Instinctive action is characterized by an unconsciousness of the psychological motive behind it; in contrast to the strictly conscious processes… instinctive action appears to be a more or less abrupt psychic occurrence, a sort of interruption of the continuity of consciousness. On this account, it is felt as an inner necessity…[11]

The power and force of this urge sets us apart from other animals. As Charles Darwin noted:

> Of all the differences between man and the lower animals, the moral sense or conscience is by far the most important […] It is summed up in

that short but imperious word ought, so full of high significance. It is the most noble of all the attributes of man, leading him without a moment's hesitation to risk his life for that of a fellow-creature; or after due deliberation, impelled simply by the deep feeling of right or duty, to sacrifice it in some great cause.[12]

Much as self-interest emerges from the subconscious as a powerful instinct which can overwhelm logical thought processes, Natural Law advocates point to such equally powerful instincts as justice, equality, and liberty which have sustained revolutionary fervor, overthrown monarchs and dictators, and motivated humans to make great personal, sometimes irrational, sacrifice. History is full of examples of individual sacrifice for Natural Law ideals. In the ultimate act of sacrificing one's life itself, such as in times of war, instinctive group values have the power to overwhelm even the instinct of self-interest. Adam Smith, in *The Theory of Moral Sentiments*, said of man and human nature:

> There are evidently some principles in his nature, which interest him in the fortunes of others, and render their happiness necessary to him, though he derives nothing from it, except the pleasure of seeing it. ... Nature, which formed men for that mutual kindness so necessary for their happiness, renders every man the peculiar object of kindness.[13]

That is a far cry from *homo economicus*, the self-serving human being described in Smith's *Wealth of Nations*.

If self-interest, justice, trust, and liberty all carry a powerful emotional component, any discipline that aims to influence human nature or decision-making—in politics, law, business management, leadership, and especially ethics—must start with a thorough understanding of the logical and emotional sides of human behavior. The central question becomes: How do emotional impulses and logical thought processes influence how people make decisions? There would be little need for an external rule-maker, or enforcer, if humans were logical in all of their actions and decisions. We all would logically come to the same conclusions and act alike. But passions also drive people. These passions fuel creativity and provide energy, ambition, and the focus necessary to self-improvement. Marc Hauser, a Harvard professor of psychology, noted:

> We should be looking at our moral psychology as an instinct [...] that unconsciously [...] generates judgments of right and wrong, and [...] why some situations tempt us to sin in the face of sensibility handed down from law, religion, and education [...] and leave us dumbfounded because the guiding principles are inaccessible, tucked away in the mind's library of unconscious knowledge.[14]

The emotional component cannot be ignored because it connects recognition to action. In all regulation of human behavior, whether on an individual or group level, there are core values or subconscious patterns that must be understood and factored into any attempt to influence behavior. Among these emotional values are: justice, liberty and the deep need to belong.

Justice as a Compelling Emotional Need

When I refer to *justice*, I mean the way both benefits and burdens are distributed among a group of people. The group may be a nation, or a business. Benefits might include wealth, power, opportunity, rewards, and fame. Burdens might include taxes and work. Does everyone get what they deserve when both the benefits and burdens are handed out? If so, this is a state of justice. One method of distribution is competition: let the strongest get all they can get. By contrast, cooperation requires putting the welfare of the group above that of any individual. It requires a social contract in which everyone agrees that the distribution of benefits and burdens is fair.

Competition and cooperation—self-interest and community interest—are two of the most powerful motivators in the business world. If Positive Law theorists are correct about human nature, when we study people experimentally, we should find that the vast majority of them are self-interested. If Natural Law proponents are correct, we should find that the interests of the group are predominant. In fact, recent research by Gintis, Bowles, Boyd and Fehr finds that human nature is a mix of four distinct character types.[15] The first is driven to compete with one another for material advantage. Their dominant motivation is self-interest. It is important to point out this is *not* the largest group, and certainly does not represent the majority. The second group is driven by the instinct to cooperate. People predisposed to cooperate are more concerned about the benefit of the whole than personal gain when they make decisions. This is a controlling instinct for a significant number of humans, but again, it is *not* the dominant instinct. The third, and smallest, group showed a predisposition to spite and envy. Finally, the largest group is what the authors called "reciprocators for whom *justice* seems to be the driving concern at first glance." This group begins by acting in the interests of the group, which looks like cooperation, but these reciprocators quickly adapt to (reciprocate) the sentiments of other players, responding in the same way they are treated. If they confront others making decisions out of self-interest, reciprocators respond the same way; if others cooperate, reciprocators respond with cooperation.

In one of hundreds of experiments corroborating these conclusions, subjects were divided into three groups for an experimental game. Each group was given $20 and asked to decide in each round of the game to contribute some portion of their money to a common account, keeping the rest for themselves. At the end of each round, the experimenter would announce how much was contributed to the common account, and what portion would be equally distributed to each group. At the end of ten rounds, the common account was again divided equally between the teams and the money was theirs to keep. If self-interest were the driving force, every team would have contributed nothing to the common account, preserving their own money while still sharing in the distributive benefits of other contributions. The results from numerous studies found that, in the early rounds, 40 to 60 percent of the private accounts were contributed to the common account, which represented a stunning act of cooperation. In later rounds, 73 percent contributed nothing. When asked about the drop in cooperation, subjects reported they would cooperate as long as the other players did so. If others acted out of self-interest, they would punish the behavior by acting selfishly in return. What they wanted was justice.

In one variation of the experiment, players were given the chance to punish others by imposing a fine on those who did not cooperate. There was a catch: players had to pay from their own account to impose the fine, which some did. Since no self-serving participant would pay to punish another selfish player (because they would lose money), the results demonstrated players were engaged in a form of justice based on retribution.

Even in experiments tied to wages and motivation, incentives are found to be less important than a sense of fairness, or justice, among workers. In games in which participants role-played employers and employees, the relationship between productivity and pay revealed that a raise in pay did not produce higher productivity. Instead, employee productivity was tied more directly to the desire for fair treatment. When employees felt their wages were set unjustly there were drops in productivity. As Nowak and Sigmund note, "The fiction of a rational *homo economicus* relentlessly optimizing material utility is giving way to bounded rational decision-makers governed by instincts and emotions [...] *homo reciprocans*."[16]

These are not just theories. Business Professor Edward Lawler cites empirical evidence that perception of fairness in setting pay in companies is critical to gaining high performance from employees. On the flip side, Lawler notes when CEO pay soars out of proportion to their job performance they, "in essence, are put in the position of appearing to be self-serving individuals who are simply getting what they can from the organization. This undermines their moral authority to lead and very much limits their ability to talk about common vision and direction for the organization."[17]

Some people behave selfishly, and some altruistically, but the largest number is concerned with justice, or equity, in their interactions with others. Importantly, the instinct for self-interest is not controlled by a rational thought process that looks far ahead to see a selfish payback, but rather by a deeply rooted passion: justice.

Brain imaging has been used to track the areas of the brain activated by different thought processes, allowing researchers to see whether a particular brain activity is rational or emotional. Using these techniques, subjects were observed playing the games described above, and researchers discovered, through CT scans of the brain, significant activation of the *anterior insula*, a part of the brain known to play a role in negative emotions. This indicates that sensitivity to injustice is more emotional than rational.

Liberty as a Compelling Emotional Need

Individuals often are caught between the dictates of authority and their own passion for justice. Suppose we lived in Atlanta in 1859 when it was illegal to help slaves escape captivity; suppose further we felt this is an unjust law. In that situation, we must decide whether to obey authority (Positive Law) or our instinct for justice (Natural Law). In other words: should one act according to conscience, or defer to the legislative body that created the law?

Our answer will depend on the level of our moral development. The highly regarded theories of American psychologist Lawrence Kohlberg place a person's ability to determine ethical duties, or Natural Law, at the top of the developmental ladder. Kohlberg places adherence to Positive Law in the middle. He begins by dividing moral development into three broad categories. The lowest level of ethical development is labeled *pre-conventional*. Here, all choices are made on the basis of selfish interest. The pre-conventional thinker asks: "Will this action benefit me, or is it necessary to avoid punishment?" The interests of others are irrelevant. The core value, which trumps everything and guides all decisions, is self-interest (examples include a 3-year-old child whose decisions are calculated to maximize pleasure and avoid pain, and a CEO inflating the value of company stock with bad financial information while selling his or her own shares at a profit).

Moving up the ladder of moral development, Kohlberg identifies a middle category he calls *conventional*. Kohlberg believes such decisions are based on the basis of the law and peer group pressure. The core value here is order. Conventional people believe order derives from obeying rules set by authorities. Unquestioning obedience to law and corporate policy is the standard for such behavior. It is the lawmakers who define morality. Such conventional thinkers are often viewed as "good team players," because the opinion of their peers is of paramount importance. Kohlberg says the vast majority of us stop our upward progress at this stage.

Kohlberg calls the highest stage of development *post-conventional*. Here, people exercise their own judgment about morality. They might ask whether a law was adopted through a fair process before deciding whether to obey it or, even higher on Kohlberg's scale, they may ask whether the law is in harmony with Natural Law. If not, these people will choose to disobey the law. The post-conventional thinker might be willing to quit a job rather than obey an unethical order.

Liberty, the freedom of individuals to act on their own judgment about ethical matters, lies at the root of the ethical tradition. Aristotle taught that to know virtue is not nearly as difficult as acting virtuously, and the only way to act virtuously is through practice. Aristotle believed that to convert theory into action required repetition: a person must think and act ethically until it becomes instinctive. Thus, a person gains no practice thinking about ethical issues if he or she always looks to some other authority for answers. Following Aristotle, Thomas Aquinas concluded that no decision is an ethical one unless it is the result of free will. Good character is based on regular choices tied to appropriate principles, and a wise person will find such principles obvious after sifting through and analyzing all relevant data.

Many philosophers have vigorously encouraged professionals to make independent judgments and to exercise their liberty (and responsibility) as independent moral agents. Justice Benjamin Cardozo said:

> As lawyers and legal scholars we can become very absorbed in the mechanics of legal reasoning, rationally connecting statutes and cases to determine the outcome of each individual case. Over time, we come to think so highly of the rational legal process that we come to believe it for its own sake, the sanctity of the law on which our orderly society depends. Judges march at times to pitiless conclusions under the prod of a remorseless logic which is supposed to leave them no alternative. They deplore the sacrificial rite. They perform it, nonetheless, with averted gaze, convinced as they plunge the knife that they obey the bidding of their office. The victim is offered up to the gods of jurisprudence on the altar of regularity.[18]

But those who watch the knife plunge are deeply offended, and they lose respect for the judge and the institution that would deprive them of the liberty of making their own moral judgments and of acting morally.

The Emotional Need To Belong

The need to belong is among the most powerful emotional needs. Kohlberg alludes to this in his descriptions of conventional development, where peer opinion and fitting-in with society's rules and conventions are a top priority. He finds this level of human development to be the most prevalent in our culture. However, the deep desire to have a seat at the table and be respected among peers is a two-edged sword: it encourages cooperation, team building, and order, but it can unleash dangerous "group think." In the words of novelist and lay theologian C.S. Lewis:

> I believe that in all men's lives at certain periods and in many men's lives at all periods between infancy and extreme old age, one of the

most dominant elements is the desire to be inside the local ring and
the terror of being left outside. ...Of all the passions the passion for
the Inner Ring is most skilful in making a man who is not yet a very
bad man do very bad things.[19]

At Nuremberg following World War II, the Allies brought Nazi war criminals
to trial arguing that individuals cannot hide behind Positive Law to escape
punishment for violating Natural Law. War criminals included Nazi judges
who followed German laws when making judgments from the bench. Per-
tinently, Nazi war criminals were not guilty of violating German law when
they persecuted and exterminated Jews. Instead, American judges sat in judgment over Germans accused of enforcing unjust, but legally made, German
laws. That is, Nazi citizens were prosecuted for horrible acts they committed
while carrying out the mandates of laws enacted through a legal process in
a sovereign country. The German people's conformity to official policy has
been attributed to this powerful emotion: the need to belong. In his book, *The
Lucifer Effect*, psychologist Philip Zimbardo reviews countless psychological
experiments and field data, including Nazi-era cruelty, the Mei Li Massacre
in Vietnam, and Iraq's Abu Ghraib prison. Zimbardo traces the cause to the
need to belong: "other people are more likely to accept us when we agree with
them than when we disagree, so we yield to their view of the world, driven by
a powerful need to belong."[20]

Conclusion

As Harvard's Marc Hauser writes, "Bottom Line: Reasoning and emotion
both play a role in our moral behavior, but neither [logic nor emotion alone]
can do complete justice to the process leading up to moral judgment."[21]
Hence, I conclude that when we ignore peoples' core ethical values we agi-
tate an emotional bomb. When we violate those core values that bomb may
explode.

In this paper I have discussed four such core values which seem to have
subconscious roots and produce powerful emotional instincts: self-interest,
justice and reciprocity, liberty, and the need to belong. Leaders of legal and
business institutions who challenge such deeply held values can damage not
only themselves but also the institutions they represent. Leaders thus must
understand human motivations on both ethical *and* emotional levels if they
expect to attract and maintain followers. The rational mind can recognize
deeply seated emotional instincts, and can distinguish instincts that are useful versus those that can be destructive. The rational mind also can reinforce
these useful instincts and try to rein in destructive ones. But the rational mind
is overmatched. If we are to have any success in ethics training, we must understand and respect the influence of subconscious emotion and the interaction
between the rational and the emotional. It is one thing for students to be able

to explain how Kant would resolve a particular ethical dilemma—because students are able to do this exercise without dealing with emotion—but it is when the students try to *act* on Kant's advice that the conflict between the rational and the emotional comes to life.

---

[1] Griswold v. Connecticut, 381 U.S. 479 (1965).

[2] Smith v. City of Jackson, Miss., 544 U.S. 228 (2005).

[3] Lawrence Summers, "Let Them Eat Pollution," *The Economist*, Feb. 8, 1992, p. 66.

[4] Robert Grandfield, "Do Law Students Abandon Their Ideals? The Crisis in the Age of Affluence," *Legal Studies Forum*, Vol. XVIII (1994), p. 53.

[5] Marc D. Hauser, *Moral Minds: How Nature Designed Our Universal Sense of Right and Wrong* (New York: HarperCollins, 2006), p. 2.

[6] Thomas Hobbes, *The Leviathan*, as reprinted in *The English Philosophers From Bacon to Mill*, Edwin A. Burtt, ed. (New York: Random House, 1939), p. 161.

[7] Adam Smith, *The Wealth of Nations* (Amherst, NY: Prometheus Books, 1991), p. 20.

[8] Ethel M. Albert, Theodore C. Denise, and Sheldon P. Peterfreund, *Great Traditions in Ethics* 6th Ed. (Wadsworth Publishing), p. 110.

[9] Daniel Goleman, *Emotional Intelligence: Why it can Matter More than IQ* (New York: Bantam Books, 1995), p. 4.

[10] Thomas Reid, *Essays on the Active Powers of Man* (Edinburgh: John Bell, 1788), p. 103.

[11] Carl G. Jung, *The Portable Jung*, Joseph Campbell, ed. (New York: Viking Penguin, 1971), pp. 48-49.

[12] Charles Darwin, *Descent of Man* (Sioux Falls, S.D.: NuVision Publications), p. 95.

[13] Adam Smith, *The Theory of Moral Sentiments* (Edinburgh, 1759), p. 1.

[14] Hauser, *Moral Minds*, supra note 5, p. 2.

[15] Herbert Gintis, Samuel Bowles, Robert Boyd and Ernst Fehr, eds., *Moral Sentiments and Material Interests: The Foundations of Cooperation in Economic Life* (Cambridge: MIT Press, 2005), pp. 151-191.

[16] Martin A. Nowak and Karl Sigmund, "Enhanced: Shrewd investments," *Science*, vol. 288, p. 819.

[17] Edward E. Lawler, *Rewarding Excellence: Pay Strategies for the New Economy* (San Francisco: Josey-Bass, 2000), p. 283.

[18] Benjamin Cardozo, *The Growth of Law* (New Haven: Yale University Press, 1924), p. 66.

[19] C.S. Lewis, "The Inner Ring," Memorial Lecture at King's College, University of London (1944)

[20] Philip Zimbardo, *The Lucifer Effect* (New York: Random House, 2007), p. 262.

[21] Hauser, *Moral Minds*, supra note 5, p. 11.

CHAPTER

In Search of Enlightened Business Leaders

by Cynthia V. Fukami

The growth of graduate business education in the U.S. over the last fifty years has been a mixed blessing. Enormous amounts of resources have been devoted to researching effective business practices, and countless students from around the world have come to American business schools to become versed in those practices. On the other hand, the dramatic growth of business schools also has invited a great deal of scrutiny and, as a result, much criticism has been leveled at the work done within their hallowed halls. Much of that criticism is well deserved. On a seemingly daily basis, we are bombarded with examples of a lack of wisdom from senior corporate leaders. From WorldCom to A.I.G., we see the aftermath of smart people making poor decisions. On a less dramatic stage, examples of bad business management also abound: in company after company, performance reviews are not conducted regularly and, when they are, they often de-motivate and demoralize the employees who receive them; business leaders seeking to reduce headcount fire long-standing employees and then give them the "opportunity" to apply for the remaining, and fewer, jobs; rather than rewarding customer service representatives for fixing customers' problems, business leaders reward those employees for selling customers more flawed services. The great comic strip "Dilbert," the popular television situation comedy, "The Office," and the independent movie, "Office Space," suggest that satirizing bad management attracts a big audience. It would appear that effective management is the exception in today's world, not the rule.

Business professors have been working diligently to develop better managers for decades. While we used to consider some management techniques as "soft" and "fuzzy," we now have a large and impressive body of evidence that certain of those practices, usually termed "high commitment," lead to better bottom-line performance for companies. Business-school coursework now places considerable emphasis on delivering these practices. For example, the mission of the Daniels College of Business is, in part, "to develop enlightened practitioners," reinforcing our recognition of the importance of effective leadership, and a review of the mission statements of other top business schools shows we are not alone in pursuing this goal. In short, today's business-school graduates ought to know how to be effective leaders; yet, once hired, they persist in ineffective courses of action. Among other things, this suggests that, while we professors might be effective in filling our students' heads with knowledge, facts, and data, we are much less effective in developing graduates who use this knowledge wisely and ethically in practice. Hence, along with being concerned with *what* we teach, perhaps we should be equally concerned with *how* we teach in business schools.

I believe that developing enlightened leaders who can link theory and practice begins with their having professors who are willing and able to act more as educators and less as professors, and who use teaching methods that support enlightened practice. In this chapter, I start by exploring the gap between management theory and practice, suggesting that ancient Greek musings on wisdom may provide a useful framework for closing this gap. Next, I explore the barriers we face in our efforts to develop enlightened, or "wise," business leaders in our classrooms and, finally, I offer suggestions on best practices for developing wise leaders for the future benefit of organizations.

The Gap between Knowing and Doing

In our current educational systems, excellence is often defined as intellectual performance.[1] Knowledge is a quantity of data to be possessed, and the professor is the means to obtaining that data. Our classrooms thus become places where professors dispense knowledge and students soak it up—to varying degrees on both sides. The student's performance in the class is evaluated on the basis of how much of this knowledge can be recalled in short run, 10-16 week assignments, and the professor's teaching performance is evaluated, at least in part, by how effectively she or he has conveyed this knowledge. What to do with this knowledge, however, is often left out of the picture. A symptom of this situation is captured by the comment sometimes heard from those who employ our graduates that *they know a lot but can't do anything.* Perhaps as a result, many excellent companies, such as Southwest Airlines, don't recruit at leading business schools, and don't show a preference for hiring MBAs.[2]

In an eye-opening essay, Stanford Professor Jeffrey Pfeffer and his research associate Christina Fong reveal that (a) there has been little assessment of the impact of business schools on either their graduates or on the profession of management, (b) what assessments do exist suggest that business schools are not particularly effective, and (c) there is little evidence that business schools have influenced management practice.[3] Others have reported similar findings. One such study reported that 73 percent of the MBA graduates surveyed indicated that they made little use of what they had learned in the classroom on their first assignments as managers.[4] Putting those findings in perspective, students must earn a minimum grade point average in order to graduate from b-school, implying that they have gained a "passing" level of knowledge. Yet, the results cited above imply that those students are unable, or unwilling, to put their knowledge into practice.

The concept of wisdom may be useful in addressing this gap between what is taught and what is practiced. Wisdom is commonly defined as "knowledge of what is true or right coupled with just judgment as to action," and implies the integration and transformation of knowledge as it is interpreted and applied appropriately within a context.[5] The difference between knowledge and wisdom, then, is that wisdom embodies and transforms knowledge into human experience[6]—as such, the application of wisdom may be said to close the gap between knowing and doing.[7]

Wisdom has been the goal of learning since the ancient Greeks first coined the term and linked it with knowledge. Over the years, we have come to associate wisdom with strong judgment, and being as prudent or astute as King Solomon.[8] Aristotle posited that there were three kinds of knowledge associated with wisdom.[9] The first is *episteme*, theoretical knowledge, or what is typically dispensed in the classroom. Episteme in a business course would include, for example, the theory of market behavior: supply intersects with demand to determine price. The second kind of knowledge is *techne*, the knowledge of making, which is the knowledge a craftsperson has. Techne in a business course would include writing programming code. The third kind of knowledge is *phronesis*, or what is thought of as "practical wisdom," the ability to interpret and adapt knowledge to a particular context, situation, or problem. An example of phronesis in a business course is investigating a performance problem and determining a course of action to address it. In addition, Aristotle introduced the concept of "virtue ethics" to indicate that intellectual virtues and practical virtues are applied *in a context*. In other words, practical wisdom can be thought of as the ability to link the other two forms of wisdom—knowledge and practice.

In this vein, some interesting research has indicated that "situation recognition" is a key difference between expert and novice leaders.[10] Virtuoso leaders recognize when rules apply, which rules to select, and when to discard or reform rules based on emergent circumstances.[11] In studies of practitioners in action, MIT's Donald Schön has found that effective problem solvers are adaptable, and have developed "honed intuition" based on practice.[12] And many scholars argue that learning is a continuous process grounded in, and tested by, experience. Thus, the mere possession of a quantity of knowledge does not create a leader who makes good judgments. Yet, in higher education, in general, and in business schools, in particular, the professoriate has focused on disseminating information and knowledge and neglected the development of wisdom. Following are a number of possible explanations for why this neglect may have occurred.

The (Low) Status of Teaching

A primary cause of the neglect of wisdom in education may be traced to the overall sense that teaching is not scholarly work, but rather the price professors must pay in order to do their "real work": research. As others have noted, this belief is symbolically conveyed in our language about teaching. For example, professors can be heard to comment about their heavy teaching "loads"[13] and, when fortunate, professors are granted "release" time. The inference is obvious—teaching is a burden to bear, and certainly not the road to glory.

As Steven Kerr noted many years ago in his classic article, "On the Folly of Rewarding A While Hoping for B," the typical university "...*hopes* that professors will not neglect their teaching responsibilities but *rewards* them almost entirely for research and publications."[14] This hope is often played out in what universities tell prospective students and their parents—that teaching matters at their institutions. But an examination of university performance and reward systems would likely reveal the opposite, specifically, that there are few significant benefits to professors who excel in teaching. Ironically, I know of at least one institution where the "reward" given to the annual "best teacher" is a year of "release" time from teaching!

Like everyone, professors are faced with allocating scarce time between teaching, research, and other obligations. Since rewards for good teaching and, conversely, punishments for poor teaching, are rare, it follows that professors would place a lower priority on teaching. Alternatively, rewards for research and punishments for failure to publish, are common in the academy. As Kerr concludes, "...it is rational for university professors to concentrate on research, even to the detriment of teaching and at the expense of their students."[15]

Focus on Teaching not Learning

Perhaps related to the lack of status accorded to teaching, there also has been more attention paid to "teaching" students than to their "learning." The difference between the two is one key to the neglect of enlightened leadership. The "teaching" model reminds me of a (very) old film I used to show on effective communication. The film depicted a model of communication called "the conveyor belt." In the conveyor belt model, one person would pluck out an idea from her or his head and deliver it into the head of the next person. This was essentially a one-way model which assumed that the sender had encoded the message appropriately, that there was no noise in the surrounding area, and that the receiver had decoded the message exactly as the sender had intended it. As most of us know, this is a wildly unrealistic model of communication. The parallel here is that many of us teach using this one-way model: we assume we are the font of all knowledge, and that our students are sponges who soak it up. Of course, we assume that they "get it," and that we have conveyed it in a way that assures their understanding, much like on the conveyor belt. In addition, this model puts all the emphasis on the teacher in the learning process. The professor is the only agent who matters in the traditional classroom and, thus, takes patriarchal control of the learning process.[16] Ironically, the Latin derivation for the word "educator" is "educa," which means "to draw forth from within." The original teaching method of Socrates of drawing from within has been largely displaced by "professing," from the Medieval Latin "professus" which means "to avow." Students are taught what the professor knows, but not how to think, write, or find their own paths.

Educators attempting to develop wise students cannot ignore the need for students to develop a deep understanding of the concepts they are attempting to convey. Knowledge is made explicit by practice, as it both sharpens understanding and clarifies misunderstanding. Like Aristotle's notion of phronesis, deep understanding requires the ability to link knowledge with action within a set of limitations and opportunities. Simply put, there is much room for improvement in student understanding, and a need to focus on students and their learning, rather than on professors and their teaching.

The Harvard-Smithsonian Center for Astrophysics, in conjunction with the Annenberg School of Communication at the University of Pennsylvania, has produced a thought-provoking video called "A Private Universe," which demonstrates this point.[17] The video begins with a group of students and professors at Harvard's commencement exercises being quizzed about a basic concept of astronomy: Why are there seasons of the year? Virtually all the graduates interviewed failed to answer the question correctly. The scene then shifts to a high school classroom where a teacher experiences great difficulty in getting bright students to move beyond their misconceptions and myths about the planets and the sun in order to gain more accurate understanding of astronomical concepts. Instead, students rely on their "private universe" of knowledge—what they already believe they know. This video reminds us that professors need to consider what is happening in the minds of our students, and to focus on their learning, not just our teaching.

Focus on Quantity not Quality

A related issue is the emphasis on the quantity of knowledge conveyed, rather than the quality with which students learn new concepts. How much knowledge is disseminated in a term? How many pounds are on a conveyor belts? How much depth is sacrificed in order to gain breadth? When I was a new Pew Scholar in the Carnegie Foundation's Academy for the Scholarship of Teaching and Learning, I met a fellow scholar who taught a course on Shakespeare. He lamented the fact that he could only teach five plays in a ten-week quarter. At the end of our two-year tenure as Pew Scholars, he was down to teaching three, and happier with the results. Rather than quickly memorizing facts that were just as easily forgotten after the class moved to the next play, his students now were able to gain a deeper understanding of fewer works.

He assessed this change by staying in contact with his students after the term was over, and having them complete surveys about what they had learned the previous quarter. The results indicated that students had retained more understanding of the plays after the end of the term when they had studied fewer rather than more plays. I have observed this same phenomenon in my own classes. I used to struggle to get at least six different theories of motivation on the table. Then, I would assess "learning" by having students compare and contrast the different theories. Although I never conducted a formal assessment, I am much more satisfied by the learning I observe by covering fewer theories and spending more class time reflecting on how motivation can be managed. Perhaps if we concentrated more on depth of understanding, and less on the number of concepts covered, business professors could deepen our students' phronesis.

Competitive Classrooms

A climate of competitiveness in the classroom is also a barrier to developing enlightened leadership. Stanford's Jeffrey Pfeffer and Bob Sutton argue "trying new things means having the confidence to learn from mistakes, and this requires driving fear out of organizations."[18] Unfortunately, a competitive classroom environment can breed fear, and thus dampen the willingness of students to take chances. A competitive classroom environment is potentially caused by several factors: grading for participation, emphasizing brutal criticism, and teaching practices that encourage competition.

One of the ways we introduce competition is by basing a substantial part of students' grades on how much they say, and how smart they sound, in class.[19] To be sure, there are valid reasons for grading students on class participation. Participation develops the skill of thinking on one's feet, expressing oneself effectively, and rewards those who prepare in advance of class. On the other hand, students may learn that they need to "sound smart" in order to gain a good grade from their professors, and to earn the respect of their peers.[20]

In addition, and perhaps more unfortunately, students learn early on in their higher education experiences that they can earn "points" in the classroom by criticizing others, sometimes quite brutally. This may be because, as part of their doctoral training, professors have been rewarded for being critical. Indeed, undergoing callous criticism is a central aspect of too many doctoral programs. Of course, to be critical, in and of itself, is not a problem. There are good outcomes to be gained from being critical and being free to express criticism. The problem is the fear that is generated in the process. A competitive classroom climate may inhibit the asking of questions that might expose a student to criticism. If students are afraid to make a mistake, or to express a controversial opinion, either because they will lose participation points or because they will suffer the pain of peer disapproval, then they will be less likely to link theory and practice and, thus, fail to develop practical wisdom.

A final way competition in the classroom is encouraged is to discourage collaboration. In general, collaboration has not been cultivated in traditional classrooms; in fact, professors typically have called collaboration "cheating."[21] That's why they have traditionally used individual, and not team, assignments. Team assignments can cause headaches for professors because group dynamics aren't always smooth or pleasant. Which professor hasn't tried to avoid students complaining about the free-rider behavior of a teammate? Sticking to individual assignments, professors are less likely to be pressed into that kind of mediation service. In the process, of course, students then will miss the opportunity to learn how to put knowledge about team dynamics to work in an actual team, and teachers will miss an opportunity to coach their students. If professors take the risk, and coach students through the very real problems of team dynamics, they and the students may learn together how to apply such knowledge to real-world situations as enlightened leaders.

On the other hand, some professors stick their toes into the water of team assignments, but don't manage them to their fullest advantage. Sometimes they don't place enough emphasis on the grade of a team assignment, so there isn't enough compensation for the amount of effort that goes into teamwork. Sometimes they don't teach, or support, effective team process in the classroom because they think that's not part of the learning they are hired to convey. And sometimes they don't hold all team members accountable for their contributions and deliverables. Suffice it to say, there is ample room for improvement in how many professors approach teaching teams. I'm suggesting that it is worth doing better because of the opportunity it presents to link knowledge and practice and, hence, to develop enlightened leaders.

Finally, there is the issue of grading "on the curve," or using a fixed distribution. In this practice, the professor limits the number of As, Bs, and so forth, to a pre-determined percentage of the class. As in other zero sum games, the key to maximizing one's outcome is to be competitive: why should I help another student get an A, when it lessens my chances of getting one? Such competitive classroom behavior reinforces and carries over to competitive organizational behavior. For example, one large, international (and quite well regarded) company has a standard practice of providing a quota on the number of employees who can receive the highest performance ratings each year. One outcome of this practice is that employees have been known to sabotage their peers, so that the odds of winning the highest ratings are improved. Why should I help a fellow employee create a report if it is going to reduce my chances of earning a top rating (and the bonus that comes with it)? Perhaps if the leaders of this company had learned the benefits of collaboration in their own business classrooms, they would encourage collaboration instead of competition among their employees.

Ignoring the "Whole Student"

Another barrier to the closing the knowing/doing gap is our reluctance to address and develop the whole person. If wisdom is an integrative aspect of human life, then it is the way of knowing, rather than knowledge itself, that matters.[22] As such, unlike episteme and techne, phronesis cannot be separated from the person.[23] But, traditionally, higher education takes a *tabula rasa* approach to students—that is, professors consider them to be "blank slates" on which they write. This assumption is debatable with respect to any student, but more so in higher education where students are adults. Students enter business schools as fairly well formed individuals with their own thoughts, opinions, values, attitudes, and beliefs. Yet, professors often avoid situations that bring their students' individuality into the classroom. We simply do not define this as part of our agenda, much as we don't want to provide "group therapy."

The Role of Professional Schools

So far, I have discussed a number of barriers to developing enlightened leaders that occur because of actions taken by individual professors. In addition, there are at least a few barriers that can be traced to the practices of business schools themselves. In the past, business school faculties were largely comprised of experienced practitioners. These were individuals who did not possess advanced academic degrees but, instead, had many years of experience on which they drew in the classroom. Over time, as business schools started producing more PhDs, experienced practitioners became less common in the classroom, and professors became more "scholarly" in the traditional sense of the word. The growth in the power of the AACSB as an accrediting body also contributed to this shift away from practitioners toward researchers, as the acceptable number of adjunct professors was capped, and the total number of refereed journal publications by a b-school's faculty was counted.

Part of the trend toward increased emphasis on research in business schools can also be attributed to the uneasy relationship between professional schools and the traditional departments in a university. At least in part, the pressure to publish has been fueled by the quest among business school professors to be taken seriously by their fellow scholars in the academy. Nonetheless, if wisdom is the marriage of knowing and doing, experienced teachers must play an important role in the classroom. In other words, can wisdom be developed by those who aren't wise themselves? As the old adage goes, "those who can, do...those who can't, teach." Would business school students be wiser if life-long practitioners, instead of life-long scholars, taught them? Perhaps, but the end product might merely be a shift from the wisdom of episteme to the wisdom of techne. Phronesis, or practical wisdom, would still be missing. So, what's to be done? Below, I turn to some avenues with the potential to enable the pursuit of wisdom in business schools.

The Scholarship of Teaching and Learning

There are some reasons for optimism about the pursuit of developing wise business school graduates, the most notable of which is the concept called the scholarship of teaching and learning (SOTL). Simply put, SOTL recognizes that teaching is an integral part of scholarship. In other words, rather than thinking about teaching as the price to be paid to do research, SOTL considers teaching to be an important part of the job of the professor. SOTL was introduced largely through the work of the late Ernest Boyer, then President of the Carnegie Foundation for the Advancement of Teaching, who argued that the role of the university professor was broader than the traditional tripartite model of research, teaching, and service. He proposed an alternative model with four separate, but overlapping, functions: the scholarship of discovery, the scholarship of integration, the scholarship of application, and the scholarship of teaching.[24]

Through this model, Boyer elevated the status of teaching by recognizing that there is a set of questions inherent to the profession that are worth pursuing as an ongoing intellectual quest. And since it is an intellectual quest, professors can use the same intellectual processes we follow in our disciplinary work to improve our teaching and our students' learning. In other words, applying the term "scholarship" to teaching implies the use of the same scientific process, and standards of evaluation, for the work of teaching that are applied to disciplinary research.

Business schools are particularly suited to SOTL because of the fundamental synergy between the substance of our scholarly disciplines and the substance of what we teach. Using my own field of management as an example, *how* we teach, and the tools we use, closely mirror important aspects of *what* we teach.[25] After all, the field of management is about understanding human behavior in organizations, as well as understanding the organizations themselves. Our classrooms thus can be thought of as organizations and, as such, provide a real-time laboratory in which to illustrate, experiment with and, more importantly, to model the most-important concepts of our discipline. This observation is not lost on our students, who often recognize the parallels between the content professors deliver about effective management, and the process professors use to manage their classroom and departments, interact with peers, and conduct their personal lives.[26] To be insensitive to this connection is to lose an opportunity to develop, and to model, wisdom.

Teaching Methods Supporting Wisdom

Once professors start to pay more attention to teaching, and to their students' learning, there is a plethora of research to draw upon that links "knowing" and "doing," including useful work on such classroom techniques as Cooperative Learning, Experiential Learning, Problem-based Learning, Internships, and the Case Method. These approaches share the common assumption that real knowledge requires personal engagement in the process of knowing.[27] Since wisdom is obtained through extensive life experience, the use of such methods are critical to the development of wise graduates.

Cooperative (sometimes called Collaborative) learning is an especially promising teaching approach to developing wisdom because it directly addresses several of the barriers to linking theory and practice outlined above.[28] It is a structured and systematic instructional strategy in which students are organized into small groups to work together in the classroom.[29] The creation of a collaborative climate in the classroom counters the competitiveness, and the resulting fear of failure, that might stifle the level of engagement required for developing wisdom. In addition, collaborative learning requires students to work in teams, a requirement that provides extensive experience in actual organizational behavior. Moreover, it demands action on the part of students (who cannot be passive observers in a successful collaborative-learning community).

A collaborative-learning community is based on five attributes that are likely to reduce the level of brutal criticism often found in a competitive classroom: 1. Positive interdependence (the members of the group perceive that they sink or swim together); 2. Promotive interaction (the members have face-to-face interactions where help, assistance, encouragement, and support are provided); 3. Individual accountability (each member is assessed on his or her individual contributions to the group); 4. Social skills (the need to develop leadership, decision-making, trust building, communication and conflict management skills within the group members); and, 5. Group process (the requirement that the group must process how they are achieving their goals, and how they are maintaining effective working relationships).[30] In essence, the use of collaborative learning methods should create a classroom that is perceived by the students as a safe haven for learning by doing.

Professors also could foster the development of wisdom by carefully designing the assignments they require of their students. Exam questions can be crafted so that answers require a link between theory and practice. Written assignments can ask students to analyze the experiences they have had with management concepts in the class. Research shows that issue framing is at the core of professional problem solving;[31] hence, professors might focus on whether students pose the right questions, rather than find the right answers.

Activities that take students out of the classroom also may prove to be fruitful avenues for developing wisdom. Internships, for example, have long been a staple in higher education, in general, and business schools, in particular. An Internship experience allows students to work in an actual organization while earning credit toward their degrees, a clear example of learning by doing.[32] At a number of business schools, MBA students are taken out of the classroom for extended learning opportunities, such as outdoor leadership training. At the Daniels College of Business, we have been providing "ropes and rocks" weekend experiences for about twenty years, where students confront problem-solving situations, challenge themselves, and have the opportunity for both introspection and reflection on these experiences.

The efficacy of the use of such teaching methods is supported by research in both cognitive science and artificial intelligence that suggests learning is best undertaken in a milieu of slow incubation, frequent practice, and in the private language of the learner.[33] In essence, the development of wisdom requires book learning and practical experience. Here, Pfeffer and Sutton draw a parallel to the training that members of life-or-death professions—soldiers, pilots, and surgeons—receive.[34] Each of those professions involves theoretical knowledge; however, those professionals-in-training also must learn by doing before they graduate from the classroom. To be sure, pilots can train in a simulator, and surgeons can practice on cadavers, but only for so long. How long is enough? Cognitive science tells us that the change from naïve understanding to seasoned performance occurs in small, gradual, almost leisurely steps using "slow modes" of thought, most likely in periods of long immersion. Obviously, the more practice, the better the performance. Improvement in performance does not follow a linear progression but, rather, like the waves of an ocean, there is forward and backward flow, with eddies and tributaries.[35] This process has been discussed in the context of artificial intelligence where even computers develop better problem solving capabilities though practice![36] To be sure, expert work has knowledge as its foundation, but it also has preparation, and incubation, as its cornerstones.[37]

The Daniels College of Business has successfully experimented with two approaches that also may be fruitful in developing wisdom in business students: an integrated curriculum, and team teaching.[38] Our integrated curriculum, between 1985-95, offered classes that were "transdisciplinary," that is, they included different disciplinary foci within one course, and were taught by professors representing different disciplinary backgrounds. This approach provided realistic preparation for the world of doing, and helped our students to make the link between theory and practice. In addition, team teaching allowed us to create synergistic combinations of "researchers" and "practitioners" in the same classroom, thus addressing the problem of having to choose between inexperienced professors and unscholarly practitioners.

A mantra that has played in my head throughout my career is that professors need to embrace their responsibilities as role models; in other words, to practice what we preach. This approach is critical in management classes, but research suggests it may also be critical to the development of practical wisdom. If wisdom is communicated by example, the professor is thus the medium of learning, and not the means for acquisition of factual knowledge. Hence, educators must be wise themselves. Whether they have developed their wisdom through personal experience in organizations, or whether they are simply scholarly facilitators and coaches of others, students will be better prepared for life's challenges if professors behave the way they want their students to act when they become managers.

The pursuit of wisdom requires a close, almost apprenticeship relationship between the learner and the expert.[39] But we must recognize the barriers to creating such a significant relationship between professors and students, not the least of which is time. That is why developing wisdom is more difficult in large classrooms, and in environments where teaching excellence is not rewarded.

I have identified a number of potential avenues to enhance the development of wisdom in our students, but none of these will be effective without recognizing that, in order to be put into action, knowledge must have a foundation in a system of values:

> Although specific practices are obviously important, such practices evolve and make sense only as part of some system that is often organized according to some philosophy or meta-theory of performance. As such, there is a knowing-doing gap in part because firms have misconstrued what they should be knowing or seeking to know in the first place.[40]

In other words, a part of what makes an individual wise is not *what* he or she does, but *why* he or she does it. Thus, a classroom that only conveys facts and data without venturing into the values that underlie one's choices misses the point of wisdom. We can teach all the skills we want to students, but that will not make them wise in their use of those skills. For example, a strong, clear sense of value has been associated with the success of many companies, such as Starbucks, Southwest Airlines, and Whole Foods. Our classrooms should aspire to develop the same approach those companies use to create a community in which all members understand how their skills contribute to the stated higher purpose, or mission, of the enterprise.

This chapter began with an implicit question: can business wisdom be taught? After reviewing the barriers, and identifying the possibilities, I conclude that enlightened leadership itself cannot be *taught*. Nonetheless, we have seen that there are avenues that can lead to enlightened applications of knowledge, and this fact leads me to be optimistic about the classroom—and workplace—of the future. In short, I believe enlightened leadership can be *learned*, and I trust that educators will create the opportunity for their students to do so.

An earlier version of this chapter was published as "Can Wisdom Be Taught?" in Eric H. Kessler and James R. Bailey (eds.) *Handbook of Organizational and Managerial Wisdom* (Los Angeles: Sage Publications, 2007), pp. 459-476.

[1] Miriam K. Martin, and Ramón Martinez de Pisón, "From knowledge to wisdom: a new challenge to the educational milieu with implications for religious education," *Religious Education* (100), 2005, at pp. 157-173.

[2] Jeffrey Pfeffer and Robert I. Sutton, "Knowing 'what' to do is not enough: turning knowledge into action," *Californial Management Review* (42), 1999, pp. 83-10.

[3] Jeffrey Pfeffer and Christina T. Fong. "The end of business schools? Less success than meets the eye," *Academy of Management Learning and Education* (1), 2002, pp. 78-95.

[4] Morgan W., McCall, Jr., Michael M. Lombardo and Ann M. Morrison *The Lessons of Experience: how successful executives develop on the job*. Lexington, MA: Lexington Books, 1988.

[5] Scott Eastham, "How is wisdom communicated? Prologue to peace studies," *Interculture* (24), 1992, pp. 1-33.

[6] Martin and de Pisón, *op. cit.*

[7] Jeffrey Pfeffer and Robert I. Sutton, *The Knowing-Doing Gap* (Boston: Harvard Business School Press, 2000).

[8] Michael W. Small, "Wisdom and now managerial wisdom: do they have a place in management development programs?" *Journal of Management Development* (23), 2004, pp. 751-764.

[9] Aristotle *The Basic Works of Aristotle*, edited by Richard McKeon (New York: Random House, 1941).

[10] Richard Halverson, "Accessing, documenting, and communicating practical wisdom: the phronesis of school leadership practice," *American Journal of Education* (111), 2004, pp. 90-121.

[11] Hubert Dreyfus and Stuart Dreyfus, *Mind over Machine: The Power of Human Intuition and Expertise in the Era of the Computer* (Oxford: Blackwell, 1986).

[12] Donald A. Schön, *The Reflective Practitioner* (Aldershot: Arena Books, 1991).

[13] Martin and de Pisón, *op. cit.*

[14] Steven Kerr, "On the folly of rewarding A, while hoping for B," *Academy of Management Journal* (18), 1975, pp. 769-783.

[15] Ibid.

[16] Martin and Martinez de Pisón, *op. cit.*

[17] M.H. Schneps and P.M Sadler, "A private universe," Video (Washington, DC: Annenberg/CPB: Pyramid Film and Video), 18 minutes, 1987.

[18] Jeffrey Pfeffer and Robert I. Sutton "Overcoming the 'knowing-doing' gap," *Corporate University Review* (8), 2000, pp. 12-15.

[19] Jeffrey Pfeffer and Robert I. Sutton "The smart-talk trap," *Harvard Business Review* (77), 1999, pp. 134-144.

[20] *Ibid.*

[21] Jerry B. Harvey "Encouraging students to cheat: One thought on the difference between teaching ethics and teaching ethically," *The Organizational Behavior Teaching Review* (9), 1984, pp. 1-13.

[22] Small, *op. cit.*

[23] Halverson, *op. cit.*

[24] Ernest L. Boyer, *Scholarship Reconsidered: Priorities of the Professoriate* (Princeton, NJ: The Carnegie Foundation for the Advancement of Teaching, 1990).

[25] Peter J. Frost and Cynthia V. Fukami "Teaching effectiveness in the organizational sciences: Recognizing and enhancing the scholarship of teaching," *Academy of Management Journal,* (40), 1997, pp. 1271-1281.

[26] Diana Bilimoria and Cynthia Fukami "The scholarship of teaching and learning in the management sciences," in Mary Taylor Huber and Sherwyn P. Morreale (eds.) *Disciplinary Styles in the Scholarship of Teaching and Learning: Exploring Common Ground* (Washington, DC: American Association for Higher Education, 2002), pp. 125-142.

[27] M. Zundel, *Itinéraire* (Paris: La Colombe, 1947).

[28] D.W. Johnson, R.T. Johnson and K.A. Smith, *Active Learning: Cooperation in the College Classroom* (Edina, MN: Interaction Books, 1991).

[29] James L. Cooper, Pamela Robinson and Molly McKinney. "Cooperative learning in the classroom," http://www.csudh.edu/SOE/cl_network/WhatisCL.html. 2002.

[30] Johnson, Johnson, and Smith, *op. cit.*

[31] Schön, *op. cit.*

[32] V.K. Narayanan, Paul Olk and Cynthia Fukami "Determinants of Internship Effectiveness: An Exploratory Model," *Academy of Management Learning and Education,* in press, 2010.

[33] Martin Talbot, "Good wine may need to mature: a critique of accelerated higher specialist training: Evidence from cognitive neuroscience," *Medical Education* (38), 2004, pp. 399-408.

[34] Pfeffer and Sutton, *op. cit.*

[35] E. De Bono, *I am Right—You are Wrong. From this to the New Renaissance: from Rock Logic to Water Logic* (London: Penguin, 1991).

[36] J. Copeland, *Artificial Intelligence; a Philosophical Introduction* (Oxford: Blackwell, 1993).

[37] Talbot, *op. cit.*

[38] C.V Fukami, M.L. Clouse, C.T. Howard, R.P. McGowan, J.W. Mullins, W.S. Silver, J.E. Sorensen, T.L. Watkins, and D.P. Wittmer, "The road less traveled: The joys and sorrows of transdisciplinary team teaching," *Journal of Management Education* (20), 1996, pp. 409-410.

[39] Talbot, *op. cit.*

[40] Pfeffer and Sutton, *op. cit.*, p. 89.

CHAPTER 5

Behavioral Ethics in Business Organizations: What the Research Teaches Us

by Dennis P. Wittmer

Do individuals in organizations always act and behave consistently with what they know or believe to be the right thing to do? While Plato may contend no one ever knowingly does evil, most of us believe individuals sometimes act contrary to what they know is right.[1] Indeed, whether viewed legally or ethically, we hold individuals accountable for their behaviors and choices, at least in part because they *should have* known better.

Even if we agree on what someone should ethically do in a given situation, most of us realize that our judgment is often clouded by other factors that cause us to act against our intuition of what good sense dictates. A manager may clearly understand signing a fraudulent accounting statement is legally and ethically wrong, yet the manager signs the document. Why? What influenced the manager to behave unethically? Once we begin to ask these questions, we are no longer inquiring about what the right thing to do is, or what a good person should do. Rather, we are attempting to understand why such an individual acted the way he or she did, trying to figure out the factors that influenced or caused the behavior. We have moved from a normative and prescriptive framework to a scientific and descriptive mode of analysis. In short, we are doing social science rather than philosophy.

This social science perspective is explored below in terms of its importance in leading organizations toward more ethical behavior. After some preliminary definitions and distinctions, some of the conceptual models and empirical research related to ethical decision-making in organizations is summarized, and the implications for leading an organization are explored. The first section goes into considerable detail about definitions and distinctions that are necessary in establishing an understanding of how behavioral ethics can better enable managers and leaders to create, and maintain, an ethical culture within an organization.

Definitions and Distinctions

Morality and ethics. Ethics and morality are terms that often are used interchangeably. When we say a person either acted unethically or immorally, we generally mean the same thing. When we say something is a moral or ethical issue, the two terms typically have the same connotation. However, I find it useful to make a distinction between ethics and morality, allowing for a more systematic approach when thinking about ethical issues. I take morality to be the starting point. With few exceptions, such as sociopaths, all humans have a moral code or some sense of morality. The term morality refers to norms, standards, or principles; the purpose of which is to provide guidance or direction for our choices and actions. All human cultures and groups have moral codes or norms. In distinction, *Ethics* connotes the study of morality from either a philosophical (normative) perspective or a behavioral (social science and descriptive) perspective. *Business* ethics is the study of morality in the sphere of business organizations, including both normative and behavioral approaches.

From the above definition of morality, we notice there are norms or expectations in every social group about the behavior of individuals. We can now see some conditions that define what it means to be a moral agent. The first is *rationality*. The existence of a set of guiding norms or principles assumes individuals can grasp a group's guiding moral principles and make decisions based on them. Lacking this capacity, individuals would not have the understanding and ability to think in a principled way. Absent reason, or the capacity to act on the basis of reason, individuals may behave only from instinct, or react irrationally or impulsively. It would be inappropriate to view a seriously brain-damaged person as a moral agent. Due to that condition, he or she would lack the capacity to reason and act on principle. In referring to a deranged killer who seemingly has no compunction, conscience, or understanding that his behavior is wrong, we might say, "He behaved like an animal," meaning he behaved impulsively and without reasoned thought.

Two other elements involved in being a moral agent are *choice* and *accountability*. To function as a moral agent is to make choices and to be held accountable for those choices by one's social group and self. An improper moral choice will result in consequences (accountability) when the actor is a fully developed, autonomous moral agent. If Johnny takes a toy from a neighbor's house because he likes the toy, his parents will view this as an opportunity for moral instruction rather than punishment for stealing—at least at certain ages and stages of the child's development. In the early stages of development, a child does not completely distinguish possession from ownership. Johnny is too young to know that what he was doing was wrong, and therefore education is a more appropriate parental response than punishment. We do not hold young children accountable until they understand moral principles and are capable of acting on the basis of those principles—until they are fully developed rational beings and complete moral agents.

Yet, the sources of moral guidance are subject to debate; lurking here is a thorny issue related to human nature itself. Some hold all humans are born good, others hew to the notion we are born evil. Some say moral principles emanate from God, while others believe there is genetic basis for moral principles adopted by humans after years of evolution. Without engaging in discussion of the validity of these theories, I suggest at least some part of morality is learned. Many ethicists begin with an assumption that learning moral norms, standards, and principles originates in a nuclear group, such as the family, and expands to larger communities, whether it be a local town, a business, or the global community. As individuals become properly socialized into their respective communities, the groups' norms and principles become their own and, in that sense, these norms ultimately become their personal morality. Of course, as individuals become fully rational and independent in their thoughts and actions, they may come to challenge or question some of the moral norms and practices of their group, perhaps rejecting some norms and adopting new or different principles. Hence, one's personal morality may be different from the particular community to which they belong.

Normative and behavioral ethics. Much as political philosophy and political science are the study of the nature of politics, political community, and political behavior, ethics can be thought of as the study of the nature or morality, moral community, and moral behavior. Business ethics can be thought of as an area of applied ethics. Business ethics is the study of moral issues in the business realm, and organizational ethics is the study of moral behavior in organizational contexts.

Whether we wish to consider ethics generally, or examine specific areas of applied ethics in business, journalism, health care, or government, there are two basic approaches to doing so: *normative* and *behavioral*. The normative approach is concerned with deciding the "right" decision or course of action. When confronted with a conflict of principles or obligations, how should one determine what is ethically correct? What is an appropriate rule for making decisions? One might reflect on the most important and fundamental moral values a leader should have. These kinds of questions are normative, or what is called action guiding. The answers in normative analyses are prescriptive; they tell us what one ought to do, or what guiding values to embrace.

As noted at the outset, some ethical questions are not about what is right or wrong, and instead are about what influences individuals to behave as they do when confronted with moral choices. Does a leader or an organization's "tone at the top" really matter in terms of the moral behavior of its employees? Do codes of conduct have an impact in terms of whether employees behave morally and ethically? Such questions fundamentally ask for descriptive or explanatory (rather than prescriptive) answers. In an important sense, this approach focuses on what is, not what ought to be; I refer to it as *behavioral* or *descriptive* ethics.

Whereas normative ethics is philosophical in character, behavioral ethics is a social science enterprise, an empirical and evidence-based approach. Included in this approach is moral psychology (focused on an individual's moral processing of information and the making of moral choices from a psychological point of view) and organizational ethics (studying individual behavior and choices in an organizational context from the perspective of social psychology). Broadly speaking, behavioral or descriptive ethics asks different questions than normative ethics, and utilizes the tools of social science to answer them.

Organizational and Behavioral Ethics: Knowledge Development

While normative ethics has a long and venerable history (as far back as ancient Greece), organizational and behavioral ethics as a discipline is, at most, a half century old. The applied area of business ethics (which utilizes survey research, theoretical modeling, and hypothesis testing) is only 30 years young. Early research on business ethics was primarily descriptive in character, summarizing data from surveys. As far back as 1961 the *Harvard Business Review* published a short article, "How Ethical Are Businessmen?" based on a survey of 1700 executives. The results confirmed, "a strong desire to improve business behavior."[2] The authors concluded, "things can't improve unless top management stands its ground and makes uncompromisingly clear that ethical methods are the only approved way of doing business."[3] The observations are certainly as true today as they were nearly 50 years ago. In 1976, during the post-Watergate era, J.S. Bowman conducted a survey comparing the ethical perceptions of business and government managers in order to get a sense of whether the two groups had different perceptions with regard to issues of ethical behavior (then, as now, there was a general crisis of confidence in all societal institutions). One of the findings was that three-quarters of those surveyed said pressures from the top caused people to compromise their beliefs. Ten years later, Waters, Bird, and Chant found, "moral considerations are very much part of everyday managerial life," and the most common moral issues were related to employees as compared to other stakeholders.[4] These empirical studies and countless others provide data that goes beyond anecdotal information or opinion.

Organizational and Behavioral Ethics: Some Conceptual Models

In the mid-1980s, social scientists began to develop models of decision-making and behavior in business organizations. Using theoretical and conceptual models, researchers generated hypotheses and tested them empirically, taking another step in adding complexity to social science methods utilized in understanding the empirical reality of business ethics.

Moral psychologist James Rest proposed one of the most important conceptual models of organizational and behavioral ethics. Following the work of Lawrence Kohlberg, Rest focused on developing measures of cognitive moral growth. He conceived of ethical decision-making in a four stage process: 1) ethical interpretation or perception of situations; 2) ethical judgment or formulation of the morally right course of action; 3) selection or actual choosing of the moral values and actions; and 4) implementation or execution of the moral course of action.

Calling attention to the lack of a comprehensive theory guiding empirical research in organizational ethics, groundbreaking work by Linda Treviño proposed a *person-situation interactionist* model. The model identifies cognitive moral development of individuals as a critical variable in explaining ethical decision-making and includes other individual variables (locus of control and ego strength) and situational variables (organizational culture and job context) as moderating variables, interacting with cognitive moral development to explain ethical decision-making.

Thomas Jones, arguing ethical decision-making outcomes are contingent on the character of the issue itself, incorporates the moral intensity of an issue as a key variable in understanding ethical decision-making in organizations. For Jones, moral intensity includes factors such as the significance of the consequences on others, the degree to which there is consensus about the issue, and the likelihood the effects and consequences will occur.

I have broadened these three conceptual models (see below). In my model, any of the four stages identified by Rest can be affected by either individual or environmental factors. Ethical decision-making is thus a function of the decision-making of individuals as moderated by individual and environmental variables. In any stage of ethical decision-making, various individual factors (for example, a disposition to comply with authority) and environmental factors (for example, an organizational culture demanding obedience to authority) can influence decision outcomes.

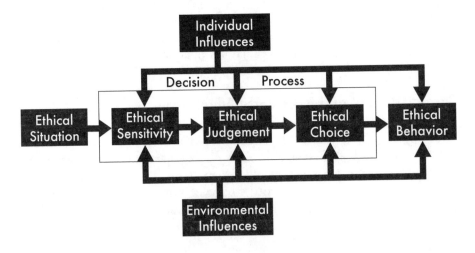

Organizational and Behavioral Ethics: Why It Matters and What We Have Learned

Leaders and managers carry models or theories about ethics and business, whether or not these are brought explicitly to consciousness. They make assumptions about what affects the behavior of their employees, and what strategies will work in terms of producing ethical behavior. Assumptions are seldom questioned, unless the outcomes are noticeably inconsistent or unsatisfactory. Social science studies of behavioral ethics provide an increasingly systematic means of testing theories and assumptions.

Imagine a leader just given responsibility for the investment banking business of a global financial enterprise. The leader is asked whether ethics is important in this new role, and how he or she plans to lead the organization to behave ethically. The leader replies ethics will be a priority, since confidence in the industry has been shaken by recent events. When pressed for specifics, the leader says codes and broad values statements are only window dressing and what matters is having clear rules and developing systems for monitoring and compliance. The leader says it is especially important to have rules in banking, since the industry is prone to unethical behavior, further stating that the size of the organization does not matter as long as there is a strong leader at the top. The leader will recruit and promote younger people in the organization since he or she believes they will be more ethical and respond better to strong leadership, compared to older employees who have their own ideas and are skeptical of changes and new leadership. She also contends that being religious is a strong indicator that people will be more ethical.

All leaders operate with such schemas and assumptions about how people function in organizations. The question is whether these ideas are solidly based on reality, or whether they are more idiosyncratic and personal. When leaders are open and curious, they can learn to test the validity of their assumptions with the aid of social science research; this matters greatly because all leaders are responsible for establishing the systems and culture within their respective organizations.

It is with this backdrop and motivation we now examine some of the findings from the discipline of behavioral and descriptive ethics. A recent review of 174 academic articles about ethical decision-making in top business journals during the period 1996-2003 revealed the following about organizational influences on ethical decisions and behavior.[5]

- "…the majority of studies support the idea that the existence of a **code of ethics** is positively related to ethical decision-making." All things being equal, having clear written statements about the fundamental values of an organization, along with clear behavioral expectations, produce more ethical organizations and more ethical employees.

- "The research generally supports the notion that **ethical climates and cultures** have positive influence on ethical decision-making." The atmosphere and ways of doing things in an organization effect ethical behavior. When ethical concerns are discussed openly, when individuals generally trust one another, and when there is a strong sense that members of the group are committed to the same principles, ethical behavior is more likely to result.

- "...no overall conclusions regarding the effect of **industry** can be drawn." There are no significant differences related to ethical behavior of individuals across various kinds of industries, even though each industry has its own peculiar sets of issues and challenges.

- "The research in this area generally suggests that **organizational size** has a detrimental effect on ethical decision-making." It is more difficult to sustain ethical behavior in large organizations; hence, leaders of such institutions should pay attention to strategies and structures that will improve the likelihood individuals will make ethical choices. For example, Johnson & Johnson (a large global corporation) makes sure everyone in the organization is educated to understand the company's famous one-page Credo, and all managers have annual training to ensure ethical issues and challenges are addressed across the organization. (see chapter 9)

- "The impact of **rewards and sanctions** is clear—rewarding unethical behavior tends to increase the frequency of such behavior, while effective sanctioning systems tend to decrease such behavior." One of the surest ways to create ethical problems is to fail to address violations of the values and standards of the organization (by overlooking and not responding to unethical behavior, or even rewarding it). On the other hand, finding ways to reward or, at least, acknowledge individuals of integrity provides dividends for the organization.

The review by O'Fallon and Butterfield also included 270 findings relating to individual factors that influence ethical decisions and behavior, including:

- **Gender**. Gender does not seem to be a strong predictor of ethical behavior. When researchers do find gender differences, women seem to heed to ethics rules slightly more often than men.

- **Philosophy/values orientation**. "More than two decades of research reveals fairly consistent findings. Idealism and deontology (duty-based orientations) are generally positively related to ethical decision-making, while relativism, teleology (decisions based on expected consequences), and other factors such as economic orientation are generally negatively related to ethical decision-making."[6] While an important driver for most decisions is the expected consequences and other relative benefits to stakeholders, this finding suggests leaders can serve the long-term interest of their organizations by establishing a culture of fundamental duties that should not be compromised, regardless of possible beneficial consequences. These include the duty of truthfulness to customers and respect for employees.

- "The research on **age** has produced mixed and inconsistent results."[7] A manager may have strong ideas about whether older and more experienced employees make wiser and more ethical decisions, or whether younger people (who are more idealistic and not jaded) make more ethical choices. However, the mixed research results would suggest one should be rather cautious about acting on these beliefs, given the uncertainty of the studies.

- "...the research generally suggests a positive relationship between CMD **[cognitive moral development]** and ethical decision-making."[8] Cognitive moral development has to do with how individuals process ethical information and arrive at decisions about what is right and wrong. Individuals at the highest levels of moral development tend to be able to put themselves in another's place and see decisions from a more universal perspective. At middle levels of development, group norms and group loyalty tend to dictate what is considered ethical, and at the lowest levels of development, individuals tend to see right and wrong from an egocentric perspective in terms of how decisions affect themselves. Leaders who understand the level of moral development of their employees can communicate with, and motivate, employees more effectively. Understanding that most individuals end up in the middle stages of development, leaders should consider the importance of establishing and reinforcing loyalty to group norms. (see chapter 3)

- "Internal **locus of control** is positively related to ethical decision-making, and external locus of control is negatively related."[9] Locus of control is essentially a measure of whether individuals believe they are in control of events in their lives (internals) or whether external events and forces determine what happens to them (externals). Research shows the more internal the orientation, the more likely a person will make ethical choices. It is unclear whether leaders can influence personal orientation; however, they can increase their sensitivity to individual orientations and preferences.

- "The results consistently suggest that **Machiavellianism** [disposition to be manipulative] is negatively related to the ethical decision-making process."[10] Individuals who are manipulative and self-centered are often very clever about how they pull strings to produce results. While leaders might be tempted to use the strengths of such individuals to achieve results, relying on them can be very risky, especially if ethical conduct is paramount to the organization.

Organizational and Behavioral Ethics: Management Implications and Further Findings

Based on their research, Linda Treviño and Gary Weaver have drawn strategies for effectively and ethically managing business organizations. They begin with a set of important questions about formal ethics programs: Do such programs really reduce unethical behavior and increase ethical behavior? Are there other positive benefits from investing in formal ethics programs? In answering, they distinguish "compliance orientation" from "values orientation" programs. Although all ethics programs are organizational control systems that "aim to create predictability in employee behavior and correspondence between specific employee behaviors and more general organizational goals and expectations," a compliance system focuses more on having clear, written rules and sanctions for violations.[11] Such an orientation is likely to be led by a corporate counsel or other attorney. A values approach is focused on gaining consensus around key core values, and is likely to be led by someone from human resources. Comparing the outcomes of the two systems as measured by increased ethical awareness, commitment to the organization, employee integrity, willingness to communicate openly about issues, willingness to report violations to management, improved decision making, willingness to seek advice, and reduced ethical conduct, Treviño and Weaver found both orientations can be effective. However, they found that the values orientation was more useful in explaining the purpose and role of ethics training. They concluded an integrated approach may be the most beneficial, utilizing a values orientation to frame the purpose and role of ethical rules and training, and a compliance orientation to ensure accountability and performance. Drawing on data from six companies, some of their other key findings include the following:

- Perception of employees that ethics programs are oriented to "protect top management from blame" has a negative effect on ethical behavior and commitment to an organization.

- Perception that a company has a formal mechanism for raising concerns and making ethics part of performance appraisal has a positive effect.

- Perception that the organization follows through and that ethics programs and policies are not mere "window dressing" has a positive effect.

- Leadership (tone at the top) was one of the most important factors contributing to positive outcomes (leaders here include supervisors).

- Perception of fair treatment was strongly and positively related to ethics outcomes (The perception of fair treatment was related positively to employee commitment and to their willingness to deliver "bad news" to management.)

- Perception that ethics is talked about and integrated into decision making was positively related to ethical outcomes.

- Perception that ethical behavior is rewarded was important and highly correlated with employee commitment and delivering "bad news" when necessary.

- Perception that the culture of the organization was one of "unquestioning obedience to authority" was negatively related to ethical outcome measures.

In another set of studies, Treviño and Weaver examine how "ethical culture" and "ethical climate" affect attitudes and ethical behavior in organizations. They defined ethical culture as "the subset of organizational culture, representing a multidimensional interplay among various formal and informal systems of behavioral control that are capable of promoting either ethical or unethical behavior" and ethical climate as the practices and procedures that have ethical content in an organization, including perceptions about whether employees have an inclination to make decisions for the benefit of the organization or for themselves, and whether there is a perception that authority can be questioned in the organization.[12] Combining both ethical climate and culture into a more general variable of ethical environment, they found that an ethical environment and climate that fosters obedience to authority were two of the strongest predictors of positive behavior. The more subjects characterized the environment as ethical, the more employees demonstrated commitment to the organization. The more an atmosphere of obedience to authority in the organization was observed, the more unethical the behavior, and the less committed employees were to the organization. In terms of ethical climate, an atmosphere fostering self-interest and protection of personal interests was negatively related to ethical behavior. In terms of organizational commitment, employees were more committed to the organization when leaders paid serious attention to ethics, when organizations "were concerned about the welfare of employees and the community."[13]

Conclusion

Sometimes it is not easy for leaders to determine the right thing to do, and competing duties and obligations can make such decisions uncertain, unclear, and untidy. Other times it is a matter of getting individuals to stay true to a common set of principles and virtues (honesty and truthfulness, fairness and equality, compassion, promise keeping, transparency, and appropriate levels of competition and self-interest). One of the jobs of leaders and managers is to create the organizational context that promotes and fosters such behavior. Empirical research confirms leaders should establish clear values and standards of conduct for their organizations. They need to model and exhibit such values themselves, reward others who exhibit the values, and sanction those who behave contrary to them. Beyond this, leaders and managers are well served by creating appropriate structures and organizational mechanisms to encourage and sustain those values.

Leaders should be attentive to the climate and culture defining their organizations. In part, this means working to establish a culture of trust and transparency; not one in which obedience to authority is the prominent expectation. Leaders and managers should encourage a culture where members of the organization are comfortable sharing bad news and reporting problems and shortcomings. Leaders and managers of ethical organizations should also create a culture in which self-interest is minimized, and professionalism and promoting the good of customers, employees, and the public are emphasized.

[1] For example in the Gorgias dialogue, Plato argues that men always seek that which "seems" good to them, even though they may be mistaken. Even choosing distasteful means, *e.g. killing*, is done for the sake of something they believe is good.

[2] R.C. Baumhart, "How ethical are businessmen?" *Harvard Business Review* (39), July-August, 1961, pp. 6-8.

[3] *Ibid.*

[4] James A. Waters, Frederick Bird, and Peter Chant, "Everyday moral issues experienced by managers," *Journal of Business Ethics* (55), 1986, pp. 373-384.

[5] Michael J. O'Fallon and Kenneth D. Butterfield, "A review of the empirical ethical decision-making literature: 1996-2003," *Journal of Business Ethics* (59), 2005, pp. 375-413.

[6] *Ibid.*

[7] *Ibid.*

[8] *Ibid.*

[9] *Ibid.*

[10] *Ibid.*

[11] Linda K. Treviño, Gary R. Weaver, *Managing Ethics in Business Organizations: Social Scientific Perspectives* (Stanford, CA: Stanford University Press, 2003.)

[12] *Ibid.*

[13] *Ibid.*

PART II

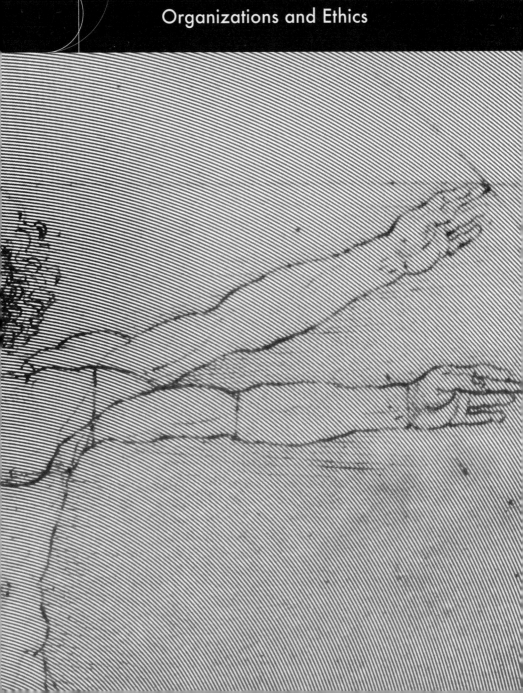

Organizations and Ethics

CHAPTER 6

Lessons from U.S. History for the 21ˢᵗ Century Corporation: The Changing Structure of Organizations and Role of Managers

by Paul Olk

History doesn't repeat itself, but it does rhyme.
—attributed to Mark Twain

The end of the first decade of the 21ˢᵗ century finds many once-dominant companies struggling, such as the Ford Motor Co. and General Motors. Even some new-economy companies are in financial trouble (Yahoo). Yet the list of thriving companies includes both older ones like IBM, and newer ones like Google. In this new century, why do some large companies do well while others do not? Much of the answer lies in the company's organizational structure and managerial skills. Hindsight offers us an understanding of historical changes in organizational structure and in the role of managers. With an eye toward what "rhymes," we then can anticipate what may occur in the future.

While the U.S. economic system continually evolves, what remains constant is the intertwined relationship of the economy, the prevailing organizational structure, and the skills needed to be effective managers. In this review, I argue that changes in (global) market opportunities and technological innovation transform the nature of economic competition among companies. In this changing context, managers with distinctive values and skills build innovative organizational structures to gain advantage within the dynamic nature of capitalism. This relationship is apparent in each historical period of the development of the U.S. economy: Merchant Capitalism (1776–1860), Industrial Capitalism (1860–1920), and Managerial Capitalism (1920–1980), as well as in the current period, which I call Network Capitalism. In the following review of these four eras, I will draw inferences about how to lead and manage in the 21ˢᵗ century.

Overview of U.S. Business Development

During each of the four eras of U.S. business history, changes in both technology and markets gradually led to a new basis of competition.[1] Each period resulted in a distinct dominant form of organizational structure that required changes in both the role of managers and the skills needed to manage effectively. For each time period, I will examine three critical dimensions: 1) general economic conditions and the nature of competition among companies; 2) the prevailing characteristics of the organizational structure of companies during the era; and, 3) the role of the manager within dominant organizations.

Economic, Organizational and Managerial Comparisons across Time Periods in U.S. History

Time Period	Nature of Competition	Dominant Organizational Structure	Role of Manager
Merchant Capitalism 1776-1860	Determined by local economic supply-and-demand conditions	Owner-craftsman with an apprentice or two	Leading through direct contact Planning based upon market transactions Organizing the layout of the factory/shop floor Controlling by watching the few employees
Industrial Capitalism 1860-1920	Determined by achieving lower means of production of commodity products	Unitary or U-Form HQ R&D — Manufacturing — Marketing	Leading through a hierarchy Planning for continous running of factories Organizing the company for efficiency Controlling for the reduction of cost

Managerial Capitalism 1920-1980	Determined by stability in sales and profits	Multidivisional or M-Form 	Leading through symbolic means Planning with different business units to achieve overall company stability and profits Organizing through the command and control of the hierarchy Controlling by evaluating
Network Capitalism 1980-Present	Determined by better innovation and speed to market as well as superior economic efficiency	Network or N-Form 	Leading through self-motivated groups Planning within and across companies Organizing through forming and reforming teams and via informal networks Controlling through consultation, personal reputation and trust

Merchant Capitalism (1776 – 1860)

The formation of the United States in 1776 coincided with the publication of Adam Smith's *The Wealth of Nations*, which was the first exposition of what we call capitalism and what Smith—who never used the term "capitalism"—called a "system of commerce." Smith wrote at a time when mercantilism was the dominant economic system. Mercantilism restricted trade between countries, and individual governments controlled which goods were imported or exported. Capitalism was a revolutionary concept, as it introduced an economic system marked by open competition in a free market. Within the free market, the means of production and distribution are privately or corporately owned and a company's growth is proportionate to its accumulation and re-investment of profits.

The new economic system Smith advocated had several critical advantages over mercantilism: A country's wealth would no longer be defined by the amount of gold it had, but, instead, by the flow of goods and services its economy could produce; ownership would be in the hands of individuals who could make better choices than governments; free trade would allow a country to establish its comparative advantage, and thus produce greater wealth; and supply and demand ("the invisible hand") would efficiently determine price and amount of goods produced. In America, Smith's ideas were adopted by Alexander Hamilton, the country's first Secretary of the Treasury, and others who ushered in the era of merchant capitalism.

In America's early days as a nation, the country's limited transportation infrastructure contributed to locally-concentrated economic activity, which took place predominantly on the Eastern Seaboard. It could take days or weeks to transport materials from a couple of hundred of miles inland to a seaport or a larger city. "Companies" were quite small, with most employing only one or two persons. For example, John Jacob Astor (1763–1848) was one of the most affluent individuals in U.S. history. He amassed his considerable wealth, first, through fur trading and, later, real estate. Yet, at the height of his career, he had only one person working for him (and Astor himself was known to stop working each day at 3:00 p.m.!)

The "Merchant Capitalism" era was characterized by an entrepreneurial organizational structure. With only a few employees to lead and few activities to plan, control, and organize, the role of the professional manager in this structure was underdeveloped compared to later periods. The American economy during this time likely came as close as it ever has to reflecting the classic free market identified by Adam Smith.

In the 1820s, the introduction of the steam locomotive and development of the railroad began to change the form of the U.S. economy. Building on earlier efforts to improve the nation's transportation infrastructure through investments in toll roads and canals, the spread of railroads reduced the time and cost of shipping resources and goods throughout the country, thus opening up new markets. Eventually, a firm like Swift and Company in Chicago could butcher Midwest-raised cattle and ship the meat in refrigerated train cars to cities in the East. Telegraph lines were laid alongside the railroad tracks to aid in coordinating train travel. Railroads and the telegraph also led to improved communication between geographically distant regions of the country. Within three decades, the total distance of U.S. railroad tracks grew from around 30 miles to approximately 30,000 miles; by 1860, the time required to travel between the middle of the country and the East Coast was reduced to a matter of days. This transformation helped set the stage for the next form of capitalism in the U.S.

Industrial Capitalism (1860–1920)

Improved transportation and communication infrastructure in the U.S. coincided with several complementary developments. First, the nation's abundant natural resources—timber, coal, oil, and farmland—were turned into commodity items that spurred economic growth. During this time, a new wave of immigrants arrived on America's shores. These immigrants tended to be poorer, less educated, and more clustered in urban centers than earlier immigrants. The result was an increased availability of centrally-located cheap labor. More important, the second industrial revolution brought about faster and cheaper ways of manufacturing existing products, as well as the creation of new ones. For example, in the steel industry, the Bessemer process permitted mass production of inexpensive steel that was used to build railroads, bridges, and buildings. The nation also witnessed the development of the telephone, the airplane, the internal combustion engine, and widespread electrification—innovations that would transform the country's ability to communicate and to transport and produce economic goods. During this time, capitalistic expansion moved at a fast pace and economic conditions were unstable with numerous booms and busts.

To meet these changing conditions, companies found the old entrepreneurial organizational structures were no longer effective—they needed a new organizational model. What emerged was the functional organization (see Table), in which divisions replicate the stages of a value chain. Under this model, companies were organized along the lines of various functional activities—such as research and development, manufacturing, and marketing—so that each division manager oversaw one distinct piece of the overall process. This structure is sometimes referred to as "U-form" (for unitary) because it is best suited for companies focused on only one product or service. For example, during the era when Andrew Carnegie's steel company successfully dominated that industry, the company made steel exclusively.[2]

The U-form structure's advantage is its high efficiency: each functional unit focuses on primarily one task or product. Since most products in the era of Industrial Capitalism were commodities (oil, steel, tin), competition was based on cost: the company that could produce the commodity at the lowest cost would likely gain the dominant market share. Thus, companies in industries that were able to employ new technologies to achieve greater economies of scale quickly developed into oligopolies, or even monopolies. Only in industries without capital-intensive technologies (clothing manufacturing, agriculture) did competition remain fragmented.

New administrative tools were developed to manage these new organizational structures. Foremost was the legal trust, created by John D. Rockefeller in 1891, which, for the first time in history, permitted a company to incorporate in one state and own shares in a company in another.[3] As a trust, Rockefeller's Standard Oil Company was able to rationalize and efficiently control its management in an unprecedented way. After acquiring competitors, often through hostile means, Rockefeller and his managers could then decide which factories were the most efficient and should remain open, and which were inefficient and should be closed. Also, the company was able to purchase in greater volume from suppliers and, thus, achieve even greater economies of scale. This sequence of (1) horizontal integration (buying up competitors), (2) rationalization (applying methods of efficiency), and (3) vertical integration (controlling the entire means of production for the industry's value chain) was replicated in other technology-intensive companies. In sum, U-form companies were able to expand their geographical reach and compete successfully against smaller local companies, often driving them out of business.

The new structure and administrative tools also brought about changes in the role of managers. Although the ruthless and illegal actions of notable individuals such as Cornelius Vanderbilt and Jay Gould seemed to justify the moniker of "robber barons," the behavior of John D. Rockefeller and Andrew Carnegie was far more typical of the era's important business leaders. Although the latter were ruthless in dealings with competitors and with labor—and both adhered to Herbert Spencer's Social Darwinism (in which the rich were considered justified in amassing great wealth because they bettered society)—each built a long-lasting, legitimate business organization. The source of their success was the U-form organizational structure they created. As business historian Alfred Chandler noted, during this time:

> [t]he visible hand of management replaced the invisible hand of market forces where and when new technology and expanded markets permitted...Modern business enterprise was thus the institutional response to the rapid pace of technological innovation and increasing consumer demand in the United States during the second half of the nineteenth century.[4]

Individuals at the top of U-forms led hierarchies that grew increasingly steep over time. Distinct from the sole proprietors or partners running small companies who were the focus of Adam Smith's economic model, these individuals were owner-managers of large organizations with thousands of employees. Their skills were organizing business processes efficiently and controlling labor and production costs. They focused on planning to make sure their factories operated continuously. They achieved economies of scale by producing at high volume and avoiding labor shutdowns. With these changes, cost accounting became important to keep track of, and reduce production costs. Within this new structure, with its requisite administrative tools and changing role of managers, lay the germ of the next stage of American corporate history.

Managerial Capitalism (1920-1980)

During the late 1800s and early 1900s, several events initiated the transition to a new industrial era. In 1890, Congress passed the Sherman Antitrust Act, which made monopolies illegal. The legislation lay dormant for many years. In 1911, it was used against Standard Oil to break the trust into numerous smaller companies. The threat of further breakups affected how other companies operated.

At roughly the same time, managers of some large companies came to see that having a monopoly led to terrific profits in a strong economy, but the monopoly would bear all of the losses in a downturn. These managers realized that to ensure more steady returns, it was beneficial to limit their market share (for many companies the ceiling was around 60 percent). By doing so, the dominant company could maintain its sales and operations during a downturn while less efficient companies would suffer. During good times, instead of trying to capture more market share, the dominant companies would invest their profits into different businesses. Thus, companies began to diversify for both legal and economic reasons.

Another major development of the era was share ownership. As the owner-founders of the large corporations arising in the late 1800s began to die, few other sole proprietors could afford to buy and manage the corporations. This led to share ownership becoming more widespread. Henceforth, many companies were managed by individuals who might not own a significant number of shares and, thus, the profession of management emerged: one could now be a manager without being an owner. The separation of management from ownership had an additional, and unintended, consequence: it made corporate leaders more risk-averse. Rather than pursuing short-term profit maximization, the professional managers at the top of corporations had an incentive to obtain a steady return to ensure the continuation of their company and their jobs. The emergence of management as a profession was aided by the rise of business schools in the late 1800s and early 1900s, and by the development of F. W. Taylor's "scientific management," which attempted to replace informal management practices with techniques based on scientific experiments.

These changes in corporate ownership and management, ushered along by the Great Depression of the 1930s and, subsequently, World War II, shifted the focus of the economy towards stability—that is, steady returns and steady employment. For example, when a strike occurred, labor and management tended to look for a quick solution that brought everyone back to work. These changes also led to a decreased rate of innovation. Many companies tended to play it safe and would make only minor modifications when updating a product. They found this economically cheaper and less risky than developing a more revolutionary product.

The experiences of the DuPont Corporation illustrate the effect of structural changes that occurred during this period. Having diversified in the early 20th century into a range of businesses (munitions and fertilizer), DuPont realized that these businesses not only had different markets (selling to governments vs. selling to farmers) but also different distribution systems which could not be managed effectively from a central office. Recognizing the company's old functional structure now contained numerous inefficiencies, DuPont's managers developed a new multidivisional (or M-form) organizational structure.[5] In this model (see Table), the organization was first split into divisions based on product areas. Next, each division was further subdivided into functional areas. This approach added a managerial layer to the organization, but it permitted each division to focus on the specific needs of its own product. This ends-orientation (as opposed to the process-orientation of the old U-form) meant that one division could make changes to its manufacturing or marketing operations without directly impacting the activities of other divisions. Thus, each division could best serve its own customers. Another advantage of this structure was the facilitation of subsequent diversification: top management could easily add or subtract business units to or from the existing decentralized structure. The chief disadvantages of this organizational form were the expensive duplication of functions like marketing and accounting, the increased need for communication between divisions to prevent conflict with one another, and a top management team focused on managing a portfolio of businesses but lacking extensive knowledge on each division's products.

DuPont's M-form was quickly adopted by Alfred Sloan's General Motors, which created five separate business lines: Buick, Cadillac, Chevrolet, Oldsmobile, and Pontiac. Sloan's professional management philosophy became the model for managers in other large corporations during this era. He emphasized that headquarters should set policy for the divisions and then evaluate their performance based on each division's internal rate of return. This approach permitted GM to pursue its goal of "a car for every purse and purpose," which was a stark contrast to the single-product Ford company, where a consumer could have "any color Model T as long as it was black." During the 1920s and 1930s, GM's success relative to Ford exemplified the benefits of the M-form in providing stable profits. Other companies, particularly after World War II, adopted the M-form and its use became extensive as many companies became conglomerates. For example, International Telephone and Telegraph (ITT) and Gulf + Western, Inc. each operated in dozens of industries in many countries. By the 1960s, the M-form structure dominated the U.S. economy, and the U.S. economy dominated the world.

The skills required of top management in M-form companies differed from those needed in U-form organizations (see Table). The earlier emphasis on direct leadership and control by an owner was replaced by symbolic leadership and by top managers overseeing other managers. In large M-form companies, most employees never met their chief executive officer, and top managers didn't need to know as much about their product lines. Instead, high-level managers needed to be skilled at analyzing figures and reports. GM's John Z. DeLorean noted that when he moved from managing the Chevrolet division of the company to a position in headquarters, he no longer saw cars being made in the factories and, sometimes, the only cars he saw at all were those on his commute to work.

Planning during this era became very complex. Some companies would engage in a six-month planning cycle to coordinate various activities across their many divisions and among the different levels within their companies. This effort was aided by the development of reasonably clear, focused performance objectives, and by a "command and control" structure in which higher levels of management typically made final decisions and evaluated subordinates' performance based upon their contributions to overall company goals.

Network Capitalism (1980–Present)

The 1970s and 1980s revealed an inherent weakness in the U.S. economy and in large U.S. corporations. Foreign competitors, who had fallen behind U.S. companies in the 1950s and 1960s, began to produce innovative, high-quality products at low prices. In the process, the incremental innovations offered by U.S. conglomerates were no longer attracting as many customers, which resulted in a struggling U.S. economy during the 1970s. Business leaders at the time offered many excuses, including rising oil prices, increased labor costs, and intrusive government regulation but, in 1980, Harvard Business School professors Robert Hayes and William Abernathy placed the blame on U.S. managers themselves, and on the type of organizations they had created. The researchers demonstrated that the dominant organizations were too vertically integrated and too diversified. Because of their enormous size and the breadth of their activities, American companies were slower than foreign companies at decision-making and adopting innovative techniques. In particular, Hayes and Abernathy argued that top-level managers lacked sufficient focus on production and operations because the skills emphasized in their rise to the top of conglomerates were financial and legal. These emphases bred top managers who did not sufficiently understand what happened in R&D or on the factory floor. Indicative of this state of affairs, statistician W. Edwards Deming championed statistical methods for improving quality in manufacturing. Using these methods often required a redesign of company operations, but eventually led to lower costs and higher quality. Deming's ideas flourished in Japan, but were generally ignored in the U.S. until after Japanese companies captured large shares of U.S. markets.

By the late 1980s, it became clear that U.S. companies needed a more dynamic organizational form to cope with the radical changes in technology and innovation in the global economy. For example, in the past, a single company could manufacture most or all of the parts to a typewriter. During the late 1980s, no one company could produce all the parts of a computer. In the new economy, successful computer companies, like Dell, focused on only a few parts of the value chain, relying on global suppliers for the rest.

As a result of globalization, many new competitors entering the U.S. domestic market brought innovative business practices that provided an advantage over traditional American management. In addition to total quality management (TQM), Japanese companies used practices like just-in-time (JIT) inventory systems to speed up operations and reduce overhead costs. Japanese and European companies also used strategic alliances with other companies—even with competitors—to introduce new products and services. Compared to vertically integrated American firms, these partnerships provided increased flexibility in adjusting to marketplace changes and led to significant innovation. In addition to efficiency, competition began to be based on speed to market and innovation.

In order to remain competitive, U.S. companies were forced to evolve. New industries, such as biotechnology and video gaming, were created in which strategic alliances were commonplace. High-performance organizations flourished, such as W.L. Gore & Associates, which develops fluoropolymer products for a variety of industries, including fabrics and its best-known product, GORE-TEX. Gore practices "non-management" in which there are no titles, job descriptions, hierarchy, or bosses. Rather, Gore uses a flat, team-based organizational model in which personal initiative, creativity, and product innovation are encouraged and rewarded.[6]

Equally dramatic in the 1990s were changes in existing companies as they began the process of flattening hierarchies, breaking down silos between divisions and functions, and forming alliances with other companies. For example, under CEO Reginald Jones in the 1970s, General Electric Co. had an elaborate, formal strategic-planning process and was considered one of America's best-managed conglomerates. After becoming CEO in the 1980s, Jack Welch set about restructuring GE and began a continual push towards creating a less formal "boundaryless" organization.[7] Under his leadership, the company competed successfully in world markets.

Across the U.S. economy, many companies followed GE's example and downsized, delayered, and outsourced. They began to focus on a small set of internally managed activities and used external alliances to leverage their capabilities. This new organizational form—the network structure (or the N-form)—is characterized by a flat organization that focuses on a narrow product offering and emphasizes sharing and transferring resources within a company and with its partners. In contrast to the M-form, the network structure stresses a core set of activities for the focal company. Popular phrases during this time like "stick to your knitting" (from Peters and Waterman's In Search of Excellence) and "the hedgehog concept" (in Collins's Good to Great) reflected the deeper concept that a company needed to develop and maintain a particular core competence.

As promoted by early "West Coast management" leaders like Robert Noyce (co-founder of the Fairchild Semiconductor Corporation and Intel Corporation) and HP's Bill Hewlett and Dave Packard, units and individuals within the N-form organization's flat structure talk directly to one another rather than relaying information up the hierarchy or through superiors. This flow of communication both allows for, and creates, higher levels of ambiguity. For example, the relatively simple chain of command that characterized Managerial Capitalism has given way to shifting leadership and virtual teams located around the globe. In the process, companies must learn how to compete and cooperate simultaneously. John Bell, head of strategic alliance planning at Royal Philips Electronics, recently observed, "How do we characterize our relationship with Sony Electronics? On some products we compete with one another, on others we collaborate, on still a third type we supply them and on a fourth, they supply us."

The new, flatter hierarchy also has altered the decision-making process. Top managers today may no longer have the skills or knowledge to make decisions, so they pass decision-making control on to lower-level managers who are better equipped to make the best decision quickly. As a result, the skills needed to be an effective manager in the N-form also have changed along the four dimensions of leading, planning, organizing, and controlling. The key skill today is to be able to lead through groups of self-motivated followers who are capable of making decisions on their own. As one CEO whose company was engaged in an integrated relationship with a supplier notes:

> At the top, executives must learn to live with a contradiction: the need to know more than ever about the company and its industry, but exercising less control as empowered and integrated teams of employees, customers and suppliers make more decisions closer to the market.[8]

Clearly, leaders today must be comfortable with letting employees make decisions since there is often not enough time to wait for approval from executives in the C-suite. However, this practice entails more than simply delegating, because top management is still ultimately responsible for the company's performance. Thus, those at the top need to maintain their expertise while, at the same time, trusting their followers to act appropriately. The followers must also evolve: they must be self-motivated and willing to inform leaders of anticipated changes before being asked to do so.

In terms of planning, companies must now coordinate both within and across organizations. Hence, planning becomes a supra-organizational challenge because a single company often cannot act unilaterally to introduce a new product or service. Instead, companies must coordinate their efforts with critical suppliers or market channel partners. For example, Toyota shares much of its production information and plans with not only its direct suppliers, but also with its suppliers' suppliers. This sharing is necessary to increase the speed of model changes: when Toyota makes changes in a model or alters production, its suppliers must be prepared. This new planning process involves two parts: first, determining what the company would like to do itself, and second, coordinating and negotiating its plans with other companies in its network. This kind of planning requires managers to communicate and coordinate laterally across organizations, as well as hierarchically within the company. Hence, managers involved in the planning process require effective consensus-building skills.

The organizing function of today's managers has changed due to the rise of strong informal relationships that provide the necessary information, advice, and knowledge for them to do their jobs. Google, according to Gary Hamel, is adept at allowing its managers to take on different roles in different projects, and one of the company's strengths is the constant forming and reforming of teams. While some efficiencies may be lost in this constant reorganization (because managers have to develop new skills for a project), it has the advantage of expanding each manager's skill set—and, thus, over time, speeding up overall decision-making in the company by building its overall leadership capacity. In organizations with deep managerial talent, all managers need to be comfortable with blurred boundaries between functions, divisions, and organizations, as well as with an authority structure in which they report to several different people on different projects. The role of top managers in these new companies is to design the organization in order to facilitate connections between and among workers, as well as to encourage the flow of knowledge and learning throughout the company.

Finally, the concept of control has changed from an earlier focus on management-by-objectives and meeting clearly defined goals, to recognizing that multiple objectives may apply for each worker. That evaluation requires multiple criteria. Since workers today often are laterally (rather than hierarchically) related to each other, they cannot rely upon formal structure and formal rewards to motivate others. Instead, they must use their personal influence, negotiation skills, and reputations to encourage others to engage in teamwork alongside them.

Summary and the Future

As this historical review demonstrates, changes in technology and global market conditions have continually altered the nature of industrial competition, the type of organizational structures that dominate in any era, and the skills needed to be an effective manager. This pattern offers a hint of what we can expect in the future. While it is safe to say that changes in technology and global market conditions will continue and inevitably lead to evolution in the nature of competition, structure of organizations, and role of the manager, predicting the direction of such changes is anyone's guess. Current technological trends emphasize user-generated content (YouTube), open systems design (Linux), and real-time and sophisticated communication forms (text messaging, Twitter). For the short-term, innovation, speed, and efficiency will continue to be important to companies and many managers will find the N-form the preferred organizational form. However, the increased emphasis on green products, sustainability, serving the "bottom of the pyramid," and related pressures for companies to enhance transparency and incorporate stakeholder considerations into decision-making are creating the need for corporate leaders to establish ethical and sustainable corporate cultures. While the long-term impact of various corporate accounting scandals over the last decade (Enron, WorldCom, Qwest), and the current crisis in the financial sector, is not yet certain, the nature of competition plausibly may shift to include ethical decision-making as well as speed, innovation, and efficiency. The future will tell whether the N-form is the best structure for this context or whether a new organizational structure—with redefined roles for managers—emerges.

In 2007, the *Harvard Business Review* reprinted the classic article, "Managing our Way to Economic Decline." Co-author Robert Hayes provided this commentary on what has happened since the article was first published in 1980:

> [I]f a new "Managing Our Way" article were written today, it would have to go beyond its call for managers to re-embrace the traditional basics—to invest, innovate, lead and create value where none existed before. It would have to encourage them to be pioneers in creating and implementing a new set of essentials to prevail in today's networked, virtual world. Companies led by such managers will advance to the forefront in the decades ahead.[9]

These observations suggest that managers themselves must be leaders in defining the role of an effective manager in the future. They must proactively anticipate social, economic, and competitive changes and then formulate the type of organizations that will be successful in those conditions. Finally, they must develop the personal and managerial skills and values needed to be effective. There is no simple road map available to point the way forward, but by looking at the experiences in the U.S. over two centuries, managers can gain perspective on which factors to monitor and attend to in charting a new course.

---

[1] This classification draws from the work of Alfred Chandler, *The Visible Hand: The Managerial Revolution in American Business* (Cambridge, MA: The Belknap Press of Harvard University Press, 1977) and Robert Heilbroner and Alan Singer, *The Economic Transformation of America: 1600 to the Present*, 4th edition (Wadsworth Publishing, 1999). It also greatly benefits from the insights of Professor Paul Tiffany, University of California, Berkeley.

[2] David Nasaw, *Andrew Carnegie* (New York: Penguin Books, 2006).

[3] Ron Chernow, *Titan: The Life of John D. Rockefeller, Sr.* (New York: Random House, 1998).

[4] Alfred Chandler, *op. cit.*

[5] Alfred Chandler, *Strategy and Structure: Chapters in the History of the American Industrial Enterprise* (Cambridge, MA: The M.I.T. Press, 1962).

[6] Gary Hamel, *The Future of Management* (Boston: Harvard Business School Press, 2007). *See also* Gore company website (www.gore.com) for details.

[7] Ron Ashkenas, Dave Ulrich, Todd Jick and Steve Kerr, *The Boundaryless Organization*, 2nd edition (San Francisco: Jossey-Bass, 2002).

[8] Charles Haggerty. Former Chairman, CEO and President of Western Digital Corporation. Undated Speech.

[9] Robert H. Hayes and William Abernathy, "Managing Our Way to Economic Decline," *Harvard Business Review*, July/August, 1980, pp. 67-77.

CHAPTER 7

What is the Purpose of the Firm?: Shareholder and Stakeholder Theories

by Michael D. Pfarrer

There are two competing theories about the purpose of the modern business firm. Each provides a framework for evaluating executive compensation policies, corporate governance procedures, and the economic and social performance of business. The first, shareholder theory, emanates from an economic perspective, focusing on the firm's purpose of creating wealth for its owners while minimizing both the importance of the firm's interaction with its other constituencies and its role in society. The second, stakeholder theory, broadens the first perspective, recognizing the importance of wealth creation as well as the firm's relationships with its multiple constituent groups—shareholders, creditors, employees, customers, suppliers, regulators, and local communities—and impact on society at large. Below, I discuss the foundations of these two theories, provide an overview of some recent developments within each theory, and conclude with some suggestions about how shareholder and stakeholder principles might be used to construct more effective frameworks for thinking about the role of the modern business firm.

Shareholder Theory

The origins of the ideas shaping shareholder theory are more than 200 years old, with roots in Adam Smith's (1776) *The Wealth of Nations*. In general, shareholder theory encompasses the idea that the main purpose of business lies in generating profits and increasing shareholder wealth. Modern proponents of shareholder theory espouse three tenets from Smith,

1. the importance of "free" markets;

2. the "invisible hand of self-regulation;" and

3. the importance of "enlightened self-interest."

Shareholder theorists call for limited government and regulatory intervention in business, believing markets are best regulated through the mechanism of the invisible hand—that is, if all firms work in their own self-interest by attempting to maximize profits, society at large will benefit. Some proponents of the shareholder view even believe that the invisible hand checks illegal activity, arguing that the market will punish, or weed out, firms that engage in illegal or unethical behavior. Therefore, they conclude that, in general, excessive oversight and regulation of industry is unnecessary.

Members of the "Austrian School" of economics were early proponents of the shareholder perspective. Such economists such as Friedrich von Hayek, Israel Kirzner, Joseph Knight, and Joseph Schumpeter advocated the idea of "laissez-faire" (literally, to "leave alone") capitalism, which focuses on the importance of self-regulation among firms, with limited government intervention.

Shareholder theory in its current form is linked most directly to the "Chicago School" of economics, most notably to Milton Friedman and his colleagues, who have argued for nearly four decades that the overriding purpose of the firm is to maximize shareholder wealth. They believe solving social problems is the responsibility of the state. Corporate philanthropy and other activities not directly related to generating shareholder wealth are both a waste of shareholders' money and, potentially, immoral because they amount to stealing from owners.

Although this last statement seems strong, Friedman believed, in short, that the business *of business is business*. Firms are created to make money, not oversee the social or moral development of society. Social and moral development, according to Friedman, is best handled by the government or (preferably) through voluntary organizations (NGOs). When firms become involved in social or public policy issues, wealth is diverted to issues outside the core expertise of their managers. This inefficient use of wealth will negatively affect society in the long run. Friedman's negative view of socially involved companies went so far as to proclaim that such actions usurped the role of democratically elected officials.

It is important to note that Friedman never espoused firms acting unethically, immorally, or illegally. In fact, while promoting the corporate goal of "maximizing shareholder wealth," he argued that this must be done within the moral, ethical, and legal boundaries of society. He asked only that government and the citizenry assume their rightful roles in creating those boundaries.

Shareholder theories today. Two influential and recent schools of thought fall under the broad umbrella of shareholder-based theories: "transaction cost economics" (TCE) and "agency theory." Like shareholder theory, each focuses on behaviors that can maximize firm efficiency: TCE focuses on the importance of corporate hierarchies and monitoring employee behavior to minimize self-interested behavior; agency theory focuses primarily on the principal vs. agent (shareowner vs. manager) relationship in publicly traded firms, and how to best align the competing interests of the two parties to maximize firm value. Both TCE and agency theory have a "gloomy vision" of human self-interest. Both assume that human beings are opportunistic, and, thus, will put their own interests before the firm's.

TCE and agency theory grew out of scholarship in the early 1970s, and both form the foundations for much of the corporate governance behavior we see today. Since both theories assume that humans are self-interested, both focus on mechanisms to 1) monitor manager behavior, and 2) provide incentives to align manager interests with those of the firm's owners (primarily, to maximize shareholder wealth). Those mechanisms constitute the primary incentive systems currently in use today in most large corporations: Because opportunism, self-interest, and shirking are assumed, public corporations have instituted boards to both monitor managers and to incentivize them. Boards hire and fire executives and set their compensation; they evaluate executive behavior and use ownership plans (the granting of stock, stock options, and bonuses) to incentivize executives to work more toward the overall interests of the firm than to increase their own personal wealth. Although these incentive systems have come under increasing fire recently, it is difficult to argue against aligning owner and manager interests through monitoring and incentive systems.

Stakeholder Theory

The idea that a company should have an expanded role and responsibilities to other stakeholders besides its owners is much newer than shareholder theory. Although tenets of shareholder and stakeholder theories differ, both are concerned with the purpose of the firm and strategies to improve its competitive position. Thus, the two theories are *not* diametrically opposed, as it sometimes appears. Each is concerned with the firm's best interests—one may say self-interest—but each differs on the most effective approach to realize those interests. For example, stakeholder theory does not view maximization of shareholder wealth as the most efficient way to generate competitive advantage for the firm. The theory holds that firms can best generate competitive advantage and wealth by taking more than just their shareholders into account.

Starting in earnest in the late 1970s and early 1980s, researchers with backgrounds in philosophy, psychology, sociology, and management began putting forth a new theory of the firm that challenged some of the basic assumptions of classic economics and shareholder theory (the term "stakeholder" is derived, perhaps irreverently, from "shareholder"). In particular, Archie Carroll and Ed Freeman theorized that by taking the interests of all the firm's stakeholders into account, the firm could do "better" (achieve greater performance) than by simply focusing on shareholder interests.

Carroll noted that corporations have four major responsibilities: economic (to generate shareholder wealth), legal (to obey laws and regulations), ethical (to recognize that the firm is part of a community, and thus has obligations to, and an impact on, others), and discretionary (to engage in philanthropy). Nonetheless, economic responsibility is still primary—that is, "the business of business is business." Similarly, Freeman espouses that profit generation should be the outcome of a well-managed company (much like Carroll and Friedman). Unlike Friedman, however, both Carroll and Freeman believe that that if a firm creates value for its stakeholders, it will create value for its shareholders, as well. Thus, unlike the assumptions of classical economics and shareholder theory (that a firm can only maximize value on one dimension), stakeholder theorists believe that taking all constituent groups into account is the better way to maximize overall firm performance.

Stakeholder theories today. A firm's stakeholders are all those diverse individuals and groups who affect or are affected by a firm's actions—including competitors, consumers, employees, investors, communities, regulators, suppliers, and governments, to name the most prominent. Stakeholders can be assigned to three categories: capital market stakeholders (e.g., financiers and shareholders); product market stakeholders (e.g., customers, suppliers, communities); and organizational stakeholders (e.g., employees). They also can also be grouped by importance, or salience. Indeed, as stakeholder theory has evolved in this century scholars are recognizing the importance for firms to understand "who counts" under what particular circumstances, as well as how this "hierarchy of salience" can change depending on the relative power of stakeholders, the legitimacy of their claims, and the urgency of their claims on the company. Hence, a firm must learn to deal with trade-offs among its stakeholders, since those groups inevitably will make competing claims in which it is likely that the firm will prefer the interests of one group over another. For example, in the wake of child labor and sweatshop allegations against its factories in Asia, Nike considered the claims of NGO, regulatory, and activist stakeholders to be most salient. During other non-crisis periods, however, shareholders, employees, and customers most likely will be treated as higher in Nike's stakeholder hierarchy. (see chapter 8)

Stakeholder theory also is influencing scholars from the communications and public relations domains who are interested in how firms interact with their environments. For example, a new theory of "symmetric" communications emphasizes the interdependence of organizations with their customers, clients, suppliers, competitors, the media, and even activists. As a result, firms are encouraged to be two-way communicators, balancing their self-interest with altruism, advocacy with accommodation, and by creating symmetry between their own interests and those of their stakeholders, even if those interests are opposed. This symmetric approach calls for compromise from both sides in order to reach a win-win zone in which the firm and its stakeholders both can benefit. Significantly, the symmetric communications perspective does not call for an end to enlightened self-interest from any side; instead, the perspective looks for a process in which firms and their stakeholders both seek their own advantage while, at the same time, respecting the needs of others.

Two other recent theories that reinforce and relate to stakeholder theory are "stewardship theory" and "social capital theory." Stewardship theory, an alternative to agency theory, assumes that human beings, in fact, may put the interests of others, including the organization, above their own self-interest. Scholars such as Lex Donaldson and Jim Davis have promoted stewardship theory as a positive approach to organizational dynamics and corporate governance, in contrast to the traditional gloomy vision of agency theory and similar economics-based perspectives.

Perhaps the most vocal critics of the shareholder model who can be viewed as members of the stakeholder (and positivist) camp are the late Sumantra Ghoshal and other proponents of social capital theory. In direct opposition to the Chicago School's emphasis on "neat mathematical models that only work when multiple assumptions are in place," and in stark contrast to the ideas of human opportunism and self-interest espoused in traditional economic views, social capital theory assumes that organizational actors also have a proclivity for goodness and self-enlightened behavior that can add value to the firm. Whereas agency theory assumes the potential for conflict between managers and owners, social capital theory assumes the potential for cooperation among employees and shareholders for the overall betterment of both the individual and the firm. Ghoshal focuses on the roles of trust, goodwill, and even good karma, in positively contributing to the firm's bottom line. Ghoshal and his followers thus challenge the economists' traditional, pessimistic vision of human nature, arguing that the assumptions of self-interest and opportunism only lead to a self-fulfilling, vicious cycle in which employees, feeling distrusted, will engage in the very opportunistic behaviors that the monitoring and governance mechanisms prescribed by traditional theories are supposed to curtail.

In contrast, social capital theory attempts to create a virtuous cycle in which organizational actors are assumed to be willing to work not for their own benefit but for the benefit of the organization as a whole. They know by doing so they will reap greater personal rewards—what economists call "psychic benefits"—in addition to monetary ones. Social capital theorists recognize that people can be self-interested and opportunistic, but they fear that the widespread use of those negative assumptions has tainted how firms run their businesses and manage their stakeholders. Instead, Ghoshal asks, "Why not assume that humans are good *and* bad?" This positivistic approach to firm-stakeholder interaction has gained great traction of late among management researchers and business leaders. The University of Michigan's Ross School of Business runs the Center for Positive Organizational Scholarship, focusing on compassion, positive identity, positive leadership, and positive social capital within the firm. Companies implementing a positivistic approach to their business decisions include Burt's Bees, Google, and Reuters. However, time will tell if this perspective makes the same impact shareholder theory has made, or stakeholder theory is beginning to make.

A final branch of stakeholder-related theory is the now near-ubiquitous field known as corporate social responsibility (CSR). As befitting a stakeholder view of the role of business in society, the study of CSR includes the actions a firm takes as it relates to other institutions and constituencies. For example, CSR can mean promoting environmental integrity, economic development, and social justice as part of the firm's overall strategy to gain competitive advantage.

CSR advocates have been trying fervently to show that a positive link exists between more inclusive stakeholder management and increased financial performance (CFP). Unfortunately, only limited progress has been made in this regard because of the intrinsic difficulty of measuring the impact of corporate actions on stakeholders other than shareholders. One clear advantage of shareholder theory is its emphasis on metrics (stock price and the bottom line) that are readily available and easily quantified. Measuring a firm's effectiveness in its interactions with stakeholders outside the capital markets is far more difficult. Indeed, several meta-analyses of the link between CSR and CFP have proved inconclusive. Some studies show a positive relationship, some negative, and some show none at all (see chapter 11).

Nevertheless, perhaps the best proof is in the pudding: that is, the ever-increasing number of companies recognizing the importance of bringing more stakeholder groups to the table, and believing that doing so can benefit their bottom line. For example, the 2009 release of the Global 100 Most Sustainable Corporations reads like a Who's Who of the world's most recognizable and profitable companies, and includes Adidas, Coca-Cola, Ericsson, Danone, and Honda. This demonstrates that stakeholder theory, and the theories like CSR that draw on it, are *management* theories intrinsically concerned with the performance of the firm.

Bridging the Shareholder-Stakeholder Gap?

A key tenet of stakeholder theory unfortunately often gets lost in the debates about its merits: taking all a firm's constituencies into account (on some level) in the process of strategy formulation can be *financially* beneficial for the firm. Too often, however, advocates of stakeholder theory have gotten away from this core intention, focusing instead on the importance of non-financial market stakeholders (employees, NGOs, local communities, and environmentalists) at the expense of the firm's owners. We must remember that both shareholder and stakeholder theories recognize the importance of the firm's financial success—they just advocate different approaches to that end. Both are theories of value creation, and both are predicated on the assumption that firms should create as much value as possible within the boundaries of the law. Stakeholder theories differ from shareholder theories, however, in recognizing that a firm can maximize value by understanding how it affects, and is affected by, all its numerous constituencies.

Shareholder theory is seemingly hostile toward actions not directly impacting the firm's bottom line, whereas stakeholder theory revolves around human decision-making and, thus, ethics. Advocates of stakeholder theory believe that it does not make sense to talk about business without ethics, and vice-versa, and it doesn't make sense to talk about either without talking about humans making choices. They thus reject the commonly held separation thesis (that economic and ethical matters in business are distinct), and provide justification for using more inclusive frameworks to think about the role of business in society. Key questions stakeholder theorists encourage managers to ask are: *For whom is value created or destroyed if this decision is made? Whose rights will be enabled or not? What kind of person will I be if I make this decision?*

None of this should be seen as anti-Friedman. After all, Milton Friedman wanted firms to maximize profits within the rules—and that *may,* or may not, include CSR-type activities—depending on the outcomes generated. The trick here is that economists traditionally have had trouble measuring value outside of the bottom-line; hence they tend to ignore what they can't (precisely) measure. In the end, they are unable to create tight mathematical models that represent the loose, real world we live in.

Generating stable and growing profits should be the outcome of a well-managed company, and stakeholder theory can help the firm get there—perhaps more effectively than shareholder theory—by measuring such soft variables as firm reputation, the quality of products and services, trustworthy suppliers, good employees, supportive communities, and cooperative financiers. In short, stakeholder theory recognizes the firm has a potential for profit in generating a strong, lasting reputation among stakeholders and through addressing real needs and interests of such groups.

Dare we then say that stakeholder theory is an extension of shareholder theory, and that its broader framework and understanding of the firm's interaction with society can actually generate better performance for the firm and thus, create more benefits for society-at-large? That is a bold assertion to be sure, but it seems to make sense in the 21st century, when greater numbers of firms are accepting the legitimacy of notions such as the triple bottom line (economic, social, and ecological), sustainability, accountability, transparency, and other soft measures of performance. It also seems sensible to assume that people can be both self-interested and self-enlightened, thus creating potential for the melding of shareholder and stakeholder approaches into one useful theory.

Resources:

Archie Carroll. "A Three-Dimensional Conceptual Model of Corporate Social Performance," *Academy of Management Review*, 4 (1979), pp. 497-505.

J.H. Davis, F.D. Schoorman, F.D., and Lex Donaldson, "Toward a stewardship theory of management," *Academy of Management Review*, 22 (1997), pp. 20-47.

R.E. Freeman, *Strategic Management: A Stakeholder Approach* (Boston: Pitman, 1984).

Milton Friedman, "The social responsibility of business is to increase its profits," *New York Times Magazine*, September 13, 1970, pp. 122-126.

M.C. Jensen, "Value maximization, stakeholder theory, and the corporate objective function," *Business Ethics Quarterly*, 12 (2002), pp. 235-247.

S. Ghoshal, "Bad management theories are destroying good management practices," *Academy of Learning & Education*, 4 (2005), pp. 75-91.

CHAPTER 8

Corporate Social Responsibility and Corporate Excellence

by Bruce Hutton and Don Mayer

Corporate social responsibility (CSR) is a concept with varied meanings, all of which seek to balance corporate strategies focused narrowly on the financial bottom line. We see CSR as a much needed antidote to an economically narrow vision of corporate possibilities focused solely on "maximizing shareholder value" in the short-term, regardless of the cost to society or a company's reputation. But rather than advancing CSR as a concept in reaction to maximizing short-term shareholder value, we propose the more expansive and pragmatic concept of *corporate excellence,* which embraces both financial and social responsibility and, thus, enhances long-term value for multiple stakeholders.

The goal of corporate excellence, as we define it, is to use corporate assets—especially human capital—to seek profits through strategies that build and enhance sustainable social and environmental systems.

Stakeholders and Stockholders: CSR the Old-Fashioned Way

Milton Friedman's oft-cited objection to traditional CSR is that corporations exist solely to create economic value for their shareholders. To Friedman, any charitable donations made by managers (to the local symphony, for example) could be justified only if the donation or action promoted the corporation's profitability. He thus insisted that (1) any charitable donations must demonstrate a positive return on investment, and (2) that nonprofit organizations (including cultural institutions) be supported only by voluntary individual donations. In contrast, advocates of CSR have encouraged managers to focus on stakeholders—in addition to shareholders—as a means to create positive value for society (see chapter 7).

Friedman himself would allow some focus on stakeholders, including a corporation's social contributions, although only in furtherance of the business's mission. While he notes that business must conform to "the basic rules of society, both those embodied in law and those embodied in ethical custom," Friedman taught that the only acceptable corporate social activities are those that enhance the bottom line. This doctrine's shortcoming is its disregard for the increasing consensus within society that the power of business must be balanced with social responsibilities. A 2005 survey by *The Economist* found that 85 percent of investors and executives said CSR was a "central" or "important" consideration in investment decisions. In a 2007 survey, two-thirds of customers said they consider a company's social practices when deciding what to buy, and 87 percent would switch brands if those activities were related to a good cause. Among employees, 72 percent want to work for companies that are involved in their communities.[1] A 2007 international survey by McKinsey & Co. found that 84 percent of executives, and 89 percent of customers, agree that companies should balance obligations between shareholders on the one hand, and the public good, on the other.

The notion of going "beyond the bottom line" to embrace numerous stakeholders has spawned several different definitions of CSR. Professor Archie Carroll defines CSR as *encompassing the economic, ethical, legal, and discretionary expectations that society has of business organizations at a given point in time.*[2] The World Business Council for Sustainable Development defines CSR as *the commitment of business to contribute to sustainable economic development, working with employees, their families, the local community, and society at large to improve their quality of life.*[3] In our view, Craig Smith says it best when he notes that businesses, like citizens in the classical sense, *cultivate a broad view of their own self-interest while searching for ways to align that self-interest with the larger public good.*[4]

In 1995, advocates of CSR applauded Aaron Feuerstein's decision to not only reconstruct his fire-destroyed Malden Mills textile factory in Lawrence, Massachusetts, but to continue paying his out-of-work employees while the factory was being rebuilt. In so doing, Feuerstein gave extraordinary moral consideration to one group of stakeholders: his employees (and by extension, the local community). Yet his generous decision turned out to be unsustainable, a situation that could have been (and was) predicted at the time he chose to rebuild. It was clear even then that the global forces of competition would undermine the profitability of the Malden Mills. Facing a world of radical change and global competition, it turned out that Feuerstein could not continue to "do good" and remain competitive. By 2001, he could not meet his payroll and make payments to creditors. In the end, the creditors took over the business.

Still, Feuerstein's focus on employees, instead of the short-term bottom line, has considerable merit *if it is part of an overall strategy for strengthening the health of the company.* After all, a company that fails has no opportunity to provide its most fundamental social benefit: jobs. But managers who merely regard employees as a drain on the bottom line will cut payroll at the slightest drop in earnings; then, because those managers have not demonstrated loyalty to their employees, they often have difficulty attracting and retaining the best people.

The experience of a popular restaurant in Denver illustrates the point: Although it employs over 100 people, it provides health insurance to all, even when doing so has a major negative impact on the bottom line. Significantly, it never has to advertise for help, and gets 20 applications a week for the rare vacancy. Most of its employees have worked there over six years. As a result, customer service ratings are consistently among the best in the city. In sum, although the restaurant's exemplary treatment of its employees is neither charity nor social activism, it represents a shift in managerial perspective by viewing employees as legitimate stakeholders to whom the company has real responsibility.

This new perspective won many converts in the 1990s, when company after company ran afoul of public opinion by failing to give adequate consideration not only to employees, but to local communities, local governments, and the moral sentiments of their customers. For example, Royal Dutch Shell Oil Co. began operations in Nigeria in 1937 under a national government license to operate. But, in the late 1980s, tribal groups (especially the Ogoni) began targeting Shell for harming the environment, failing to address crushing poverty, and for a pattern of breaking promises of community development. These protests turned increasingly violent, culminating in the killing of four Ogoni leaders and the execution of Ken Saro-Wiwa, a well-known Nigerian novelist and environmental activist.

Shell adopted a hands-off stance in response to the protests, publicly stating that it would not interfere with the legal or political prerogatives of the Nigerian government. This stance proved to be a disaster for Shell; unions, environmental groups, human rights organizations, and churches all over the world accused the company of abetting Nigeria's military regime. In light of these protests, Shell revised its business model in 1997 and, among other actions, came out strongly in support of advocating human rights as a legitimate role of business, as well as addressing a variety of environmental and community issues. Even so, the past has haunted Shell: in 2009, the company had to answer charges of crimes against humanity for human rights abuses that took place in the 1990s in connection with the death of Ken Saro-Wiwa. Shell agreed to pay $15.5 million to settle the case.[5]

Even with good intentions, hard realities can make some CSR initiatives counter-productive. When William Clay Ford, Jr. became chairman of Ford in 1999, he was an ardent environmentalist who broke with Detroit traditions by recognizing global warming as a real and serious problem. He stated Ford's commitment to improve the fuel efficiency of Ford's high powered and popular SUVs. Yet Ford's promises did not bear significant fruit, as the company met few, if any, of its environmental goals. Over the past decade, there was little improvement in fuel efficiency, and Ford vehicles remain among the most carbon intensive of all vehicles sold in America. Although Ford made progress in greening its manufacturing processes at the River Rouge plant, company lobbyists simultaneously fought increases in fuel economy standards. One explanation for this contradictory behavior is that Ford must satisfy three main constituencies—customers, shareholders, and the U.A.W.—none of which are concerned much about fuel economy.

Ford is still struggling with the challenge of meeting its earlier commitments. In contrast, Toyota has created a coherent business strategy that integrates business profitability and environmental issues. Early on, Toyota accepted the reality that no company exists outside of its legal, political, and social milieu. As true as it is that "no man is an island," a business firm is similarly an integral part of a complex interdependent political, social, and economic system. A 2006 article in the *McKinsey Quarterly* concludes that companies must find a way to incorporate an awareness of socio-political issues more systematically into their core strategic decisions, and to see the social and political dimensions in which they operate not only as risks, but also as opportunities.[6] To facilitate this, the authors of the article advocate an increased emphasis on partnerships and alliances among nonprofits, civil society, governments, and other businesses as a growing necessity for effective strategic planning. This increasingly collaborative behavior is a function of the changing, and progressively more interdependent, roles of governments, businesses, and civil society.

The 2002 Earth Summit in Johannesburg, South Africa was a good example of this collaborative spirit on the global front. Attended by representatives of over 100 national governments, multinational businesses, and non-governmental organizations (NGOs), the summit was singularly important because of the number of cross-sector partnerships that emerged. By contrast, the 1992 International Conference on Environment and Development in Rio de Janeiro had focused on various non-binding treaties and principles. Very few business leaders attended, and a sharp divide emerged between governments and NGOs. But ten years later, in Johannesburg, instead of forming new agreements between governments, the focus was on the more than 300 cross-sector partnership initiatives established to achieve Millennium Development Goals. For example, the Alliance for Rural Energy in Africa has ten partners, including BP Solar, the World Business Council for Sustainable Development, Totalfina (France), the UN Development Program, and the Agency for Environment and Energy Management. The primary objective of the alliance is to pool the resources of participants in order to meet the energy needs of rural Africa.

A good example of a successful cross-sector alliance is OneCoast, a partnership between Sun Microsystems, the government of Australia, three UN agencies, and more than ten nonprofits (including six universities) focused on sustainable and restorative practices in oceans and seas. A second example is EU Water for Life, a tri-sector partnership involving governments (European Union), nonprofits (WWF, Green Cross International, UN Environment

Program), and private industry (Suez, Vivendi) working together to provide clean water for the developing world.

Domestically, Michael Porter advocates moving from the "welfare model" to a "development model" that builds community capacity through coordinating actions of business, government, and nonprofits.[7] For example, the Timberland company recognizes the value of such collaboration in achieving public good and business benefit. CEO Jeffery Swartz says, "Timberland is on this earth to make superior boots, shoes, clothing, and accessories—but that's not all we can do. We can create enhanced value. We can take a short-term impact, long-term solutions approach to improving the neighborhoods around us, and improve our business at the same time."[8] One of the most successful and visible ways Swartz accomplished this vision is through a partnership with the nonprofit City Year, whose purpose is to engage young people in civic service projects across America. Together, this partnership has generated more than 250,000 hours of volunteer services by young people.

Still, it is one thing for businesses to find "win-win" scenarios through partnering with governments, NGOs, and civic organizations, and another thing to meet the demands of social or environmental activists that they save the planet, preserve cultures, and nurture social capital. Particularly in a global context, it is nearly paralyzing for a profit-oriented firm to think that it must give equal consideration to the needs of all its numerous stakeholders, for example by sacrificing profits in order to uphold human rights. Once a company leaves behind the seeming certainty of "maximizing shareholder value," an almost endless array of stakeholders—and their conflicting desires—confronts the corporation. Since no company can satisfy all of its constituencies at all times, how, then, to choose the "right" socially responsible actions?

CSR as a Core Business Strategy

To answer this question, we turn to the advice of the late Peter Drucker, the pre-eminent thinker on corporate management, who emphasized the need for companies to stick with their core competencies. He argued that there must be a meaningful synergy between organizational competence, reality, and societal needs—that is, between the mission of the enterprise and its relation to society.[9] Hence, a robust corporate strategy must include CSR *without diluting the long-term value of the firm as it relates to all its stakeholders*. Careful deliberation on the needs and preferences of stakeholders can help a firm to create long-term value; the challenge lies in identifying where the corporation can have the most significant influence and then establishing appropriate boundaries so as not to exceed its core competencies.

The arenas where a company has clear social responsibilities are those related to its core operations; that is, labor standards, health and safety practices, and product safety. Companies also have direct responsibility—and leverage—in the areas of corporate governance, financial reporting, and shareholder relations, and control of their relationships with host communities in such areas as pollution control, corruption, and bribery. Moving outward from the core, businesses may partner with government and other businesses to set industry-wide norms for labor standards, indigenous people's rights, and social equity.

Ultimately, incorporating social issues as an integral part of strategic planning entails an expansive, outside-the-box look at the non-market factors that affect profitability (we call them "non-market" factors because they are not directly related to price, product quality, market positioning, actions of competitors, marketing, or branding). Such factors include the threat of potential costs of customer boycotts for perceived unethical practices, brand issues resulting from negative media attention, failure of self-regulation leading to inefficient government regulation, and product recall losses as a result of inadequate attention to supplier and subcontractor ethics and standards.

A corporate strategy that includes such issues does not require noble motives, altruism, or the sacrifice of corporate self-interest. In fact, social or environmental concerns cannot survive as viable parts of corporate strategy if they do require sacrificing short-term profitability or if they undermine long-term sustainability. Milton Friedman was not wrong to insist on profitability; instead, he was too dismissive of corporate social responsibility as an integral part of a firm's strategy to attain long-term profitability. Ian Davis argues the "business of business is business" mantra tends to obscure the reality that social issues are not tangential to business but are, instead, fundamental to it.[10] Ignoring public sentiment makes a company vulnerable to attack on social concerns (Nike's labor practices in the developing world, for example) and including environmental issues and opportunities can create important market advantages (witness Toyota's Prius). CSR need not be seen as a defensive strategy but, rather, can be a proactive way for companies to create value with one's values. As Michael Porter notes:

> The prevailing approaches to CSR are so fragmented and disconnected from business and strategy that they obscure many of the greatest opportunities for companies to benefit society. If, instead, corporations were to analyze their prospects for social responsibility using the same frameworks that guide their core business choices, they would discover that CSR can be much more than a cost, a constraint, or a charitable deed. It can be a source of opportunity, innovation, and competitive advantage.[11]

Clearly, a company cannot be all things to all people, nor can it do what it has no competency to do. In several different contexts, Drucker has made it clear that organizations have a responsibility to try to find an approach to social problems that fits their basic competence, making the social problem into an opportunity for the organization. Equally, it is not a responsibility of business to "act where it lacks competence; to do so is not responsibility but irresponsibility."[12] It follows that the best opportunities for a company to make socially responsible contributions always relate to its mission, goals, and core competencies.

Kurucz, Colbert, and Wheeler suggest that the business case for CSR (and sustainability) can be made in four strategic areas.[13] First, in the reduction of costs and risks, because the demands of stakeholders present potential threats to the firm (regulation, boycotts and so forth). Thus, the firm stands to gain advantage by acting to mitigate the threats. Second, the firm can also take actions that increase advantage over competitors. In a world where it is increasingly difficult to differentiate brands on functional attributes, CSR strategies can provide differentiation (for example, promoting social awareness by supporting local community groups). Third, activities related to reputation enhancement, including socially responsible investing, and cause-related marketing programs. Fourth, sustainable development policies that connect economic, social, and environmental opportunities into one coherent strategy.

Perhaps the best contemporary example of an integrated, coherent strategy is GE's Ecomagination. Introduced in 2005, Ecomagination is GE's commitment to developing pioneering technologies that meet customers' environmental and financial needs. At the time, CEO Jeff Immelt said GE's aim was to "focus our unique energy, technology, manufacturing, and infrastructure capabilities to develop tomorrow's solutions such as solar energy, hybrid locomotives, fuel cells, lower-emission aircraft engines, lighter and stronger materials, efficient lighting, and water purification technology."[14] If successful, GE will be a world leader in helping to solve some of the most serious environmental issues facing the planet and humanity, such as access to fresh water and reduction of greenhouse gases. But, first and foremost, Immelt sees this move as a substantial business opportunity to grow the company and create value for shareholders. GE's position is that clean technology and innovation resonate in the marketplace. Moreover, by cutting internal costs and reducing energy, water usage, and emissions, GE strengthens its competitive position. Although implementing the plan has not been easy, early returns are promising: originally, the goal was to increase revenues from Ecomagination products to $20 billion by 2010. Revenues from its environmental portfolio topped $14 billion in 2007, up more than 15 percent from 2006. 2008 revenues were expected to grow over 20 percent to $17 billion. Forecasts for 2009 indicate that revenues could surpass $20 billion, allowing GE to reach its goal ahead of schedule.

From Crisis to Opportunity: The Road to CSR

Sometimes, a company must be in crisis to see the opportunities latent in CSR. Nike is an example of a company that was slow to understand the responsibilities that society increasingly places on business. Nike became the poster child for sweatshop labor and child exploitation partly because the company left social and environmental issues out of its business model and strategic planning process. The company outsourced all manufacturing and claimed no responsibility for the actions of its contractors. The money saved from outsourcing flowed into Nike's marketing effort, creating one of the world's strongest brands. But outsourcing also produced an inviting target for activist NGOs who were beginning to track labor issues in developing countries in the early 1990s. Nike soon became the subject of negative articles in the media. For example, a 1996 editorial in *Business Week* noted:

> Too few executives understand that the clamor for ethical sourcing isn't going to disappear with the wave of a magic press release. They have protested disingenuously, that conditions at factories run by subcontractors are beyond their control. Such attitudes won't wash anymore. As the industry gropes for solutions, Nike will be a key company to watch.[15]

After years of continuing NGO pressure, Nike finally did "just do it." In 1998, it established a Corporate Responsibility department in recognition of the fact that responsible business entails much more than simple legal compliance; they found that social actions must be managed like any other part of a business. Nike then became a leader in addressing public policy issues. Nike grew deeply involved with the Fair Labor Association, the organization responsible for setting standards for the Apparel Industry with regard to global labor practices.[16] Also, Nike was the only U.S. company represented at the launch of the UN Global Compact, a multi-stakeholder initiative to promote responsible business.[17] Today, the company has turned its reputation around and is now considered a role model and leader in the social arena.

Several lessons can be learned from Nike's experience, the most important of which is the potentially negative impact of social and environmental issues on organizational performance and reputation when they are not dealt with as part of the company's core business strategy. Simon Zadek chronicles the Nike story and suggests that a company's journey to corporate responsibility involves combining two factors—organizational and societal—to create a strategic opportunity. In fact, organizational learning at Nike occurred in several stages. At the lowest level, the organization was dismissive of human rights issues, such as child labor in off-shore plants, claiming they were simply legal or communications problems. Nike insisted child labor was not *their* problem because contractors, and not Nike, were responsible for managing the factories where shoes were made. In the next stage, Nike saw the issue as a "cost of doing business," which resulted in a minimal compliance effort, expending just enough money, time, and effort to reduce litigation and maintain Nike's reputation. Neither of those approaches was sufficient to reduce pressure from NGOs, and customers began to take notice.

Consequently, Nike entered a third stage: recognition that child labor was a long-term issue that needed to be managed as part of its core business strategy. Once addressing child labor became part of the overall strategic process within Nike, managers began to see that the organization could gain competitive advantage by aligning labor issues with overall company strategy. The final stage of learning occurred with the recognition that the entire industry needed to address problems of child labor and other human rights issues. At this stage, Nike led the effort to set industry standards.

Zadek suggests that the reason companies go through such a long, and costly, learning process is that corporate awareness grows slowly and lags behind changes in social values. Initially, the American public was largely unaware of the social and environmental issues in off-shore plants in developing countries. Because those issues also were not on their radar screens, Nike's managers failed to consider them when making key decisions. But in the 1990s, NGOs and the media began compiling data on the labor practices of subcontractors in the developing world. The public—and Nike customers—caught on quickly, resulting in protests, negative publicity, and even litigation. This led to a delayed response culminating in the development of the company's new business practices and industry-wide voluntary standards of conduct. Ultimately, Nike's response to the issue became institutionalized, norms of ethical behavior were established, and the company began to achieve "corporate excellence."

Corporate Excellence:
the New Mandate in an Interconnected World

We live in a time of radical change: the world today is technologically complex, ecologically fragile, socially fragmented, and fraught with both opportunities and threats. Indeed, we live in a perfect storm of uncertainty—geopolitically, economically, and environmentally. In such a storm, ostrich-like reactions must yield to creativity. At a minimum, business leaders must proactively look at the needs of their many constituencies to identify strategies that both promote profits and enhance the social and natural environment.

Developing such strategies requires forsaking models that put the organization and its immediate needs at the center of reality. A more realistic model is one in which there is constructive engagement of all parts of society, public and private. From this perspective, companies may see that social and environmental problems create entrepreneurial opportunities. As a *Business Week* story put it in 2007, "Imagine a World in which socially responsible and eco-friendly practices actually boost a company's bottom line. It's closer than you think."[18] As Unilever's CEO, Patrick Cescau, says, "You can't ignore the impact your company has on the community and environment." He goes on to say that issues such as poverty, water scarcity, and climate change used to be framed in the context of moral responsibilities, but now they are also sources of growth and innovation: "In the future, it will be the only way to do business." Such a view should not be surprising from the CEO of a company where 40 percent of sales, and the majority of its growth, takes place in developing nations.

Interface, a billion-dollar manufacturer of carpets and textiles, similarly found opportunity in social and environmental challenges. CEO Ray Anderson's growing concern for the environment triggered a profitable change in how he defined his business: from selling carpets (then) to providing environmentally sustainable flooring (now). Avon put finding a cure for breast cancer at the heart of its business, and consequently boosted employee morale and retention. Green Mountain Coffee adopted "fair trade" practices and made a profitable business by working with small family vendors in the developing world who previously had been exploited by Green Mountain's competitors. The company has been working for fifteen years (considerably longer than either Dunkin' Donuts or Starbucks) to perfect a business model that sustains small farm communities.

Every company is faced with social issues, whether internal (supplier relations, workforce productivity, loyalty, diversity) or external (community relations, emissions, promoting sound public policy to create effective market systems). The decision they must make is whether to (a) ignore them, (b) treat them as a cost of doing business, or (c) capitalize on them as a legitimate opportunity to create value. The success of companies like Interface, Avon, Green Mountain Coffee, and GE depends on their ability not only to see opportunities, but also on their skill at deciding which opportunities to capitalize on, and which to forego. Generally, the decision rules for social issues are not much different than for other business decisions: those opportunities providing the best "bang for the buck" will probably lead to the best strategy. As in any strategic plan, assessing a company's core competencies, its customer base, its location, and its current cash flow all need to be part of the process of deciding which social issues to tackle.

Globalization and the spread of free market capitalism have greatly altered the terms of the social contract by which American businesses operate in the less developed world, for example, by altering relationships and responsibilities between and among sectors. In the past, business, labor, civil society, and government had well-defined roles: business could focus on the "economic bottom line," with a nod to community and good works to enhance reputations. Like it or not, business leaders cannot realistically think in the same manner today. Multinational companies operating in developing countries often have to do things that government ordinarily does in the more developed world. A local community may demand that a private company build roads, hospitals, or schools. As Shell painfully learned in Nigeria, multinational corporations (MNCs) can no longer fulfill social contract simply by "obeying the law." Legal compliance, especially in developing countries, is a non-starter as a substitute for corporate social responsibility. Indeed, expectations of MNCs are highest where public governance is weakest. Hence, a license to operate an oil, gas, or mining operation from a central government does not bestow legitimacy on a company in a community in great need of schools, jobs, and health care. Instead, companies must work to achieve support from local communities through collaboration (see Chapters 11 and 13).

Nowhere is this more apparent than in developing countries where multinational mining companies deal with weak national governments. For many years, Newmont Mining, the second largest gold mining company in the world, suffered the same fate as many extractive companies as it became a target of environmental and human rights NGOs, local communities, and government regulators. Today, Newmont Mining is the only gold mining company listed on the Dow Jones Sustainability Index. A substantial part of this transformation is due to Newmont's purposeful consideration of gaining a credible "social license to operate" (SLTO) from local communities through strategically acting out an appropriate social role within the developing countries where it operates.

Of course, obtaining a SLTO is no easy matter: fulfilling social obligations and meeting community demands can be like taking aim at a moving target.[19] A company operating in a developing country may believe it knows which activities are appropriate for a private company, and which are better suited as responsibilities of nonprofits and governments, but it's likely that community expectations will be considerably different. A small village in Africa without a formal school and hospital, and lacking clean water, may see the presence of a company like Newmont as its one opportunity to meet its fundamental needs. Regardless of which sector is theoretically supposed to meet those needs, to the villagers, Newmont looks like a government, business, and NGO all rolled into one resource opportunity.

Newmont's goal is to be viewed as a friend of the country and community where it operates by creating value, bridging cultures, and by being trustworthy, dependable, and engaged. At the same time, it must not be seen, or treated, as an agent of the national government. Walking this fine line requires purposeful planning and time to build relationships with a full range of stakeholders, including tribal community leaders, relevant NGOs, and government agencies.

Newmont's strategy in Ghana is successful in this regard. In order not to be perceived as a "government" offering handouts, Newmont established a foundation to which it contributes money for community projects. A local board directs the foundation and makes decisions on the allocation of all funds. Thus, if the community needs a school, its members do not go to Newmont for the money, or ask Newmont to build it. Instead, the local board evaluates the proposal and makes funding decisions. In short, Newmont avoids playing the decision-making role of government, while fulfilling its obligation to the community as a valued partner.

Corporate Excellence

As Milton Friedman wrote, the responsibility of business is to conduct itself in accordance with the desires of its owners while, "conforming to the basic rules of society, both those embodied in law and those embodied in ethical custom."[20] It is clear that, for the last 20 years or so, society has spoken on the need for new rules that demand greater social responsibility on the part of business. Successive—and increasingly frequent—market meltdowns since the 1980s create ever-stronger demand for a business sector that is more responsible to wider society. The question for today is not whether businesses should be socially responsible, but rather how they should go about doing so.

Conceptually, CSR has been viewed as imposing social, economic, and environmental obligations on businesses that necessarily limit financial performance. As such, we believe CSR has a limited shelf life. Far more promising is the concept of corporate excellence, which embraces economic profitability through strategies that maintain and enhance social and environmental integrity. Corporate excellence is not merely the old mantra that "good ethics is good business." Instead, an increasing number of companies are carefully measuring their strengths and positions within complex political, legal, social, cultural, and environmental milieus and adopting strategies that are sustainable, responsible, *and profitable*.

---

[1] Emily Tan, "Survey: Good is the New Black," *Advertising Age*, July 12, 2007, available at http://adage.com/results?endeca=1&return=endeca&search_offset=0&search_order_by=score&search_phrase=07/12/2007.

[2] Archie Carroll, "A Three-Dimensional Conceptual Model of Corporate Social Performance," *Academy of Management Review* (4), 1979, pp. 497-505.

[3] Lloyd Timberlake, (ed.) 2002. "The Business Case for Sustainable Development," World Business Council for Sustainable Development.

[4] Craig Smith, "The New Corporate Philanthropy," *Harvard Business Review*, 72(3), May-June, 1994, pp. 105-116.

[5] Jad Mouawad, "Shell to Pay $15.5 Million to Settle Nigerian Case," *New York Times*, June 9, 2009.

[6] Ian Davis & Elizabeth Stephenson, "Ten Trends to Watch in 2006," *The McKinsey Quarterly*, January, 2006.

[7] Michael E. Porter, "The Competitive Advantage of the Inner City," *Harvard Business Review* (73), May-June, 1995.

[8] Christine Arena, *Cause for Success* (Novato, CA New World Library, 2004), pp. 78-97.

[9] Peter Drucker, *Management Challenges for the 21st Century* (New York: Harper-Collins, 1999).

[10] Ian Davis, "What is the Business of Business?" *The McKinsey Quarterly*, No. 3. 2005.

[11] Michael E. Porter and Mark R. Kramer, "The Competitive Advantage of Corporate Philanthropy," *Harvard Business Review* (80), December, 2002, pp. 57-68.

[12] Peter Drucker, *The Frontiers of Management: Where Tomorrow's Decisions Are Being Shaped Today* (New York: Penguin, 1986), p. 187.

[13] Elizabeth Kurucz, Barry Colbert, & David Wheeler, "The Business Case for Corporate Social Responsibility," *The Oxford Handbook of Corporate Social Responsibility* (Oxford: Oxford University Press, 2008), pp. 83-112.

[14] Joel Makower, "Ecomagination: Inside GE's Power Play," WorldChanging.com, May 8, 2005, available at www.worldchanging.com\archives\002669.html.

[15] M.L. Clifford, "Commentary: Keep the Heat on Sweatshops," *BusinessWeek*, December 23, 1996, p. 90.

[16] SA8000 is based on the United Nations' Universal Declaration of Human Rights, the Convention on the Rights of the Child, and various International Labour Organization (ILO) conventions. The SA8000 standards cover issues of child labor, forced labor, workplace safety and health standards, non-discrimination, fair wages, and abusive working conditions.

[17] Simon Zadek, "The Path to Corporate Responsibility," *Harvard Business Review*, December, 2004, pp. 125-132.

[18] Pete Engardio, "Beyond the Green Corporation," *BusinessWeek*, January 29, 2007. pp. 50-64.

[19] John Zinkin, "Maximizing the License to Operate," *Journal of Corporate Citizenship*, Summer, 2004, pp. 67-79.

[20] Milton Friedman, "The social responsibility of business is to increase its profits," *New York Times Magazine*, September 13, 1970, pp. 122-126.

CHAPTER 9

Doing Good Business: Leadership, and Sustainable Corporate Cultures

by James O'Toole

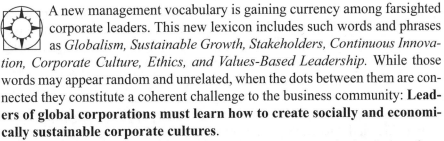 A new management vocabulary is gaining currency among farsighted corporate leaders. This new lexicon includes such words and phrases as *Globalism, Sustainable Growth, Stakeholders, Continuous Innovation, Corporate Culture, Ethics, and Values-Based Leadership.* While those words may appear random and unrelated, when the dots between them are connected they constitute a coherent challenge to the business community: **Leaders of global corporations must learn how to create socially and economically sustainable corporate cultures**.

This challenge is as complex as it is important. Its complexity derives from the fact that it contains numerous and disparate elements, few of which seem complementary:

- The manifest need to protect the environment by using natural resources wisely, and by proactively addressing issues of global warming and pollution;

- The moral imperative to treat workers in developing nations with respect and dignity, a responsibility that includes preparing them through training and education to contribute to the long-term development of their home nations;

- Implicit social responsibilities to all a corporation's domestic stakeholders—including employees, customers, suppliers, dealers, and host communities;

- The legal imperative to obey all the laws in every country where a company operates—including regulatory compliance and accounting and reporting procedures—extending

beyond where the law ends to include ethical governance and
business practices.

Last, but not least, there is the requirement of long-term profitability—no matter how well a company may perform its non-economic functions, it will be
viewed as a failure if it fails to fulfill its basic task of providing customers
with goods and services they need at prices they are willing to pay. To do that
requires an effective business strategy along with the appropriate internal management practices needed to create continuous organizational self-renewal, innovation, and customer responsiveness—all of which are needed for sustainable long-term growth. In sum, doing Good Business is a tall order.

The Red Ball of Profit

While the centrality of this complex set of challenges has become increasingly
clear in recent years, it is far from new. In 1975, the CEO of pharmaceutical giant Johnson&Johnson presented his executive team with exactly those
challenges. He sent the team on a two-day retreat to discuss the company's
founding document, the J&J Credo, which had hung unheeded and yellowing
on company walls for decades after the company's founder had penned it. The
Credo outlines specific responsibilities to all J&J's stakeholders, starting with
its customers—the doctors, nurses, patients and mothers of sick children who
buy the company's medicines—on through to their suppliers, employees, host
communities and, finally, the company's share owners.

Toward the end of the meeting, one of J&J's top executives summarized
what he saw as the reality of corporate life. He said being an executive in a
large company was like being a circus juggler, attempting to keep five balls
in the air simultaneously. Four of those balls were white (representing customers, suppliers, employees and communities), and the fifth ball was red
(representing shareholders). To the approval of most of his colleagues in the
room—and reflecting the beliefs of the vast majority of corporate managers at
the time—the executive said it was possible to drop one of the white balls and
still survive, but it was fatal to let the red ball of profit fall. At that point, the
company's president, James Burke, spoke up and said: "My friend, I am afraid
you are wrong. Today, *all the balls are red.*"[1]

By being the first corporate leader to acknowledge this new reality, and to
accept the challenge of balancing the legitimate needs of all of J&J's stakeholders, Burke went on to become one of the most successful CEOs in America. When his European competitors paid bribes to win business in developing markets, he refused to do so. When it was discovered that eight people
had died from ingesting cyanide-laced Tylenol capsules (a J&J product), he
immediately assumed full responsibility for the deaths, pulling $100 million
worth of the analgesic off drugstore shelves. He then opened the company's
executive suite to the media and dealt with the issue in a transparent manner

that, to this day, stands as the model of effective crisis management. Yet, at the time, critics in the financial community said Burke's transparency was foolish: instead, he should "stonewall," or else his candor would cause the company to go bankrupt. The critics urged him to put J&J shareholders' interests first: *Remember the red ball!*

Later, it was discovered that a psychopath had placed the poisoned bottles on the shelves of only a few stores in one city and, therefore, the company was not responsible for the deaths. But by going public before it was known who was responsible, J&J built a strong reputation for integrity, Tylenol sales recovered quickly, and the company went on to new heights of profitability.

In short, Burke did what was unthinkable in U.S. big business in the 1980s and 90s: he sacrificed short-term profits to do the right thing for his company's stakeholders in the conviction that *it is the long term that counts.* That lesson finally is being accepted in the executive suites of many large American companies. Clearly, it is accepted in Europe at such companies as IKEA, in Japan at Toyota, and even in the developing world at companies like India's Tata. In progressive global companies on almost all continents, leaders are seeking to create and maintain responsible, healthy, and ethical corporate cultures.

Research shows that transforming a traditional company culture into a Good Business is extremely difficult. In fact, it is an exceedingly rare leadership feat to truly change any large, established company's strategy, structure, systems, and behaviors. A large part of the problem is that leaders in large companies traditionally have used centralized power and controls to direct, and to change, their large, bureaucratic, and hierarchical organizations. But that form of organization—and that type of leadership—are no longer the norm in the business world (see chapter 6). As a result of the recent confluence of changing social and workplace values, globalization, information technology, and advancing managerial knowledge, many large global companies today are becoming dynamic, organic, decentralized organizations in which leaders utilize shared values, mission, and purpose to gain alignment with corporate goals. Under those conditions, it is far easier for leaders to create strategies that lead to continual innovation, sustainable profitability, and sensitivity to stakeholder needs.

Let me offer an "improbable" example of such leadership. I call it improbable because it concerns an old-line company in a dirty, unglamorous industry. Alcoa is a global producer of aluminum and other metal products, with 130,000 employees at 436 locations in 43 countries. Traditionally, companies in the mining and metal processing industries have had miserable records in terms of environmental degradation, particularly in the developing world and in terms of the effects of their operations on worker health and safety. Indeed, when Paul O'Neil became CEO of Alcoa in 1986, there was no gainsaying the fact that the company's workers around the globe were routinely injured, maimed, and killed on the job, and a great many suffered long-term health effects from job-related diseases. The company's manufacturing practices also put the health of residents in host communities at risk of being compromised through air and water pollution and the inappropriate disposal of solid waste.

O'Neil took the CEO's job at Alcoa on one condition: that worker safety and health become the company's number one priority, and that the company establish as their primary goals zero days lost to injury, zero fatalities, and zero work-related illnesses. In effect, O'Neil made safety as important as the red ball of profit. To meet those high standards he had to change Alcoa's entire corporate culture, as well as the expectations of Wall Street. He had to involve workers at all levels, and unions in all the nations where the company operated. Employees participated in thousands of local health and safety initiatives over the next decade, for which Alcoa had to develop new education programs, performance measures, and rewards. They even changed the way meetings were conducted. No matter how many people were present, and at whatever organizational level, all meetings began with a safety review. O'Neil also had to convince investors that such actions were necessary to create a sustainable future for Alcoa.[2]

O'Neil is now long gone from the company, but his commitment to the priority of health and safety has become institutionalized at Alcoa. To this day, the company reports real-time data on its public website relating to injuries and days lost. The company's practices now are copied around the world by businesses seeking to become good corporate citizens.

New Ways of Thinking

If an old-line company in an extractive industry is capable of such change, there is good reason to believe companies in cleaner industries are capable of making similar transformations. Yet, during the same era when O'Neil was transforming Alcoa's culture, leaders at such American companies as General Motors, Chrysler, and Ford were saying they could not change their practices, claiming they were prisoners of competitive market forces, slaves to union contracts, and stuck with current technologies. Perhaps, but motorcycle manufacturer Harley-Davidson did business in the same markets as the Big Three automakers, had a similarly strong union, and used similar technologies and, despite those impediments (and unlike the car manufacturers) it underwent a remarkable transformation in recent years.

In 1989, Harley was on the brink of bankruptcy, offering products no one wanted to buy, and saddled with union contracts that made them uncompetitive against Asian manufacturers employing cheaper labor. That year, Richard Teerlink took over the handlebars as Harley's CEO and immediately began listening to customers and motivating his employees to efficiently produce the high-quality motorbikes those customers said they wanted. He renegotiated the union contract and put all 5,000 company workers on incentive compensation, rewarding them for their ideas and efforts to improve product quality and customer service. This was rather un-American of him in that he did not lay off workers to demonstrate to Wall St. how tough he was, export jobs offshore, grandstand by engaging in a high-profile merger or spinoff, or lock himself up in the executive suite with a team of accountants and finance experts who would not know a motorcycle from a bicycle. At the beginning of the current Great Recession, employment at Harley had doubled to nearly 10,000 workers as company sales, profits, and exports grew. Over the same period, the Big Three automakers lost significant market share and laid off over two-thirds of their workforce, all-the-while their leaders claimed it impossible for them to do the very things Teerlink was doing at Harley.[3] As Albert Einstein said, "You can't solve a problem from the same consciousness that created it. You must learn to see the world anew."

We can see how the thinking at Harley is different from traditionally managed industrial firms, but do all the non-traditional companies that practice Good Business—such as Harley, Alcoa, IKEA, Toyota, and Tata—have anything in common? While the national cultures of the United States, Sweden, Japan, and India are unique from one another, the corporate cultures of each of those companies turn out to be remarkably similar. The culture of each is characterized by a credible belief system and clearly articulated values (together with a commitment to live and practice those values in all their activities and operations around the globe). One key value they all share is *community,* both in the sense that their employees experience the security and support of their entire organizations, and in the sense that these companies are part of the local communities where operations are located. They also acknowledge their membership in the global community: planet earth. All these companies are decentralized organizations marked by high levels of employee involvement (where workers see they can make a difference in company performance, and are rewarded for doing so); all have managerial processes that impose discipline by fixing decision rights and accountability (insuring alignment between overall strategic goals and the actions of front-line business units); all are transparent organizations in which people feel free to express their ideas; and all have systems that reward continuous change and innovation.

Let me offer another improbable example of such Good Business: a global company with no hierarchy, no bosses, no job descriptions, no titles, and no rules! W.L. Gore and Associates is a $1.5 billion company with six thousand employees and a line of over a thousand different chemical-based products. Since its founding in 1958, the company has practiced what its founder called "non-management." To nurture a sense of community and facilitate communication, the organization is broken down into units of about 150 workers each at which a new hire is assigned to a team and simply told, "Go find something useful to do." Each year, all team members evaluate each other's performance to determine compensation, and all share in company profits. Employees spend roughly ten percent of their time developing long-term, speculative product ideas and are given the resources to commercialize them when they can attract a team to work with them. Thus, team leadership is continually shifting, with Joe leading a team this year, but next year serving on a team led by Mary.

The purpose of this non-management is to liberate employees to innovate and make fast decisions without needing the approval of layers of management. *Chaos,* some would say but, in place of inflexible rules, W.L. Gore and Associates has four governing principles that create organizational alignment:

1. Try to be fair to all associates, suppliers, and customers.

2. Allow, help, and encourage all associates to grow in knowledge, skill, and scope of responsibility.

3. Make commitments and keep them.

4. Consult with others before making high-risk decisions that would endanger the enterprise.[4]

Ethos and Ethics

These four principles are, are base, ethical precepts. It is significant that the word ethics has the same etymological root as the Greek word for culture, *ethos*. The element common to the two is **character**. Ethics refers to the moral character of individuals, while ethos refers to the moral character of a group or organization.

It is useful to examine the relationship between these two ethical concepts with reference to corporate culture of retailer Costco—whose main competitor, Sam's Club, is a subsidiary of global giant Wal-Mart. Wal-Mart is a non-union, low-wage company offering scant health insurance to hourly employees, and investing little in their training and development; Costco is unionized, high-wage, provides high-benefits and invests heavily in employee training and development. In 2004, the average Wal-Mart employee earned $24,000 per year, while the average at Costco was $33,000. Significantly, total labor costs at Costco were far lower than at Wal-Mart because Costco workers were more productive, committed to the organization, needed less supervision, had lower rates of turnover, and contributed their efforts and ideas to improve operational efficiency and customer service. Like many traditionally managed U.S. firms, Wal-Mart is convinced they have no choice but to pay low wages to keep prices of goods low for consumers. They ignore the fact that what really counts is *total* labor costs, not *unit* labor costs.[5] As early as the 1980s, Peter Drucker had called attention to the fact workers should be seen as resources to invest in, rather than costs of doing business, but Wal-Mart has never accepted that fact.

What is truly different about Costco and Wal-Mart is their cultures. Costco's culture stresses the importance of each employee. The company trains—then trusts—employees to make decisions, solve problems, and take initiative in the absence of supervisors and rules. This has consequences beyond high worker productivity: it positively affects the *character* of employees. A few years ago, a motorist in Los Angeles drove his SUV onto railroad tracks in the path of an oncoming commuter train. He jumped from his car at the last second, but the ensuing crash was terrible: hundreds of passengers were injured, and several killed. The collision occurred outside a Costco store. Hearing the crash, Costco employees immediately organized themselves into a rescue brigade. Loading first aid equipment and fire extinguishers on their backhoes and forklift trucks, they set to work freeing trapped passengers and administering aid before professional "first responders" arrived on the scene.

This initiative was not coincidental to the nature of the Costco corporate culture. Experience shows that workers in high-involvement organizations like Costco, Alcoa, and W.L. Gore tend to be more active as citizens and parents than those who work in low-involvement organizations like Wal-Mart. The former are more likely to vote, participate in their children's PTA, contribute to local charities, and be involved in civic activities. Hence, the Greeks had it right about ethos: the character of individuals is related to the character of the group to which they belong.

Environmental Sustainability

Companies with high-involvement cultures also are likely to be leaders in protecting the environment. In the early 1980s, California-headquartered Patagonia was the first company to practice what is today called fair trade. Patagonia imports fabrics and finished goods from developing countries, and has long insisted on paying fair wages to foreign workers, fair prices to suppliers, and making sure local communities share in the benefits of international commerce. Patagonia donates one percent of its profits to grassroots environmental organizations, and grants employees up to two months paid leave to volunteer at NGOs (it even allows California employees to take time off during working hours to go to the beach when the surf is up, trusting them to make up lost time at their discretion).

Organic food retailer, Whole Foods, is perhaps the nation's leader in terms of supporting environmental NGOs and protecting the planet. Employees of Whole Foods share in the ownership, management, and profits of the company to an unusually high degree. In the typical American company, 75 percent of stock options go to the CEO, 15 percent to the next fifty highest-compensated executives, and only 10 percent to all other employees. At Whole Foods, 85 percent of stock options go to non-executives. In large U.S. corporations, CEOs typically earn at least 400 times their average worker, but at Whole Foods the ratio is just 19:1.[6]

Significantly, the leaders of Costco and Whole Foods are solid capitalists who are adamant on the point that they are not running charities. Indeed, all the companies I have cited are highly profitable, and those that are multinational are effective in competing in world markets. Starbucks is perhaps the most widely known of these new global champions. Starbucks is a leader in fair trade, environmental practices, and how it treats employees. In the United States, hardly any employees of fast-food chains earn above the minimum wage, and practically none have employer-provided health insurance; but even part-time Starbucks workers are eligible for health care, stock options, pensions, and college tuition reimbursement. These practices were recently dismissed by the CEO of a conventionally managed company, "Well, if I could charge the equivalent of $4.00 for a cup of coffee for my products, I could afford to take care of my employees as lavishly as Starbucks does." Starbucks' CEO, Howard Schultz, quickly answered, "You don't understand. You have it backwards: I am able to charge $4.00 for a cup of coffee *because* of the way I treat my employees." When faced with hard times and declining profits during the recent Great Recession, Costco and Starbucks did not abandon their commitments to employees and other company stakeholders.

High-Involvement Cultures

There is solid research to support Schultz's theory that high-involvement cultures lead to high productivity. In the only scientifically valid study of the motivations of a cross-section of the entire U.S. workforce, researchers unveiled the secret behind why the leaders of such companies as Starbucks, Gore, Costco, and Harley-Davidson have been able to create working conditions that effectively tap into the deep wellspring of worker motivation. This 2002 survey of 3,000 workers (undertaken by the U.S. Census Bureau) links employee motivation, loyalty, commitment, and productivity, on the one hand, with employee participation in decision making and in the economic returns of the organization, on the other. Researchers found employees were more loyal, committed, and productive when given more freedom to make decisions. And, workers who had the opportunity to participate in company financial gains— through profit sharing, stock ownership, stock options, and the like—were also the most loyal and committed. When the two sources of participation were combined the effect was intensified: the higher the level of employee involvement in both decision making and financial gains, the more positive their behavior. Significantly, the study found that higher levels of participation also led to more ethical behavior. Employees in high-involvement cultures were the most willing to intervene when a co-worker under-performed or misbehaved.[7]

There is an ethical principle underlying these scientific findings: Participation in decision-making without participation in financial gains is *unjust* because employees are not compensated for their contributions to the bottom line; participation in financial gains without participation in decision making is also *unjust* because workers are powerless to influence conditions determining the size of their paychecks. Thus, the two forms of participation are positively linked, morally and practically.

The link has long been recognized in reward systems designed for top executives, and now has been shown to motivate lower-level employees, as well. SRC Holdings has been operating for several decades by what its founder, Jack Stack, calls "open book management." When Stack purchased the bankrupt re-manufacturer of diesel engines, he bought a company with old technology and facilities and a disgruntled workforce with relatively low levels of education. He proceeded to teach those workers everything he had learned in business school, giving them the equivalent of an MBA by teaching them how to read balance sheets and income statements. He then shared the company's managerial and financial information with his employees, and involved them in profit sharing and decision making. Soon, employees were finding ways to make the company more efficient and profitable. This unusual culture of trust, accountability, fairness, and transparency not only has had positive business consequences, the company has never experienced any ethical shenanigans. In the Enron era, SRC's CFO commented, "It is like having a thousand internal auditors out there." Jan Carlzon, former CEO of Scandinavian Airlines, explains the source of this ethical phenomenon: "An individual without information cannot take responsibility; an individual who is given information cannot help but to take responsibility."[8]

Employee Development

The most important product of the cultures I have cited is a shared feeling of *trust* which is the glue that holds communities together willingly and without need of coercion. That sense of community is fueled by a company's investments in the development of its employees, and the making of such investments is perhaps the clearest and strongest moral obligation any company has. Since Aristotle, it has been known that the greatest life satisfaction comes when people are engaged in realizing the potential with which they were born. Because modern corporate employees invest the largest part of their waking lives at work, for them the workplace is the only venue where they have the opportunity to realize their potential. Hence, when given the opportunity for development on the job, they almost always respond gratefully through enhanced productivity and loyalty.

And that is why workers in developed countries *can* compete successfully with those in low-wage countries, but only *if* their employers provide them with the right conditions—participative cultures in which they have opportunities to grow by making a difference, that is, by "adding value" in economic terms. The greater the opportunity workers have to add value—as they can at Costco, SRC Holdings, and W.L.Gore—the more innovative and productive they will be. By adding value through their own ideas and efforts, workers in high-involvement America companies actually *earn* the higher wages they receive, while their less-educated, less-productive counterparts in the developing world are paid less for adding less value. For example, the Wisconsin-based Trek company is able to export bicycles to the world because its American workers are empowered—and rewarded—to make continual improvements to their products and work processes. Trek employees are educated men and women who love to ride bikes and do not for a moment think of themselves as industrial workers, even though they build bikes mainly by hand. They instead see themselves as self-managing innovators working on important matters, on things that are meaningful to them. The result is that Trek's workplace system creates a constant stream of new products that forces the poorly paid, under-educated, and micro-managed workers making copy-cat bikes in South Asian factories continually to play catch up.

The Trek approach is, of course, the norm in American high-tech industries where computer nerds are rewarded for constantly tinkering and innovating. At both low-tech Trek and at high-tech companies, the result is continuous product improvement, innovation, and growth. And there is strong evidence that the comparative advantage of having educated, motivated, and committed workers like those at Trek can be duplicated at a wide variety of businesses. But that can happen only in companies where leaders choose to implement organizational practices that create communities in which employees are encouraged to take initiative, and in which they are rewarded for adding value.

A Unified Theory

We now can see how the disparate elements of the new management lexicon add up to a unified theory of Good Business: In essence, the values of business leaders are the primary drivers of the culture of an organization. That ethos (manifested in organizational purpose, structure, design, and rewards) influences behavior, as measured by the extent to which employees are motivated, identify with company mission and goals, and are committed to innovate and to serve customer and stakeholder needs. And such employee behavior yields positive results, whether measured financially in terms of profits, or socially as observed through responsible and ethical global citizenship.

Thus, it all begins with the values of leaders—that is, how they want their contributions to society to be measured. It is those values that ultimately determine the behavior and results of an organization. What we learn from the examples cited above is that the more leaders create values-based cultures that build a strong sense of community through employee involvement, the less need there is for them to exercise central controls, and the more likely it is that their companies will respond appropriately and continuously to the changing needs of their global stakeholders. Now, we can connect the dots of the new management lexicon:

Values-Based Leadership→Robust Corporate Cultures→Productive,

Innovative, and Ethical Behavior→Sustainable Growth = Good Business.

A version of this chapter appears on-line in the <u>iveybusinessjournal.com</u>, September/ October, 2009

[1] James O'Toole, *Vanguard Management*, Doubleday, 1985

[2] James O'Toole and Edward E. Lawler III, *The New American Workplace*, Palgrave Macmillan, 2006

[3] *Ibid.*

[4] *Ibid.*

[5] *Ibid.*

[6] *Ibid.*

[7] *Ibid.*

[8] Jan Carlzon, *Moments of Truth*, Harper & Row, 1987

PART III

Corporations, Public Policy, and Global Citizenship

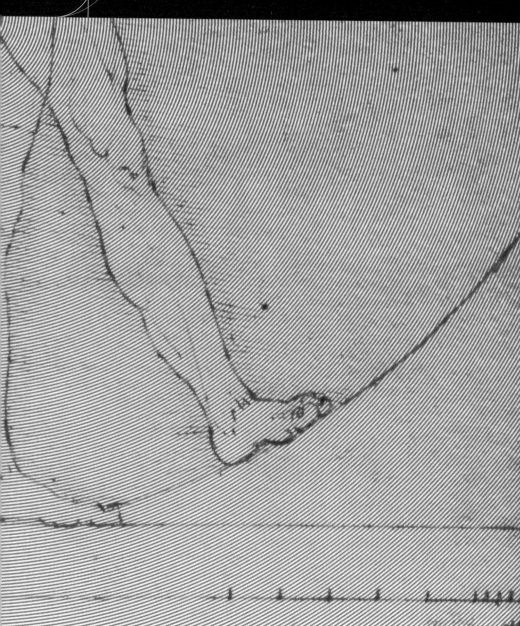

CHAPTER 10

The Post-Enron Regulatory Environment: Encouraging Ethical Leadership

by Elizabeth C. Stapp, Kevin O. O'Brien and Stephen R. Martin II

The current economic crisis, coming hard on the heels of the Enron, WorldCom, and Tyco scandals, has diminished public trust in both corporate executives and the business professionals—accountants and lawyers—who advise and serve them. At the same time there is a growing societal demand that corporations, and their agents, have a moral obligation to do no harm, which falls not solely on the corporation but, more specifically, on those who manage it.

Until recently, the regulatory environment—or lack thereof—was complicit in the unethical behavior of corporate officers and employees. Officers legally could claim ignorance, hide behind the corporate veil, and eschew personal responsibility for corporate misdeeds. Honesty, transparency, and responsibility all but disappeared in such an environment. An ensuing culture emerged in which employees were hesitant to speak the truth. Distrusting their bosses, employees feared retaliation, firing, or worse. Out of a perverse sense of loyalty, employees and managers of giant corporations tacitly agreed to a code of silence, even when facing glaring legal, ethical, and financial crises.

This culture of opaqueness, rather than transparency, contributed to the ethical scandals early in this millennium. The current regulatory environment attempts to address this culture of opacity by casting light on the inner-workings of corporations. As the result of recent actions by Congress, the Securities and Exchange Commission (SEC), and the United States Sentencing Commission (together, regulatory bodies) it is no longer *legally* permissible for an officer or director of a publicly held company to ignore fraud. This is an important and dramatic shift: the law is beginning to codify elements of ethical leadership, rewarding it when it's present, and penalizing those who choose to ignore it.

Moreover, in the current regulatory environment it is safer for employees down the corporate ladder to point out looming troubles. Companies are now rewarded for encouraging legal compliance and ethical decision-making.

Rather than "no good deed goes unpunished," good deeds now are rewarded. For example, if a company supports internal whistle blowing and then self-reports a violation to the Justice Department, the company's financial penalty will be eliminated, or substantially reduced.

This chapter focuses on the post-Enron regulatory environment and—more specifically—the passage and implications of the Sarbanes-Oxley Act (hereafter SOX, but also called the "Public Company Accounting Reform and Investor Protection Act of 2002"). It addresses some tough questions facing post-Enron corporate officers, their lawyers, and accountants, such as: What is the precise duty owed by corporate officers (or business professionals) to prevent a company from harming others? Even if not legally obligated, does the law protect employees from retaliation by their peers if they choose to blow the whistle on corporate fraud? And, how has the law changed to encourage ethical leadership in publicly traded companies?

Sarbanes-Oxley and its Mandate for Ethical Leadership

Society's mistrust of corporations is widely attributable to failures in the nation's economic regulatory system and the lapsing ethical standards of the legal and accounting professions. That is why SOX focused on closing gaps in the legal environment that permitted the infamous, unethical conduct at corporations such as Enron, WorldCom, and Adelphia. While there is clear evidence that regulatory reform and improved professional ethics are essential to restoring public trust in business, we believe they are insufficient. While SOX was an appropriate *legal* response to the problems, we believe that regulatory bodies alone cannot create a wave of *ethical* leadership in corporate America. All the new laws and ethical training in the world will not, in and of themselves, lead to virtuous corporate behavior.

In the pages that follow, we argue that ethical leadership was the missing ingredient pre-Enron. We believe there will continue to be ethical lapses in corporate America until executives realize that, along with their financial and strategic responsibilities, one of their primary obligations is to create ethical organizational cultures. The good news is that, if for no other reason than the fear of retribution in the form of fines and possible jail time, executive behavior in this regard appears to be changing.

In response to the Enron/Arthur Andersen debacle, Congress held extensive hearings aimed at unearthing the root causes of the accounting scandals. It attempted to create a law that encouraged, and rewarded, legal and ethical compliance while simultaneously increasing executive and professional (lawyers and accountants) responsibilities and punishments absent compliance. In crafting SOX, Congress attempted to regulate corporate behavior in four ways: through increased professional reporting requirements, increased prison terms and amended federal sentencing guidelines for wrongdoers, enhanced corporate compliance programs, and stronger protections for internal whistle-blowers.

Increased Reporting Requirements

In legislating increased officer/director penalties for misleading the public, Congress ultimately focused on establishing *effective deterrents* for white-collar criminals. First, Congress successfully increased punishment with respect to securities fraud and insider trading. For example, SOX includes an "obstruction measure," which criminalizes the destruction or alteration of documents when such actions impair federal agency investigations. It also directs the SEC to enact civil remedies—as opposed to criminal—so that injured parties themselves can sue corporate officers who break the law.

Perhaps the most controversial directive of SOX is aimed at chief financial and executive officers. Section 906(a) addresses the "willful blindness problem" of such officers by specifically requiring them to review corporate records, and then to issue statements certifying that the information contained in their companies' financial reports properly reflects the financial condition of those companies. Through SOX, the SEC requires chief financial and executive officers to certify the accuracy of quarterly and annual financial reports—something that until the passage of SOX they did not have to do. In sum, post-SOX, CEOs now are criminally responsible for misleading or fraudulent financial reports.

Now that CFOs and CEOs must investigate and certify the accuracy of financial statements given to the public, SOX calls for steep criminal penalties of ten to twenty years in prison if executives know that the financial statements do not fairly represent the financial condition of their companies. Since individuals and institutions invest money in companies based on published information, post-Enron, the investing public became reluctant to place their trust in corporate America. Pre-SOX, corporate officers who acted without knowledge of accounting irregularities were not held liable—which only encouraged the type of organizational opacity described above. Executives, like Enron's Ken Lay, tried to stick their heads in the sand to avoid learning about financial malfeasance within their companies. In an attempt to restore public faith, SOX now requires such "hear no evil, see no evil" corporate officers to face substantial fines and possible jail time.

Congress also recognized that professionals—lawyers and accountants, both external and internal—were complicit in "window dressing" companies' financial statements. Fearing retaliation if they spoke up or opposed such shenanigans, ancillary professionals became complicit in the bad actions of executives—and, in the process, violated their basic, professional ethical obligation to refuse to subordinate their judgment to that of a client or employer. Thus, SOX provisions reflect the hard-earned lessons from Enron: independent corporate lawyers and CPAs are essential to ethical behavior. Indeed, it is the lawyers and CPAs working on the ground floors of corporations who often are the first to see problems as they brew. In the worse cases, those professionals provide the "seal of approval" needed to successfully dupe the public. Thus, SOX creates a framework of government oversight of the accounting profession and its practices, and imposes reporting duties on lawyers, as well.

In an attempt to restore trust, Congress hoped to improve the quality of the financial information that public companies report to investors by increasing transparency. To do so, SOX makes not only accountants, but also lawyers, *gatekeepers* for the public. The law now imposes significant limitations on the kinds of relationships that accounting firms can have with the companies they audit. For example, to avoid conflicts of interest, an accounting firm no longer can act as a consultant to the same company whose financial statements its accountants certify. Congress noted that Arthur Andersen may have had difficulty in saying no to Enron's questionable accounting practices during their audit because the firm's consulting revenue from Enron was scheduled to be $100 million, while their audit fee was only $4 million.

Congress also established the Public Company Accounting Oversight Board (PCAOB), which now oversees the audits of publicly traded companies. This oversight is designed to protect the interests of investors and the public interest by encouraging CPAs to prepare informative, fair, and independent audit reports.

For lawyers and accountants, SOX also sets minimum standards of professional conduct for those who appear and practice before the SEC. In the new regulatory environment, a violation of any SOX provisions now also constitutes a violation of the Securities Exchange Act of 1934. Such a violation can give rise not only to monetary penalties, but also to an order disbarring an attorney or accountant from practicing before the SEC. These SEC's sanctions are not the only regulatory enforcement provisions in place. In addition, all states require that SEC-sanctioned attorneys and accountants report their federal violations to the state that has licensed them. Doing so will likely be followed by disciplinary proceedings before the relevant state authorities governing the conduct of attorneys and accountants, who then may impose the ultimate penalty: the loss of the professional's license to practice.

To strengthen SOX's impact, Congress imposed prison terms on the professional aiders and abettors of SEC violations—lawyers and accountants—to the same extent as corporate officers. For example, SOX now punishes both executives and the professionals who aid them in committing insider trading with the identical potential twenty-five year prison term. Before SOX, executives faced a ten-year term for insider trading, while lawyers and accountants faced a five-year term for aiding and abetting insider trading or any other SEC violation. SOX substantially increased all SEC-related prison terms for executives, and required that professionals face the same increased prison terms as executives.

Amended Sentencing Guidelines

Congress also passed a portion of SOX known as the "Corporate Fraud Accountability Act of 2002," the goal of which was to create harsher prison terms when judges sentence executives who commit fraud. Congress enacted these new Federal Sentencing Guidelines in the belief that the strongest deterrent to executive malfeasance is the threat of a substantial loss of freedom. A conviction under SOX without such an enhanced criminal sentence would have vitiated the deterrent effect of the legislation, particularly given the fact that corporate officers (and their professional staffs) have the resources and ability to mount lengthy, rigorous, and often successful legal defenses. For example, Qwest's (a Colorado-based company) former CEO Joe Nacchio's 2007 criminal insider trading conviction resulted in a six-year prison term under the prior guidelines, but under the new guidelines that took effect after he committed insider trading, he would have faced several years more of imprisonment.

Congress also wanted to ensure that criminal sentencing guidelines relating to organizations would properly deter and punish their criminal misconduct. Thus, in 2004, the United States Sentencing Commission voted unanimously to amend the United States Federal Sentencing Guidelines, including substantial amendments to the section of the Guidelines regarding organizations. In the past, when executives broke the law, they faced individual fines and imprisonment; now, corporations themselves can be charged, convicted, and fined. This change reflects a shift from requiring mere legal compliance toward a broader requirement for organizations to create ethical cultures.

The new Organizational Guidelines encourage corporate boards to make concerted efforts to prevent wrongdoing by providing an incentive to establish good organizational practices and behavior. For example, if a corporation breaks the law, a judge (or a regulator through a settlement) is now empowered to impose reduced fines *if* the corporation can show that it had taken specific actions to prevent wrongdoing. The Organizational Guidelines provide an eight-point "culpability score" for organizations that sentencing judges must consider when imposing fines, four which may increase the ultimate punishment, and four that may mitigate it. The increasing factors are the involvement in, or tolerance of, criminal activity; the prior history of the organization; the violation of a court order; and obstruction of justice. The decreasing factors are self-reporting of a violation; cooperation with regulatory authorities; acceptance of responsibility; and the existence of an effective compliance and ethics program (ECEP).

In the post-Enron regulatory environment, corporate silence is no longer an option. Instead, cooperating with the government, accepting responsibility for a crime, promoting ethical compliance, and establishing an effective compliance program are now encouraged. SOX thus closes the pre-Enron legal loophole that allowed a corporate board of directors to play absentee landlord which, in turn, allowed officers to turn a blind eye towards fraud, deception, and abuses of the public trust.

Meaningful Compliance and Ethics Programs

Although the application of the Organizational Guidelines by judges is not mandatory, many executives view them as the *de facto* standards for what constitute an effective compliance program. For example, the guidelines require companies to evaluate and measure the effectiveness of their compliance programs, and place greater responsibility on boards of directors and executives for oversight and management of ECEPs. While some companies have attempted to "window dress" such programs, SOX is clear that merely having an ECEP (and/or simply self-reporting a violation) is not sufficient to warrant a reduction in penalties for crimes committed. To promote and restore honesty, cooperation, and trust in corporate America, the new Organizational Guidelines expressly state that an organization will not be eligible to receive reduced penalties *if* the organization delays reporting an offense, or *if* individuals at certain levels of the organization turned a blind eye, tacitly approved, or participated in, the offense.

We believe the amended Organizational Guidelines have succeeded in creating a dramatic shift from mere compliance towards creating a true ethical environment in some corporations. The effect of SOX has been to establish legal compliance as a *minimum* threshold rather than the ultimate standard for ethical behavior. Where that has occurred, SOX has succeeded in its effort to foster the kind of ethical decision-making that is less likely to result in compliance failure.

Moreover, the burden of setting the "ethical tone" for a company now falls squarely on the shoulders of those at the top. The Organizational Guidelines are clear that directors and executives must now take an active role in establishing the content and implementation of an ECEP. In addition, they must attempt to prevent and detect criminal conduct themselves, and they must promote a culture that encourages ethical conduct and compliance with the law throughout the organization.

The new legislation attempts to shatter the "silence is golden" mode of corporate conduct. Effective compliance and ethics training is now a requirement for *all* employees within the context of an ECEP. Additionally, an organization's compliance and ethics officers must be given adequate authority and resources to carry out their duties. This includes reporting directly, and having access to, top executives and the Board of Directors (usually through the Audit Committee).

Moreover, the amended Organizational Guidelines expressly provide—as an essential component of the design, implementation, and modification of an effective compliance program—that all companies must periodically assess the risk that criminal conduct will occur in their organizations. In other words, good business now dictates that companies identify risk areas where criminal violations may occur, and be proactive in preventing them. Organizations also must demonstrate the use of auditing and monitoring systems to detect criminal conduct, and undertake periodic evaluations of the effectiveness of their compliance programs.

The Organizational Guidelines focus on individual responsibility for corporate behavior regardless of one's position, knowledge, or stature within an organization. To this end, they define seven minimum requirements for an effective compliance program:

1. Prevention and Detection Procedures: Standards and procedures are established to prevent and detect criminal conduct;

2. High-Level Oversight: High-level personnel are assigned overall responsibility to oversee compliance, and provided adequate resources and authority to carry out such responsibility;

3. Due Care: Reasonable efforts are made to exclude high-level individuals who engage in illegal activities or other improper conduct;

4. Training and Communication: Effective compliance and ethics training is effectively required for all employees and agents, including those in upper levels, and this obligation is ongoing, with required periodic updates;

5. Monitoring: Reasonable steps are taken to achieve compliance by detecting criminal conduct, and providing systems to anonymously report (and seek guidance) regarding potential or actual criminal conduct;

6. Consistent Enforcement: Compliance is enforced and encouraged through disciplinary measures and appropriate incentives; and

7. Response and Prevention: Reasonable steps are taken to prevent criminal conduct.

While we recognize that many organizations have yet to reach these standards, we believe that, through them, SOX has begun to incrementally change the tide towards more ethical behavior.

Enhanced Internal Whistle-Blowing Protection

In enacting SOX, Congress wanted to change the corporate environment "from the inside out" in order to prevent wrongdoing from occurring in the first instance. When Enron's Sherron Watkins attempted to call attention to the fraud at Enron, she was ignored. Yet, in so doing, she ultimately proved that the best way to prevent corporate fraud was to encourage those witnessing it to speak up. Unfortunately, in most companies, lower management employees are encouraged to fix, rather than report, such problems. Top executives do not want to hear bad news; what they want is for their employees to deliver on the projected financial figures they promised to Wall Street. This internal pressure leads to the potential for compromised decision-making in which urgent short-term actions replace a long-term, ethical, perspective. As the pressure on managers to perform mounts, their tendency to ignore ethical ramifications of their actions grows.

In this environment, whistle blowers, who often serve as the lone voice of organizational morality, are under tremendous pressure, and usually fare poorly at the hands of their company: They may be denied promotions, fired, or even blackballed within their industry. Thus, those who consider making a firm's wrongdoings public are aware of the high likelihood that they will be condemned for their efforts by others in the organization. Because the consequences for whistle blowers are often so disastrous, such actions are not to be taken lightly. That is why SOX increases protection for employees who witness, and report, accounting misstatements, fraud, and other wrongdoing. Although SOX does not *require* employees of publicly traded companies to whistle blow externally to the SEC, the Act *encourages* them to do so because it requires the board of directors of publicly traded companies to create anonymous reporting procedures to protect the identity of whistle blowers.

SOX also requires company attorneys to pay attention to their intuition when they see something is awry—and does not allow them to hide behind the privilege of attorney/client confidentiality. In other words, attorneys must now blow the whistle on corporate fraud. In addition, SOX compels the SEC to adopt new rules of professional conduct applicable to attorneys practicing before the agency. These rules *require* an attorney to report evidence of legal violations by any agent of the company to the company's legal counsel and audit committee, and this applies to both corporate in-house attorneys and to outside counsel.

These rules have potentially far reaching effects because, in the past, the assumption has been that what one says to one's lawyer stays with one's lawyer. SOX changes this rule. If there is evidence of legal violations, any attorney retained by a publicly traded corporation must now report those facts to the company's audit committee. It should be noted that an attorney is not required to report to the SEC if the company then fails to fix the problem; however, the American Bar Association now permits an attorney under these circumstances to whistle blow externally without violating confidentiality concerns.

Whistle-blowing accountants are subject to protection by the rules of professional conduct and ethics promulgated by the state boards of accountancy where they practice, and by the American Institute of Certified Public Accountants (AICPA). Yet, many internal CPAs are nonetheless reluctant to whistle blow both internally and externally to the SEC, fearing retaliation by their employers. Congress was particularly sensitive to the fact that Enron's Sherron Watkins was effectively demoted after her whistle-blowing meeting with Ken Lay. Consequently, it granted all whistle blowers, including accountants, sweeping protections under SOX, which enhances existing state protections such as the right of the terminated whistle blower to sue under the tort of wrongful discharge under the public policy exception. Specifically, SOX provides whistle-blower-protection for internal accountants for any disclosures to a supervisor or regulatory body.

This protection is multi-layered. First, the Department of Labor requires an employer to reinstate fired whistle blowers to their prior positions if their terminations are deemed illegitimate. Although, the Department of Labor has not been very successful in compelling employers to do this, the law is at least on the books. Second, SOX provides a full spectrum of damages for an employee who is wrongfully fired for blowing the whistle in good faith. Third, it requires prosecution and imprisonment for up to ten years for any company supervisor who retaliates against an employee for truthful whistle blowing to law enforcement agencies, such as the FBI and Department of Justice. This last provision punishes executives who pressure their lawyers and accountants to "subordinate their judgment" and accept management's perspective on the treatment of questionable accounting practices. Finally, SOX requires companies to have an independent audit committee that establishes, maintains and oversees whistle-blowing procedures.

In all, there is now a real opportunity for companies to adopt clear and effective whistle-blowing procedures. We believe corporate boards should consider requiring employees to whistle blow internally first, before going to the SEC or Congress. This would allow a company to properly and timely correct or mitigate the problem or damage, as well as to report any legal violations under the Organizational Guidelines. Corporate boards also should consider requiring in-house accountants to whistle blow internally when there is material departure from Generally Accepted Accounting Principles (GAAP) in the presentation of financial statements. While some states require in-house accountants to whistle blow internally, most states do not expressly require it.

Conclusion

Corporate America cannot run on ignorance and mistrust, and SOX has made great strides in fostering ethical behavior among corporate executives, their attorneys, and their accountants. While SOX does not ensure ethical leadership, without doubt it encourages and rewards it. Moreover, while SOX does not solve all of the ethical problems brought to light by Enron, WorldCom, and those involved in the recent financial industry meltdown, it does demonstrate the regulatory environment's ability to act swiftly in an attempt to steer the ship back on course. But, in the final analysis, public trust in corporations will continue to depend on business leaders who *earn it* though virtuous and ethical behavior. Laws can do only so much. While taking the cue from the new regulatory environment, executives nonetheless must *choose* the path of ethical leadership. If they do so, their employees will follow them and act in the best interests of the company. When leaders choose this path, they will see enhanced profitability and sustainability over the long term.

CHAPTER 11

Value Creation: The Promise of Sustainable Development

by Bruce Hutton and Dave Cox

Sustainable development is the only intellectually coherent, sufficiently inclusive, potentially mind-changing concept that gets even half way close to capturing the true nature and urgency of the challenges that now confront the world. There really is no alternative.

—J. Porritt, "The Only Game in Town"

In his keynote address at the 2008 Business for Social Responsibility International Conference, Chairman and CEO of General Electric, Jeffrey Immelt, warned against characterizing the most recent economic crisis as part of the traditional business cycle. He said the economic crisis, in conjunction with the effects of globalization, climate change, and political instability, requires a "reset" in how business is done: Restructuring the financial industry, increasing transparency and accountability of companies to multiple stakeholders, and fostering new interactions between government, business, and civil society are all critical in reshaping the role of business for generations to come. Immelt concluded, "It is the sustained ability to change that really counts."[1]

Immelt is suggesting the economic crisis is not a single event but, rather, part of what Malcolm Gladwell calls a "tipping point," in which a game is changed forever. The emerging rules of this new global game are being established in real time amid great change, and with significant uncertainty. The environment in which the game will be played out is a kind of perfect storm characterized by geopolitical uncertainties, a colossal failure of corporate governance and ethics, global economic uncertainty, accelerating environmental challenges, and a rock bottom loss of public confidence in our institutions— business, government, and civil society. As Klaus Schwab, President of the World Economic Forum, said in 2003:

> Never before in the 33 years of the World Economic Forum's history
> has the situation in the world been so fragile, as complex and danger-
> ous as this year. We feel that we are living in a new world—with new
> rules and new dangers—but certainly also with new opportunities...
> Today we need a new and enlarged concept of business leadership."[2]

In short, business leaders must change their thinking. The introduction to *Massive Change*, a book exploring innovation and designs for the future, begins with this question: "Now that we can do anything, what will we do?"[3] The question suggests that the proper responses to the perfect storm are not so much about technology but about time frames, political will, and moral responsibility. In the recent past, the time frame for political leaders too often has been the next election; for business leaders, quarterly earnings; for leaders of NGOs, the next donation. Leaders in all three sectors of society have responded with delaying actions, fake debates, and cosmetic solutions. However, there is another force at work today, an optimism that sees challenges as opportunities, and brings hope, creativity, and action to the game. This force goes by a variety of names, but we refer to it here as sustainable development, and call those organizations following its processes and principles sustainable enterprises. In a sustainable enterprise economy a spirit of innovation, creativity, problem solving, and respect for life drives the community—thereby producing wealth, preserving the natural environment, and providing social equity.

Current Realities

The case for thinking differently about what we value and how we behave is increasingly convincing. A 2007 McKinsey Global Survey of business executives found that a number of social and environmental issues are expected to have an important impact on global business decisions over the next five years. Among those issues rated "very important" or "important" are the growing number of consumers in emerging markets (84 percent), an increasing global labor pool (81 percent), and increasing constraints on the supply and use of natural resources (73 percent). In a 2008 international survey, GlobeScan reports that 57 percent of experts agree the term sustainable development is increasingly potent in influencing government and industry decision makers. They believe the highest potential for addressing social and environmental issues includes the greening of supply chains (81 percent), eco-efficiency (79 percent), corporate social responsibility (63 percent), industrial ecology (62 percent), and triple-bottom line reporting (59 percent). While these experts believe progress is being made in these and other aspects of sustainability, a majority rate the performance of businesses with regard to those issues as poor, especially at the global level (74 percent). Here is some evidence of the urgent need to turn around that poor performance:[4]

- The U.S. economy consumes 100 billion tons of raw materials a year, 90 percent being discarded as waste. This averages out to a ton of waste per day per U.S. citizen.

- The Asian Brown Cloud, a result of industrial pollution, is blamed for 500,000 deaths per year from respiratory illness in India alone.

- Renewable resources are disappearing at alarming rates with more than 20 percent of the world's population lacking access to safe drinking water, 70 percent of the world's fish stocks in danger of collapse, and one-third of the world's forests having disappeared in the last 50 years.

- The average income of the richest twenty countries is 37 times that of the poorest twenty (a ratio that has doubled in just 20 years). More than one billion people are barely surviving on less than a dollar a day.

- More than 43 million people are living with HIV/AIDS, 39 million of them in developing countries.

- 11 million children under the age of five are dying every year from easily preventable and treatable causes.

Such facts illustrate the challenges the world faces in a variety of forms: economic (tensions stemming from the widening income gap between rich and poor create pressure for short-term results); social (the challenges manifest themselves in the domains of education, health care, and community stability); ecological (as environments become increasingly uninhabitable, there will be more displacement of populations with resulting conflicts); and political (stresses increasingly arise from societies in conflict over resources and power). Inevitably, the tensions arising from failing ecosystems, social unrest, and economic uncertainties will compound one another because they are inextricably linked. To turn such challenges into opportunities requires, at a minimum, a better understanding and adjustment of the current business model to create a sense of balance between long- and short-term priorities, and among the interdependent economic, social, and environmental components of the global system.

Evolution of an Ethic
The concept of sustainable development addresses both the challenges of short-termism and systems interdependency. While the jargon is contemporary, by

no means does the underlying concept represent new thinking. For example, the oral constitution, Gayanashagowa, which created the Iroquois Confederacy (circa 1150 A.D.) states that, in all tribal deliberations, the impact of every decision must be considered on "the next seven generations."[5] In the 1949 classic, *A Sand County Almanac*, Aldo Leopold describes a kind of ethical sequencing for human history: the first ethic to evolve dealt with relations between individuals, the second, between individuals and society, and the third—which he posits has yet to be fully adopted—deals with humanity's relation to nature. Leopold argued the current relationship between man and nature is purely economic, entailing privileges without obligations. He believed all truly sustainable and viable human ethics have evolved from the premise that the individual is a member of a community comprised of interdependent parts. He concluded that the adoption of a "land ethic" is crucial because it changes the role of humans from conquerors of the land to members/citizens of a community in which both people and the environment are treated with respect and care.[6]

The same ideas were reintroduced in 1987, when the World Commission on Environment and Development issued *Our Common Future*, which became a catalyst for the sustainability movement. The report offered a global agenda for change, calling for cooperation across national boundaries, coordinated political action, and the engagement of the private sector as a major driver of innovative solutions for a broad array of environmental, social, economic, and security challenges. While the Commission's early focus was on environmental concerns (especially the negative impacts of economic growth), they quickly recognized the environment does not exist independently from human actions, needs, and ambitions. Hence, a re-definition of sustainable development was needed that embraced an integrated, interdisciplinary approach to global concerns. This definition recognized the interdependency of three factors: economic development, environmental integrity, and social justice. The Commission thus acknowledged the important impact ecological stress has on the ability to grow economically. Per Lindblom, a member of the Commission, stated:

> The problems of today do not come with a tag marked energy or economy or CO2 or demography, nor with a label indicating a country or a region. The problems are multi-disciplinary and transnational or global. The problems are not primarily scientific and technological. In science we have the knowledge and in technology the tools. The problems are basically political, economic, and cultural.[7]

The Commission defined sustainability as, "development that meets the needs of the present without compromising the ability of future generations to meet their own needs."[8] This suggests sustainable development is not a fixed state of harmony but, instead, a continual process of accommodation to meet changing current and future needs. Therefore, companies have social responsibilities to both the present and future, just as they have obligations to provide value to shareholders both now and over the long term. Indeed, the political process of taking painful short-term actions today in order to ensure a healthy environment for the future is similar to the struggle business managers encounter when balancing pressures for quarterly earnings, on the one hand, and creating long-term value, on the other. Such processes are not easy or straightforward and often entail difficult tradeoffs, particularly in the short run. Consequently, whether one is talking about the sustainability of the planet or of a company, ultimate success often rests on political or managerial will.

Over the years, the business case for sustainable development has continued to grow, although not as fast as many have hoped. The good news is some business leaders have begun to see the connection between sustaining the planet and sustaining their enterprises, specifically the required balancing acts between long- and short-term thinking and among the varied interests of numerous stakeholders. What has prevented this thinking from spreading is the absence of a forward-looking perspective among the majority of corporate leaders. Companies that live only in the present are less likely to innovate and to notice disruptive technologies and events on the horizon. However, banking solely on future prospects, as dotcom leaders did in the 1990s, can be equally disastrous. It seems market pressures for short-term quarterly earnings have produced a kind of myopia in the decision processes of many business leaders, causing them to ignore the complexities of today's global business environment.

In light of the rapid pace of technological advances, uncertain and changing political landscapes, globalization, and instantaneous communications, more business leaders are beginning to recognize that static strategies carry more risk and less reward than at any time in the recent past.[9] Hence, the critical question today is how to build sustainable development processes into the overall strategy of firms in order to create real value in the long term.

As noted in chapter 8, corporate social responsibility (CSR) represents one way a firm can engage in practices that align organizational self-interest with the greater public good. While the CSR concept lacks a universal definition, it typically connects the goals of business success with ethical behavior and respect for people, communities, and the natural environment. Business professor Archie Carroll captures the essence of this concept in four dimensions: The foundation of a responsible company is to be **profitable**, but not at any cost. Society demands the company **obey the law**, expects it to act in an **ethical** manner toward all stakeholders, and to be a good **corporate citizen** in the communities in which it lives and operates.

As with sustainable development, the future acceptance of strategic corporate responsibility is said to depend on demonstrating its impact on financial performance. Evidence of such a linkage continues to grow, although the results are not conclusive. Some argue the lack of a developed theory of social responsibility and issues of measurement have hindered acceptance of the concept,[10] but University of California professor David Vogel, in *The Market for Virtue,* makes a different, perhaps stronger, case. He argues that current evidence does not support the conclusion that more responsible firms always are more profitable; however, he says this does not mean there is no business case for social responsibility. In his view, the case for particular firms must be more nuanced than simply saying "virtue pays." In other words, the value of a responsible corporate action depends on circumstances and the specific business strategy of a firm. Thus, it is in the context of *strategy* that options for creating value through socially responsible actions can be assessed, implemented, and measured.

A number of research studies conclude that a positive business case can be made for CSR activities. One study comparing higher- to lower-yielding companies across ten industries from 1977 to 1988 found the financially more successful companies placed higher value on stakeholder interests, fairness, and leadership than did lower-yielding companies.[11] A 1985 study of 81 high-growth companies found that they tended to have a well-articulated set of guiding principles, a strong sense of shared values, and leaders who were more motivated to "make a difference."[12] Harvard professor Lynne Paine suggests that the best perspective on the issue of values and economic performance is contained in a review of 95 academic studies examining the relationship between economic and social performance. Employing a variety of methodologies, 55 of those studies found a positive correlation between financial and social performance, and only five found a negative relationship. A 2003 study found that firms with a high "governance index" rating (strong stakeholder rights) had higher firm value, profits, sales growth, and lower capital expenditures than companies with lower ratings.[13] Governance Metrics tracked returns on firms listed on the S&P 500 index, and found those scoring high on corporate responsibility metrics outperformed the overall index on average stock price increase, return on assets, return on investment, and return on capital. Comparably, the United Kingdom's Institute of Business Ethics compared companies in the FTSE 250 on the strength of their ethics codes and related factors, finding companies scoring highest on ethics also had higher Earned Value Management (EVM) and Market Value Margin (MVM), in addition to higher profits.

The growing correlation between corporate responsibility and positive financial performance seems to be occurring for a number of reasons, starting with improved efficiency. For example, efforts to reduce waste and production inefficiencies often have positive environmental impact and lower costs. A number of studies have shown a relationship between social responsibility, on the one hand, and higher product quality, productivity, and innovative workforces, on the other.[14]

Responsible companies seem to benefit from enjoying enhanced reputations in the marketplace, which then may lead to access to new markets.

Responsible actions also can reduce such costly risks as being subjected to new regulations, being pressured to change policies by special-interest stakeholders, and being affected by higher business costs due to externalities (such as forces of nature or civil conflict). A 2001 comprehensive study by SustainAbility positively linked measures of business success such as shareholder value, reputation, and risk profile with sustainable development indicators of good ethics, environmental processes, and human rights records.

Sustainable Development Merges with Business Strategy

Although some progress has been made in connecting sustainable development to value creation for a firm (through enhanced eco-efficiency, employee development programs, reputation, and community goodwill), rarely are such actions connected to core business objectives. This inability, or reluctance, on the part of corporate executives, to fully integrate sustainable development practices with their business strategies can be tracked to the evolving nature of the sustainability concept. As noted, the original definition of sustainable development in the 1987 report, *Our Common Future*, dealt with the interaction of three systems: environmental, social, and economic. However, one of the unintended outcomes of the subsequent Earth Summit in 1992 was the virtual ascendancy of the environmental dimension relative to the economic and social dimensions, and the related dominance of environmental non-governmental organizations (NGOs) in all matters related to sustainable development. The sustainability movement consequently has become trapped in a "save the environment first" mode, and risks making the same mistakes business has made with its own narrow focus on financial wealth creation at the expense of other systems (social and environmental).

Judith Samuelson, director of the Aspen Institute's Business & Society Program, has addressed this proclivity to focus on just one system to the detriment of other systems (as well as to the whole). She calls for new thinking that recognizes the interdependencies of the economic, social, and environmental systems, and the connections between social and environmental challenges, on the one hand, and firm level growth and innovation, on the other. She couples this with corporate strategies designed to create value for the future, as well as the next quarter.

William McDonough and Michael Braungart see the issues raised by Samuelson as a fundamental design problem. In their book, *Cradle to Cradle: Remaking the Way We Make Things,* they use the Titanic as a metaphor for the Industrial Revolution and its consequences. The Titanic was a massive ship thought to be impervious to the forces of nature, a state-of-the-art technological marvel powered by artificial sources of energy that spewed out waste and pollution, all designed for the pleasure of the wealthy. Although seemingly

Sustainable Development

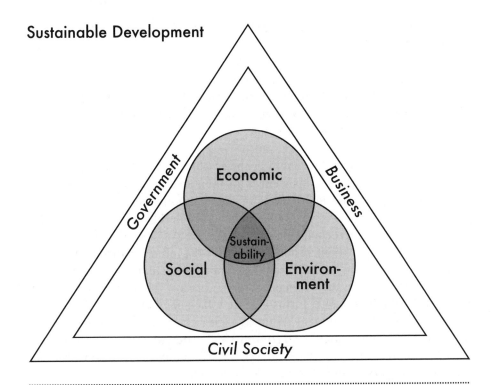

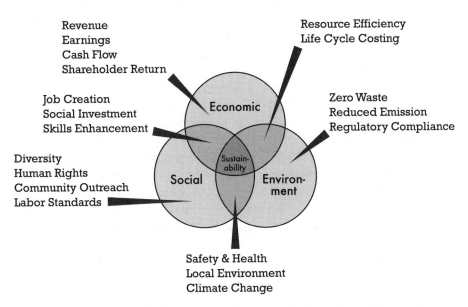

invincible, fundamental flaws in the Titanic's design led to disaster. Hence, both Samuelson and McDonough/Braungart suggest the necessary context for sustainable development is strategic: that is, embedded in a firm's core business plan and operating processes. A new definition of sustainable development by the International Institute for Sustainable Development supports this strategic orientation:

> Sustainable development is the adoption of strategies and activities that meet the needs of the enterprise and its stakeholders today while protecting, sustaining, and enhancing the human and natural resources that will be needed in the future.[15]

The conceptual model below captures the essence of how firms can embrace sustainable development consistent with their overall business strategies. The diagram shows the interactions of the economic, social, and environmental systems and gives examples of measurable business variables that reflect the natural interdependencies between the systems. The triangle bordering the "interdependent systems" indicates the influence different sectors of society can have on the firm's ability to operate sustainably. For example, government provides such things as regulatory oversight, incentives, and the legal license to operate. Firms also may face conflicting messages from different parts of government (from agencies charged with environmental protection, consumer safety, and so forth) and different levels of jurisdiction (local, state, national, and inter-governmental). Similarly, civil institutions are many and varied, and often at odds with each other in terms of what they want from a firm (environmental protection versus job creation). In addition, the actions of an individual firm are often shaped by others within their industry, acting through trade associations, industry principles of conduct, and so forth.

The extent to which sustainability will move from the margin of business practice to the mainstream of business strategy will depend upon its ability to create value for an enterprise. While there has been a good deal of discussion in the past regarding the value of "triple bottom line" reporting (social, environmental, and economic metrics), the fact is that a private sector business is ultimately held accountable based on a single bottom line: profitability. Hence, what firms must come to recognize (and an increasing number have) is that strategic environmental and social actions can enhance profitability through environmental stewardship and through promoting social equity in ways that serve both shareholders and the larger public good. When that occurs, the value of a firm is increased through enhanced reputation, performance, and brand image among key stakeholders.

Creating Sustainable Value

Sustainable development for a private sector enterprise comes down to strategically aligning a company's products and services with society's values and needs. It is important to understand that neither societal values nor societal needs are fixed. Therefore, it is essential that sustainability not be considered as an end state for the firm but, rather, as part of an ongoing strategic process continuously recalibrated to meet the shifting needs and expectations of society and the changing environment.

The sustainable strategies employed by a company thus will vary over time and circumstance, and across the spectrum of its operations and stakeholders, the objective of which is to align business practices with stakeholder value while balancing short and long-term considerations. When this alignment is achieved, shareholder value is created, leading to a virtuous circle in which companies will be incentivized to invest more in sustainable activities to the benefit of both shareholders and other stakeholders.

Identifying a firm's opportunities for sustainable practices is not especially difficult. The greater leadership challenge is how to choose among the virtually limitless options given the inescapable limitations on a firm's budget, time, expertise, and the often conflicting values and motives of its stakeholders. Perhaps the best way for leaders to make such choices is to weigh the value creation potential of various options within the context of their strategic plan. For example, the report, *Single Bottom Line Sustainability*, identifies four primary drivers of value creation:[16]

1. Margin improvement. This can be achieved through actions that increase operational effectiveness, such as eco-efficiency measures and creating premium pricing opportunities through enhanced customer loyalty, product differentiation, and gaining access to new market segments.

2. Risk reduction. Sustainability actions can reduce both financial risk and protect corporate and brand reputations through actions that create positive stakeholder relationships, generate community support, and increase employee loyalty; thereby reducing the risk of delay in new product introductions and negative shareholder resolutions.

3. Growth enhancement. This may be accomplished through product and process innovation, and also by developing capacity in new markets, motivating employees, and increasing sales of existing products.

4. Capital efficiency. Return on investment can be improved by reducing working capital requirements, replacing products with service, or materials with knowledge.

Savvy companies can implement strategies that affect more than one of these value-creation drivers. For example, when DuPont Performance Coatings, a division of the chemical giant providing auto paint, redefined its business from

"selling paint" to "selling the service of painting," there was significant reduction of paint needed per vehicle, resulting in reduced waste and increased
margins. Essentially, DuPont Performance Coatings substituted a service (the
expertise of their workforce in painting) for a product (paint) to grow their
business and improve margins.

The company Interface offers perhaps the best example of redefining a
business around the principles of sustainability. The world's largest manufacturer of commercial carpet tiles, Interface was confronted by the fact that their
manufacturing processes generated toxic pollutants, large amounts of waste-
water, high emissions, and a product that ultimately ends up in landfills. In
light of this, the company's founder and Chairman, Ray Anderson, vowed in
1994 to make the entire company "sustainable," meaning profitable over the
long term. The change process he initiated began with re-conceptualizing the
mission of the business from "selling carpet" to "covering floors." This simple repositioning opened new avenues for growth, including increased sales
to existing clients, as well as attracting new business. Looking to improve
margins, the company saw that reductions in resource and energy use could
save money. They thus conceived Solenium, a floor covering product that uses
one-third less material and energy than standard floor covers and is fully re-
cyclable. They then developed such other new products as polytrimethylene
terephthalate, a carpet fiber that is resistant enough to use in hospitals. Since
these carpets are produced as tiles, replacing worn sections became easier,
increasing the useful life of the less-worn tiles and saving customers money
(which, in turn, increased brand loyalty). As a result, employees became more
motivated because the new product was less toxic, and because they felt part
of a company that was "making a difference" in the world. Today, Interface
continues to innovate by proactively managing its innovation process around
sustainable solutions.

Of course, not every innovation succeeds. A case in point is Monsanto's
pioneering work in the development of genetically modified crops (GM). GM
crops promised what economist Joseph Schumpter called "creative destruction," that is, an innovation that changes the game so drastically that it offers
opportunities for new businesses and poses threats to existing ones. However,
Monsanto mistook technological innovation for sustainable development.
While many farmers and food producers saw the value in GM crops, other
stakeholders did not. Environmental, safety, and anti-globalization groups
raised concerns about 1) gene transfer from GM crops to wild plant species, 2)
pest resistance, and 3) over-dependence on seed companies by local farmers.
Thus, while Monsanto framed the innovation as a scientific issue, stakeholders
saw it as a moral, cultural, social, and environmental one. Monsanto's GM
crops backfired in the end, and the company continues to struggle to regain
both its image and financial performance.

One of the important lessons from the Monsanto experience is the value of
understanding, and working with, all of a company's stakeholders. Farsighted

companies today are finding ways to create value through collaboration and partnerships, even with organizations that might have been viewed as adversaries in the past. Such activities reduce the risk of conflict and strengthen corporate and brand reputation. For example, Avon Products, the largest corporate supporter of women's breast cancer research and education, works closely with nonprofit partners to advance that cause. McDonalds partners with Conservation International around rainforest conservation (that NGO is now helping McDonalds build a more sustainable supply chain by creating a self-assessment scorecard for suppliers, measuring their performance in water, air, energy, and waste). McDonalds also works with the NGO Environmental Defense to stop poultry farmers from using antibiotics to increase chicken growth. Home Depot supports Habitat for Humanity and KaBoom (an NGO that builds playgrounds), both of which are perfect fits for a company in the home improvement and construction supply industry. Such positive collaborations provide growth enhancement through increased sales and customer and employee loyalty.

Such collaborations also entail risks. Differences between corporate and nonprofit values, poor inter-organizational communications, perceived lack of transparency, and cultural misunderstandings can lead to a mutual lack of trust. Hence, corporations need to reduce such potential risks by being strategic in their choice of partners. For example, Novartis Argentina decided to institute a drug donation program in Argentine communities. In order to determine which organizations to collaborate with, they enlisted the help of Argentine Catholic University, which provided research and advice that led to finding a nonprofit partner for Novartis that fit in terms of common values and experience.

There is good reason why many companies are looking for strategic ways to become sustainable organizations. Aside from the dollars saved through eco-efficiency, tapping new markets, and creating new products, there is increasing recognition of the importance of "intangible value." Research shows that the proportion of total company market value exceeding book value has risen from 40 percent in the early 1980s to more than 80 percent at the turn of the century.[17] That is, the majority of a company's market value today is based more on its brand and reputation than on its tangible assets.

That is why Enterprise Rent-a-Car is establishing its brand position around sustainability. Half of Enterprise's rental fleet now gets more than 28 miles per gallon. It is adding thousands of hybrids and flexi-fuel cars to the fleet, and undertaking research in the area of alternative fuels. In this way, the company hopes to save money in the short term, and build its reputation in the long term.

General Electric has made serious moves to rebuild its reputation and brand (and find new revenue streams) by introducing a variety of environmental initiatives. Launched in 2005, Ecomagination is the company's platform for innovative technologies and brand positioning centered around helping customers solve environmental problems (see chapter 8). The company's portfolio of environmentally-oriented products and services has gone from 17 to more than 60 in three years, and revenues are exceeding goals. Even Wal-Mart, the company so many love to shop at and hate at the same time, has announced it is pursuing sustainability as a core business strategy. Thus far, it is getting good grades on environmental initiatives—using renewable energy, creating less waste, stocking environmentally-friendly products, reducing green house gases, and greening its supply chain. Because its weaker social agenda is still subject to criticism, Wal-Mart exemplifies the fact that sustainability is a journey, not an end state.

Conclusion

In January 2007, the cover of *BusinessWeek* challenged readers to "Imagine a World in which socially responsible and eco-friendly practices actually boost a company's bottom line. It's closer than you think." The article captures the promise—and identifies various pitfalls—associated with going sustainable. A major theme of the article is that increasing numbers of corporate leaders are becoming committed to the idea of sustainable development. The article ends with a conclusion that seems particularly appropriate for a world in the most serious economic crisis since the Great Depression: "Such laudable (sustainable) efforts, even if successful, may not help managers make their numbers next quarter. But, amid turbulent global challenges, they could help investors sort long-term survivors from the dinosaurs."[18]

The leadership challenge is finding ways to create both a sustainable and prosperous future. Business guru Peter Senge submits three guiding principles for doing so.[19] First, viable strategies must take into account the needs of future generations. Aside from the moral obligation to meet those needs, the next generation will be the customers of tomorrow's businesses. Second, both new leadership and new kinds of leadership are required. Because the actions of business, government, and civil organizations can affect the ability of a firm to survive and thrive, outmoded assumptions that encourage sectors to act independently under a set of well-defined, non-overlapping roles must disappear. For a business to act sustainably, it will need to be aligned with actors in the other sectors. Third, the profound change needed will require new ways of thinking and perceiving. For example, the concept of "interconnectivity" is key in thinking about the major variables at play (energy and transportation, food and conflict, water and health, prosperity and environment/social justice), and understanding the "interdependency" of systems (economic, social, environmental) is key to successful strategy formulation.

Perhaps the most important issue moving forward originated some 900 years ago, with the Iroquois Confederacy's constitution calling for consideration of "the next seven generations" in all decisions. In our age of hyper competition, immediate gratification, and individualism, will it be possible for businesses and governments to make decisions today that will ensure the sustainability of the planet for future generations? The answer may have been provided at the 1992 Earth Summit by Oren Lyons, chief spiritual leader of the Iroquois nation.

At dinner with Lyons, several of us were bemoaning the poor results of the conference. Representatives of the private sector had left before the conference even started, and the NGO community was physically and philosophically disconnected from government policymakers (who had been largely concerned with making grand declarations with little thought to practical enforcement). Lyons responded to our despondent mood by offering the Iroquois philosophy for action as an alternative to the hand-wringing at the table. He said it does no good to worry about whether humanity ultimately will be the cause of the demise of the planet. The key, he said, was *to not let it happen on your watch*. He meant that if all of us do what we can to save the planet each day, we will put the inevitable off into infinity, which is the heart of the seven generations philosophy.

---

[1] Jeffrey Immelt, Plenary Address to the Business for Social Responsibility Conference, San Francisco, CA, 2008 (author's notes).

[2] Klaus Schwab, President, World Economic Forum, as cited in Ira Jackson and Jane Nelson, *Profits with Principles: Seven Strategies for Delivering Value with Values* (New York: Random House, 2004), p. 1.

[3] Bruce Mau, Jennifer Leonard, the Institute Without Boundaries, *Massive Change* (New York: Phaidon Press, 2004), p. 15.

[4] Peter Senge, Brian Smith, Nina Kruschwitz, Joe Laur, Sarah Schley, *The Necessary Revolution: How Individuals and Organizations are Working Together to Create a Sustainable World* (New York: Doubleday, 2008).

[5] Bill Baue, "Brundtland Report Celebrates 20th Anniversary Since Coining Sustainable Development," SocialFunds.com, June 11, 2007. Available at http://www.socialfunds.com/news/article.cgi/2308.html

[6] Aldo Leopold, *A Sand County Almanac* (NewYork: Oxford University Press 1949), p. 240.

[7] Per Lindblom, WCED Public Hearing, Oslo, Norway, June 24-25, 1985, as cited in The World Commission on Environment and Development, *Our Common Future* (Oxford: Oxford University Press, 1987), p. 342.

[8] *Ibid.*, p. 19.

[9] Chad Holliday, Stephan Schmidheiny, and Philip Watts, *Walking the Talk: The Business Case for Sustainable Development* (San Francisco: Berrett-Koehler Publishers, 2002).

[10] Abigail McWilliams and Donald Siegel, "Corporate Responsibility and Financial Performance: Correlation or Misspecification?" *Strategic Management Journal*, 21, (2000), pp. 603-609.

[11] John P. Kotter and James L. Heskett, *Corporate Culture and Performance* (New York: Simon & Schuster, 1992).

[12] Donald K. Clifford and Richard E. Cavanaugh, *The Winning Performance: How America's High Growth Companies Succeed* (New York: Bantam Books, 1985).

[13] Paul A. Gompers, Joy L. Ishii, and Andrew Metrick, "Corporate Governance and Equity Prices," *Quarterly Journal of Economics* (118), Feb. 2003, pp. 107-155.

[14] See, among others, Lynn S. Paine, *Values Shift* (New York: McGraw Hill, 2003); T. Amabile, "How to Kill Creativity," *Harvard Business Review*, Sept-Oct, 1997, pp. 77-87; and W. Kim and R. Mauborgne, "Making Global Strategies Work," *Sloan Management Review*, Spring 1993, pp. 11-27.

[15] International Institute for Sustainable Development, *Global Green Standards: ISO and Sustainable Development* (Winnipeg, Manitoba, 1992), p 8.

[16] Paul Gilding, Murray Hogarth, and Don Reed, *Single Bottom Line Sustainability: How a Values Centered Approach to Corporate Sustainability Can Pay Off for Shareholders and Society* (Sydney, Australia: Ecos Corporation, 2002), pp. 18-19. Available at http://www.shapenz.org.nz/_attachments/Single_Bottom_Line_Sustainability.pdf

[17] Juergen H. Daum, *Intangible Assets and Value Creation* (Chichester, U.K.: John Wiley & Sons, 2002).

[18] Pete Engardio, "Beyond the Green Corporation," *Business Week*, Jan. 29, 2007, p. 50.

[19] Senge, et al., *The Necessary Revolution* (2008). *op. cit.*

CHAPTER 12

Business and Public Policy

by John M. Holcomb

Any company that ignores public policy in this day and age does so at its peril. The collapse of the financial and auto sectors in 2008-09 has fostered an unprecedented intrusion of government into American corporate decision-making. As part of the bailouts and structured bankruptcies of General Motors and Chrysler, as well as through the bank rescue operations under the Troubled Asset Relief Program (TARP), the federal government has imposed conditions on those companies heretofore unseen in American capitalism. Whether by unilateral actions of the President and regulators, or through legislation passed by Congress, the government has (1) imposed limits on executive compensation, (2) restructured boards of directors and replaced CEOs, (3) pressured companies like Bank of America and Merrill Lynch to merge, (4) re-shaped the corporate strategy of auto companies, (5) acquired major ownership interests in companies such as AIG and Citigroup, and (6) announced that it would pursue a more aggressive antitrust policy in restructuring other industries.

These steps are not totally without parallel and have a certain foundation in American history, but we have never gone this far with government intervention in the past: The nation's first Secretary of the Treasury, Alexander Hamilton, advocated a business-government partnership to aid certain industries and advance economic development; President Theodore Roosevelt created a strong role for government as a "trust-buster" and regulator of specific industries; President Richard Nixon pursued such "centrist" Republican policies as promoting minority business development and instituting wage and price controls. None of these government actions, however, included the degree or kind of restrictions on managerial prerogatives included in today's government initiatives.

Historically, waves of government intervention in business activities and the market occurred more frequently than episodes of government retrenchment, but activism typically plateaued before the next wave of intervention. Growth in intervention often correlates with periods of economic distress, demands by organized social movements, and periods of Democratic rule. However, government intervention can increase during Republican Administrations, and government retrenchment can occur during Democratic Administrations. The period of the late 1970s through the early 1990s, for instance, witnessed a wave of deregulation of the economy in order to promote competition and eliminate bureaucratic excesses and inefficiencies. That period included the Reagan era, but was bookended by the Carter and Clinton Administrations. The Carter years saw the deregulation of transportation industries, and the early Clinton years witnessed the centrist, or neo-liberal, agenda of limited privatization and reinvention of government to more efficiently deliver public services.

These various waves of government intervention, with occasional retrenchment, pose several lessons for business strategy. Business must learn to "think politically," as Irving Kristol once advised. It must anticipate, advocate, and then adapt. During times of economic distress and major shifts in the political landscape, business must anticipate new forms of government intervention. It then can advocate policies that advance its own interests, which hopefully coincide with the public interest. Most often, business will seek assistance from government while also resisting incursions into its own managerial decision-making. It will utilize common political tools and tactics—such as lobbying, political advocacy, and campaign contributions—but will simultaneously seek to cooperate with Congressional and agency policy-makers by providing ideas and information. Once political bargains have been struck with other interest groups and policy-makers, it is up to business to adapt to the final package of policies. Occasionally, it will do so only grudgingly and after exhausting other remedies, such as car dealers recently did in mounting judicial challenges against provisions in the auto bankruptcy provisions.

Beyond exploring the public policy and regulatory landscape in greater depth, this chapter explores another recent challenge to business, that of private politics that bypass the formal institutions of government. Especially since the 1990s, business has been targeted by direct citizen activism and protest. Organized interests and non-governmental organizations (NGOs) have been the source of such pressures. After their relatively unsuccessful experiences in influencing public policy in the 1960s and '70s, citizen activists grew skeptical of government's ability to respond rapidly and effectively; in the process, these activists discovered they could often accomplish more by *directly* influencing corporate policies. These activist organizations both have confronted and collaborated with corporations in order to foster change. For example, NGOs have targeted major brands and leveraged their influence up and down the supply chain to maximize their effectiveness.

Some Definitions

When business leaders hear the term public policy, they may first think of laws and government decisions. However, the term encompasses much more than that. To demonstrate that public policy goes well beyond specific laws and regulations, a leading political scientist defined public policy as the "authoritative allocation of values." That is, when government attempts to advance the collective good, it does so not only by passing laws and regulations, but by pressuring or exhorting business to act, providing negative and positive incentives that shape business decisions, and by exposing wrong-doing through congressional hearings, executive speeches, and pronouncements. Similarly, as the concept of stakeholder management evolved, it has come to include several constituencies beyond government that are important in shaping and developing public policy, including political interest groups, the news media, and public opinion—all key elements in the nonmarket environment that significantly affect business operations and strategic decisions.

A more expansive definition of public policy might include elements of private politics because when a business considers its nonmarket environment, it weighs actions by such private actors as organized interest groups and the media. In fact, since 1990, business has had to respond to influences in the private political realm more than to those in the halls of government. As noted, organized groups of "citizen activists," have found private pressure often to be more effective in influencing business decisions than the longer and more cumbersome process of lobbying government to influence business.

Public Policy Cycle

As government's role in American business affairs continues to grow over time, and with business and government increasingly intertwined, corporate leaders must be more involved than ever in anticipating, advocating, and then adapting to public policy. In particular, leaders need to be aware of the public policy cycle, which is a concept that goes beyond the mere existence of laws and regulations and includes such steps in the legislative and administrative process as agenda setting, and policy development, formulation, implementation, and evaluation. Business can be effectively involved in the public policy process at any or all of those stages, but experience shows it is usually wise for it to enter at the earliest possible stage when its zone of discretion is widest. If business waits until policy is implemented or evaluated, it has foregone the opportunity to frame the issue as it is being advanced, or to shape it at the development stage.

It may be instructive to specify the potential roles of business and other private actors at various stages of the public policy cycle. Typically, a major event or crisis moves an issue on to the public policy agenda where it will galvanize public attention and support for government action. Even without such an event, political interest groups and/or the media might force an issue to the attention of government policy-makers. Additionally, leaders of interest groups and, often, journalists often assist in the development of legislative proposals and then lobby for the passage of laws. Once laws are sent to regulatory agencies to be implemented, business and other private actors once again enter the fray by (a) commenting on the regulations prior to ultimate adoption, (b) participating on agency advisory committees, or (c) suing the agency for abusing its discretion or invading the rights of the private actors. Once a policy is implemented, its effectiveness must be evaluated. At this stage, interest groups and think tanks may develop their own "impact" studies of the public policy and may testify at Congressional oversight hearings on the accomplishments and gaps in the legislation and enforcement rules.

The global aspects of business bring additional dimensions to the public policy cycle. For example, the entire process is often repeated, at a later time, in other countries. The time line on foreign bribery and corruption, for instance, started in the U.S. in the mid-1970s, culminating in the passage of the Foreign Corrupt Practices Act, but did not really enter the global arena until the 1990s with the passage of the anti-corruption guidelines of the Organization of Economic Cooperation and Development (OECD) and the founding of Transparency International. Given the complex global dimensions of certain issues, business therefore may need to enter the debate at different times in different regions of the world. Further, studies show that policy could be developed at one level of government (for example, by the European Union) but implemented at a different level (by nation states). Hence, business must address issues earlier in time at one level of government than at an other. Again, experience has shown it is prudent for business to enter at the earliest, agenda-setting, stage.

Public Policy Actors

The most prominent actors involved in traditional public policy decisions are the formal institutions of government. These include the three major branches—legislative, executive, and judicial—as well as the all-important fourth branch of government, the regulatory agencies. Business must monitor and respond to decisions by all of these institutions. They often lobby, or present their views, to legislative committees and staff and at the White House and relevant cabinet departments, and also interact with two types of regulatory agencies: executive agencies such as the Occupational Health and Safety Administration (OSHA) that are part of cabinet departments, and independent regulatory commissions, such as the Federal Communications Commission (FCC), that generally regulate the economic conduct of specific industries or sectors.

While businesses find dealing with public policy at the national level daunting in itself, the American system of federalism gives state governments wide-ranging jurisdiction, as well. For instance, more climate change regulations have been passed by state and local governments than by the federal government. Business, therefore, must keep track of the fabric of complex and often conflicting laws and regulations at the state and local levels. In some cases, states pass laws to meet standards established by federal legislation in a system often referred to as cooperative federalism. Hence, it is important for business people to understand the roles played by both the federal and state governments, and when it makes sense for them to advocate action taken at one level rather than another. In many cases, business has found that it is more sensible for the federal government to pre-empt an area of policy-making so there is only one uniform body of law and regulations to comply with, rather than conflicting standards from fifty state governments.

Beyond the formal institutions of government, an array of informal institutions is increasingly involved in the arenas of both public-sector politics and private politics. Political scientist Jack Walker found a huge spike in the growth of NGOs starting in the 1960s, following on the heels of the numerous social movements born in that era. Each social movement—civil rights, women's rights, the consumer and environmental movements—gave rise to a new constellation of single-issue and multi-issue interest groups, ranging in size from organizations with large memberships to some with virtually no members (supported by foundations or wealthy donors). Typically, interest groups based in Washington, D.C., and New York have fewer members with funding bases composed of large donors, while state and local groups typically tend to receive funding from large numbers of grassroots members and smaller donors. Some groups are able to become financially self-sustaining by providing selective benefits in the form of information, training, and products only available to their members. Business needs to understand the constituencies and support bases of these groups before deciding how to respond to them.

When it comes to political tactics, some public-interest groups are more confrontational, and some are more collaborative. Nascent groups trend to be more aggressive, while groups with longer histories, or those who evolved from earlier social movements into part of the political establishment, tend to be more moderate. Some NGOs have a narrow range of tactics, while others have a broad-ranging arsenal; some engage only in lobbying, while others combine that with litigation, research, and political contributions to candidates. Often, within any particular interest group sector, such as environmentalists, there will be a division of labor among groups, with some engaging only in litigation while others pursue research or lobbying. These facts have important implications for how business can most effectively respond. In order to meet the political challenges of NGOs, initially, business will imitate their tactics and division of labor. For instance, the Ford Foundation sparked the liberal public-interest law movement in the early 1970s, and business and conservative foundations responded by financing a counter-movement of conservative litigation groups and think tanks in the late 1970s. Business also imitated the grassroots lobbying tactics and coalition building of NGOs.

Beyond traditional political tactics, NGOs also have developed new tactics to pressure business. For example, organizers Saul Alinsky and Ralph Nader pioneered the use of shareholder resolutions to protest such corporate actions as discriminatory hiring, investment in South Africa, nuclear power, environmental pollution, and campaign donations. Since the 1970s, religious organizations, most prominently the Interfaith Center on Corporate Responsibility, have been the chief sponsors of such resolutions. More recently, they have been joined by mainstream shareholder groups, such as large institutional investors and pension funds, in calling for major changes in corporate governance. This movement has accelerated its pace of activism since the corporate scandals at the turn of the century.

As NGOs evolved and matured, they have embraced two new tactics: cross-sector coalitions and collaboration with corporations. In the former, activist groups from one sector have joined forces with groups in another sector to present a broad front in opposition to particular business practices. For instance, health, migrant labor, environmental, and even religious groups now work together on the issue of pesticides. Often an effective division of labor emerges, with unions and labor groups providing the lobbying muscle, health and environmental groups providing scientific research, and religious groups providing moral rectitude and vocal outrage. Obviously, such cross-sector coalitions can pose enormous challenges to business.

When NGOs find that confrontation is counter-productive, and government lobbying is protracted and ineffective, they often turn to collaboration with business to resolve issues. Indeed, as both sides have matured and grown less combative, business and NGOs have learned to work together to resolve problems. There are many examples of such productive collaboration, the most prominent of which have emerged on the environmental front: the Environmental Defense organization has successfully worked with a number of corporations, and the Rainforest Action Network (RAN) has worked with Home Depot, Lowes, and several timber companies in an initiative to protect old-growth forests. RAN and Greenpeace both combine elements of activist, and even militant, protest along with peaceful collaboration, making them particularly challenging partners for business.

Increasingly, corporate managers must appreciate the importance of another informal actor (or external stakeholder): the news media. The media provide a number of vital functions for both society and business: they help set the public policy agenda by filtering interest-group demands into a coherent set of issues and policy proposals; they serve as watchdogs over both business and government, exposing the damaging and unethical practices of each institution (investigative reporters and blog sites may be especially helpful in surfacing potential business or government scandals); they work closely with NGOs in disseminating information about harmful business practices, and in exposing private and public corruption. In general, the news media and, increasingly, internet sources, promote a more transparent and accountable corporate sector. Without such independent voices, democracy would not function as well.

Of course, the media also are businesses in search of wider audiences and greater profits and, thus, may hype stories of little significance and disseminate inaccurate information or "junk science." In so doing, the media may do great damage to corporate reputations. Hence, businesses must constantly monitor the media for such overreaching and be ready to respond with accurate information. In particular, since the media is usually a pivotal actor in any corporate crisis, company crisis management plans must include steps for dealing appropriately with the media and other critics.

Global corporations face the most complex array of formal and informal public policy actors. The best estimate is that there are currently 30,000 to 40,000 NGOs globally, and that number keeps expanding as those groups enjoy more support and legitimacy from their host countries and populations. Human rights and environmental organizations, in particular, are becoming global players. Regional and international organizations, as well as inter-governmental bodies, are increasingly important players in the policy arena. For example, the World Trade Organization (WTO) has become an active player and referee of global trade. Corporations often interact with NGOs through such international networks as the UN Global Compact and through such functionally specific organizations as the Apparel Industry Partnership—a coalition of businesses, unions, and NGOs established to promote voluntary standards in the battle against sweatshop labor conditions in developing countries. International politics expert Francis Fukuyama has advocated the further development of such organizations as part of his concept of "multi-multilateralism," in order to compensate for the weaknesses of global institutions like the United Nations.

Political Power Structure

In defending its position in the global political arena, it is important for business to understand the competing schools of thought with regard to political power. Business critics, such as the late sociologist C. Wright Mills, sometimes base their critiques on Marxist premises, concluding that a "power elite" rules society and the world. Recently, in his book *Superclass*, David Rothkopf argues for the existence of a global power elite that includes the most prominent leaders of multinational corporations, policy organizations, and governmental bodies. Opposed to those from the sociological school, political scientists such as Arthur Bentley, David Truman, and Robert Dahl have developed a much more business-friendly school of thought known as pluralism. They developed their theory based on the primacy of interest groups in American politics, arguing that: (1) a coalition of minority interests rules on most issues; (2) different interests rule on different issues; (3) the power of any given interest fluctu-ates over time; (4) power flows from different sources, not just money; and (5) business is not a monolithic interest, but one in which factions within the business community are often at odds with each other. Their overall conclu-sion is that business is not a power elite, but, instead, is one of many forces in a pluralist constellation.

A third school of thought attempts to bridge the gap between the two de-scribed above, arguing that some groups are continually more powerful than others due to their resources and the functions they provide in society. For example, Charles Lindblom, in his landmark *Politics and Markets*, finds cor-porate power flowing from the crucial benefits that business provides society in the form of jobs, products, and innovation. Business is not powerful due to any power grab, according to Lindblom but, instead, because government must often defer to the political wishes of business in order for society to function. Obviously, the dominance of one of these three competing schools at any time and place can have enormous implications for the role of business in public affairs and, thus, business leaders who understand these theories are better able to pose effective defenses against their critics.

Business-Government Relations

Within the traditional boundaries of business and public policy—that is, deci-sions solely involving government—there lay a host of complex relationships that managers need to understand. The most primary one is that of state owner-ship, common in socialist systems but uncommon in the U.S. (until the nation-alization of AIG in 2008) where more typically the preferred model has been government authorized and/or partially financed corporations, such as Am-trak, the U.S. Postal Service, and Fannie Mae. Such businesses usually provide unique public functions and are especially accountable to the government to meet their important social obligations. Leaders of these quasi-private organi-zations need to be aware of their heightened public responsibilities, to see the government as their highest priority stakeholder, and to practice a high level of ethics when influencing the government and fulfilling their public functions.

Another form of relationship between business and government involves government procurement. Because the government is the sole purchaser of weapons in the American system of national defense, Lindblom has dubbed this relationship "pentagon capitalism." Since there is only a very limited market for defense production, and high stakes involved, both the government and de-fense contractors have a special responsibility to behave effectively, efficiently, and ethically. Even before the corporate scandals of the 21st century prompted legislation mandating ethics officers and training in publicly traded companies, an earlier defense procurement scandal in 1985 (involving General Dynamics) led to legislation that mandated ethics programs for defense contractors.

A third type of business-government relationship involves various forms of what is called corporate welfare. Lindblom maintains that business is often most interested in limiting government intrusion in its decision-making prerogatives while, at the same time, gaining financial support from government. This tradition goes back to Alexander Hamilton, the nation's first advocate of close ties between business and government for the sake of advancing business concerns. The most common modern manifestations of corporate welfare include government subsidies, trade protection, and bailouts for certain companies or industries. Some business leaders and politicians call for public support of new, innovative companies or "sunrise industries," but most often it is the entrenched and politically powerful "sunset industries" of the past that are able to squeeze protection (or subsidies) out of government. This is of great concern to a sector of libertarian think tanks, such as the Cato Institute and Competitive Enterprise Institute, which oppose any form of corporate welfare or government regulation.

Government Regulation and Antitrust

There are two major forms of government regulation of business—economic and social—and each is quite different. Economic regulation is generally easier for companies to comply with: in fact, some companies have learned to benefit from it. Even some critics of the free market have long advocated economic deregulation because of the influence business has been able to exercise over economic regulatory agencies. Economist Joseph Stigler won a Nobel Prize in economics largely based on development of the "capture theory" of regulation. According to his analysis, an iron triangle often exists between (1) an economic regulatory agency, (2) relevant Congressional committees, and (3) the industry the agency was established to regulate. In this kind of relationship, the dominant firms in an industry "capture" an agency that is supposed to protect the public through incentives that the industry provides to the regulators. For example, many regulators are happily caught in a revolving door between business and government, succumbing to the financial incentives to take higher paying jobs with industry after they have left a government agency. Their long-run financial interests therefore are best served by complying with the wishes and suggestions of business while they serve as regulators—leading to decisions that are friendly to the dominant firms in the industry, but promote inefficiencies and impede competition from new entrants. Dominant firms subject to industry-specific economic regulation obviously will view (and influence) an agency differently than smaller potential entrants, which might prefer less regulation, or even deregulation. Studies showing that economic regulation often favors business (at the expense of consumer welfare) led to a wave of economic deregulation in the late 1970s and early '80s, during the Carter and Reagan Administrations.

While economic regulation may present economic *benefits* to certain firms in an industry, social regulation creates more in the way of economic *costs*. The politics of social regulation make it nearly impossible for business to capture, or dominate, a social regulatory agency because such an agency has an economy-wide scope, regulating many industries and, thus, lowering the incentive for any particular company to expend resources and effort to influence it. For instance, because the Environmental Protection Administration (EPA) may spend only a few days a year on regulations that affect the paper industry, there is little incentive for that industry to influence EPA regulators. Meanwhile, environmental NGOs have a continual stake in every action taken by the EPA, giving them an incentive to try to participate in agency deliberations on a continual basis.

Public attention is greater to media stories on the social impacts of business because they tend to be more dramatic and emotional than the more esoteric and technical stories about economic regulation. Hence, the media also is a strong counterforce to business in the politics of social regulation. Between the influence of NGOs and the media, the ability of business to influence social agencies such as the EPA and the Equal Employment Opportunity Commission (EEOC) is thus far more limited than its ability to influence economic regulatory agencies. Business will likely never capture the EPA in the way the transportation industry once captured the Interstate Commerce Commission, or as the airline industry once captured the Civil Aeronautics Board.

There are many players in the complex political environment of regulatory agencies—including influential members of Congress, the Administration, and the courts—and business needs to take them into account, as well. Nevertheless, through the jobs it can bestow on regulators, and the campaign contributions it can shower on political candidates, business has great power over economic regulatory agencies. It took a powerful case for deregulation (built by economists) to break the ability of corporations to capture economic regulators. The economic case against social regulation is weaker and, due to the forces of political influence surrounding social regulatory agencies, business has less power to capture those agencies. Thus, business can only hope to make social regulations more efficient and less costly by lobbying for sensible reforms using such tools as cost-benefit analysis.

Often, antitrust pressures are less threatening to business than are regulatory pressures. While regulators may substitute their own prerogatives for those of business managers and, thus, may interfere with free market results (sometimes to benefit the public, but other times not), many antitrust laws aim merely to make the market work rather than to interfere with its workings. A classic example is the law against price fixing. In such instances, when "competitors" are interfering with the law of supply and demand by setting prices, government merely corrects for industry inefficiencies when it enforces anti-trust law. Hence, when the government enforces such "behavioral" antitrust laws, it usually enjoys a broad consensus of support from the public, economists, and even most elements of the business community. In these areas, businesses have found it is wise to establish stringent internal controls to comply with such laws, rather than argue for their repeal or reform.

The situation is somewhat different when it comes to the so-called "structural" aspects of antitrust—those laws designed to restrict mergers or to alter the structure of industries. The aim of these laws is to alleviate the negative impacts of oligopolies (industries where a few firms control overwhelming shares of the market). Structural antitrust advocates believe that industries in which there is a high level of market concentration will inevitably lead to collusion and, thus, harm consumer welfare. They also believe that large firms in concentrated markets wield more political power than firms in a competitive marketplace (a concern, it is worth noting, that is not widely shared in American courts). The costs and benefits of concentrated markets are widely debated among policy analysts, economists, and legal scholars—which leaves room for a business to enter the debate and either embrace or contest the structural view depending on its stake in a particular law or enforcement action. For example, a large firm in an oligopolistic market seeking to merge with another firm will take a different view than a firm that opposes such a merger as anticompetitive and damaging to its own economic fortunes.

Further complicating the structural antitrust debate are the different approaches taken in different areas of the globe, chiefly between the U.S. and Europe. To simplify matters somewhat, the prevalent view in the U.S. is the behavioral view, which is that government should crack down on anticompetitive behavior, like price fixing, but be more permissive when it comes to mergers. While the E.U. is tough on anticompetitive behavior, it also is tough on mergers. Hence, while the U.S. Department of Justice (DOJ) approved a proposed merger between General Electric and Honeywell, the same merger was opposed and successfully blocked by the E.U. Competition Commission. That same E.U. Commission also has meted out stronger sanctions against Microsoft for monopolistic practices than have the courts and the DOJ in the U.S.

These national differences in antitrust policies have major implications for business. First, global enterprises need to communicate with antitrust enforcement bodies in various countries to determine the legal risks before making any final merger or acquisition decisions across national borders. Second, business may want to engage in the debate over the need for greater convergence in antitrust standards among all nations to avoid the perils of approval by one nation and disapproval by another.

Business Responses to Public Policy

Prudent and mature businesses recognize the need to engage in the public policy process and to interact with both the formal institutions of government, and the informal institutions involved in public policy-making and private politics. The aforementioned example of Microsoft indicates the dangers of ignoring the public policy process. The U.S. antitrust case against Microsoft awakened the company to the prudence of engaging with key political and regulatory actors. Prior to the case, the company had no presence in Washington, DC, made no political contributions, had limited engagement with stakeholders, and had an unsystematic corporate philanthropy program. Since that case, the company has dramatically ramped up all of its political and social initiatives. In contrast, the learning curve for Google has been much less steep because it has engaged, almost from its founding, in campaign contributions, emphasized business-government cooperation, and built public policy coalitions.

In responding to the formal institutions of government, a company often engages in one or more of a litany of traditional political tactics, including participation in regulatory agency proceedings and litigation in the courts; direct and indirect lobbying of Congress and state legislatures; and lobbying the legislature and executive branch agencies directly through its own government relations specialists, industry trade associations, consultants, or a combination of all those avenues. It also may engage in indirect, or grassroots, lobbying by appealing to its own employees, stakeholders, and the general public to make their views known to policy makers. In order to build a broad grassroots constituency, business may utilize "issue advertising" campaigns, or purchase issue ads in the media that target public policy-makers and Washington insiders, as the Mobil Corporation once pioneered. Business should be aware that orchestrated e-mail or letter-writing campaigns can leave an impression of "Astroturf" lobbying, as opposed to spontaneous pressure from the grassroots, which may undermine the cause of the sponsoring corporation.

Business may engage in both defensive lobbying (defending its own freedom from government regulation) and social lobbying (where it supports the views of NGOs or other partners to advance the public interest, and where it may also have long-term benefits to the firm with few short-term costs). For example, chemical companies occasionally have joined environmental NGOs in lobbying for an increased budget for the EPA, and retailers have joined consumer groups in pressuring the Consumer Product Safety Commission to adopt more stringent product safety standards. Corporations that show a willingness to join such public interest coalitions may gain reputational rewards from NGOs, the media, and public policy-makers.

Beyond lobbying, businesses also make contributions to political candidates. There are a range of avenues companies use in making such contributions, but the most legitimate is that of forming a political action committee (PAC) to which their employees' voluntary contributions are amassed and then given in legally limited amounts to selected candidates. Not surprisingly, larger firms in regulated industries, or in industries exposed to greater political risk, use PACs more often than other firms. Those companies find it more important to establish relationships with political candidates. Because it relates to lobbying, campaign finance is one of the most complex areas of regulatory law and, thus, it is important for executives to understand the justifications for such laws, as well as their gaps and weaknesses. Campaign finance is an area rife with ethical implications and shortcomings—and new regulations and court challenges emerge on a regular basis—thus any business that makes political contributions must keep abreast of current legal developments. Beyond contributing to political candidates (where firms face strict legal regulations and limits), businesses also advertise on ballot measure campaigns that they support or oppose, and those contributions can come from corporate assets (and are subject to almost no legal limitations).

In meeting challenges from informal actors like NGOs and the media, business may respond in a variety of ways, including: (1) Confrontation: it may aggressively attack either the message or the messenger—this course of action may not be either ethical or politically prudent but, in extreme cases, some businesses have felt justified in suing critics for libel; (2) Imitation: business often has successfully adopted the tactics of its adversaries in the public policy process when critics are ahead of the curve in terms of political innovation (as NGOs were in developing think tanks and legal foundations in the 1970s); (3) Participation: business may develop coalitions or partnerships with NGOs, as Merck did in combating AIDS, or as Nike did with the Apparel Industry Partnership to enforce fair labor practices; (4) Anticipation: business may adopt issues management programs to forecast emerging issues and to adjust business practices in advance of the passage of stringent laws or regulations.

Conclusion and Business Implications

Based on the public policy concepts examined above, several implications emerge for business:

- Corporations are most effective when they engage an issue at the earliest possible stage of the public policy cycle.

- Global corporations must anticipate that the same issue will follow a different time line in different areas of the world, and must be prepared to cope with different variations of the same issue as they emerge (and even recycle) a number of times and in different places.

- Within America, state and local governments may be more activist than the federal government on certain issues, and corporations may often find it to their advantage to seek refuge in federal pre-emption.

- In cases of private politics, businesses must adapt to the different styles of operation, tactics, and ranges of accountability embraced by various NGOs. Corporations sometimes face cross-sector coalitions across the table or across the political battleground, but in some cases must join them.

- Collaboration, rather than confrontation, usually yields the best results.

- While recognizing the value of the media as a legitimate institution in a democracy, corporations must have crisis management plans in place to prepare for unfair treatment.

- In responding to public policy challenges, businesses can use a wide range of political tactics to anticipate, advocate, and adapt to public policy.

- While the level of government intervention in the American economy has occasionally declined in the past, corporations may now be facing an era of unprecedented government intervention and supervision of managerial decision-making.

Resources:

Baumol, William J.; Litan, Robert E.; and Schramm, Carl J. (2007) *Good Capitalism, Bad Capitalism: and the Economics of Growth and Prosperity*. New Haven, CT: Yale University Press.

Berry, Jeffrey. (1999) *The New Liberalism: The Rising Power of Citizen Groups*. Washington, DC: The Brookings Institution.

Dahl, Robert. (1961) *Who Governs? Democracy and Power in an American City*. New Haven, CT: Yale University Press.

Lindblom, Charles E. (1977) *Politics and Markets, The World's Political-Economic Systems*. New York: Basic Books.

Olson, Mancur. (1965) *The Logic of Collective Action*. Boston: Harvard University Press.

Rothkopf, David. (2008) *Superclass: The Global Power Elite and the World They Are Making*. New York: Farrar, Straus and Giroux.

Vogel, David. (1989) *Fluctuating Fortunes: The Political Power of Business in America*. New York: Basic Books.

Walker, Jack. (1991) *Mobilizing Interest Groups in America: Patrons, Professions, and Social Movements*. Ann Arbor: University of Michigan Press.

The Legal and Ethical Environment for Multinational Corporations

by Don Mayer and Ruth Jebe

Every company doing business abroad faces numerous legal and ethical issues. The multinational corporation (MNC) faces legal issues raised by "home country" laws, "host country" laws, regional regulations or directives, bilateral and multilateral treaties, and international standards and certifications. Ethical issues become entwined in various legal options, and local customs and norms add another layer of complexity to the question of how to act both legally and ethically in an unfamiliar environment. This chapter offers general guidance on these complexities. We contend that MNCs are wise to focus on four kinds of ethical challenges: these are (1) bribery, competition, cronyism and public governance as they relate to supporting competitive market capitalism; (2) human rights issues; (3) environmental issues; and (4) social equity issues. While failure to focus on these can result in significant legal and reputational consequences, paying proper attention to them can improve corporate performance and enhance the functioning of economies that embrace capitalism.

After a brief summary of international law and the market system, this chapter reviews the four main ethical challenge areas for MNCs. Each challenge area should receive careful deliberation by multinational managers who wish to maintain a company's legal and reputational balance.

International Law

The salient features of international law are relatively simple: companies operating internationally are subject to bilateral and multilateral treaties ratified by nations involved in global trade, and also are subject to the specific laws of the host countries where they operate. When companies do business in host countries, they also may be required to obey the laws of their home nations: In addition to the right to make and enforce laws within their territory, all nation-states reserve the right to make and enforce laws that apply to its citizens (or "nationals"), wherever they may be located or do business. For MNCs based in the United States, this means that U.S. antitrust, anti-bribery, and equal employment opportunity laws often apply to their operations abroad.

When U.S. companies do business internationally they often find that host country laws and regulations are far more lenient in areas of environmental protection, human rights, and health and safety labor standards than they are in the United States. To some managers, this warrants a morally relativistic approach of "When in Rome, do as the Romans do." However, when an MNC is introducing a new type of enterprise in a host country, there may be no local standards or customs to follow. Moreover, when MNCs doing business in developing nations with relatively weak regulatory regimes fail to follow widely recognized standards of labor standards, environmental care, and human rights, they can generate local antagonism—regardless of legalities—as well as adverse reactions from non-governmental organizations (NGOs) and others, resulting in reputational loss, or even their ability to operate within a given host country. Also, failing to give serious deliberation to such ethical challenges can result in criminal prosecution, either in the MNC's home country or host country. In other cases, civil lawsuits may create significant liability or, at the least, prove to be unprofitable distractions.

The Market System and International Law

Capitalism has many forms and variations.[1] But in all of its manifestations, some concept of a "free market" stands at the center: that is, individuals and business organizations exchange goods, services, and various forms of payment with minimal government restrictions. Where people freely transact business with adequate information, "the market" is said to deliver an optimal mix of goods and services to society. The ethics of such a system depend on the application of such notions as free will, consent, choice, rationality, competition, merit, and due diligence.

Economists posit that a perfectly competitive market would have an absence of "negative externalities," an adequate supply of "public goods," and many buyers and sellers with "few barriers to market entry." Negative externalities are the costs imposed on people who have not freely chosen to assume them, such as bystanders who suffer ill-effects from pollution. The public goods essential to a properly functioning free market system include a state-sponsored system of dispute resolution (courts and established legal rules), a system of titles for various kinds of property (real and personal), and a physical infrastructure that can support the movement of goods across interstate and international borders. Barriers to entry can be public (such as tariffs, or public subsidies that make it more difficult for new technologies or competitors to emerge), or private (such as monopolies and cartels that deliberately restrain competition).

For many reasons, including politics and human nature, governments even in most developed nation-states have not completely aligned their policies and practices with these basic principles of perfectly competitive markets. Economists call this "market failure." Even in the United States, where there is a relatively sound legal and physical infrastructure for business, there remain significant instances of anti-competitive behavior, negative externalities, subsidies that distort competition, and lack of adequate information (or information asymmetries, in which sellers generally have more information than buyers). And international law offers even greater opportunities for companies to engage in profitable acts that violate the principles underlying free market systems. In sum, both in the domestic and international context, the principles of the perfectly competitive system that economists prize are often subverted in practice: a firm may monopolize an entire industry and exercise its market power to throttle potential competition, divide up a market with a competitor, or fix prices with one or more competitors so as to wrest the maximum profit from unsuspecting consumers. For example, some pharmaceutical companies market drugs approved for one use for another (unapproved) use, or provide financial incentives to doctors to prescribe drugs that may not be the most efficacious.

Because even the myriad U.S. fair trade laws, in addition to U.S. antitrust and European competition laws, cannot put a stop to all such practices, below we explore how profit-seeking actions by MNCs can undermine the capitalist system through political and market manipulations, bribery, and tax evasion. In the areas of environmental protection, human rights, and social equity, we show how legal systems provide numerous opportunities for MNCs to profit while generating negative externalities, infringing human rights, or neglecting important social needs in various host countries. Put positively, we argue that when corporations engage in fair competition, encourage sound public governance, respect human rights and community values, and protect the natural environment, they can create lasting value for themselves and for the system we call capitalism.

Fair Competition and Good Governance

Good business requires adequate public goods and fair, well-enforced rules of competition, all of which can be subverted by bribery, corporate tax evasion, market manipulations, and the exercise of political power for private profit. Let us begin with bribery.

The practice of bribery undermines competition, and does so in the most direct possible way. For example, after W.S. Kirkpatrick Company won a large contract in Nigeria in 1981 by bribing a public official, another U.S.

company, Environmental Tectonics, learned that its competitive bid had never been seriously considered. Hence, competition in terms of quality and cost did not matter in the transaction; the bribe was the determining factor as to which company was awarded the contract. U.S. anti-racketeering laws applied in this instance (since both companies were U.S. "nationals"); moreover, the underlying act also violated the basic premises of competitive capitalism: that initiative, industry, diligence, and merit will be rewarded, and the best product or service will "win" in the marketplace. Kirkpatrick did not need to offer the best product, process, or project—it just needed to offer the biggest bribe. In any competitive bidding for contracts, true competition does not exist when a greatly inferior product "wins" via bribery. The act may create value for the bribing company but, otherwise, the market is distorted: the product costs too much (to cover the bribe), is of inferior quantity, or both. Innovative firms that would compete on merit are discouraged. In addition, the higher cost to governments of inferior products or services is a drain on the scarce public resources in the developing world and undermines confidence in both capitalism and democracy. Yet bribery remains a very potent force in global business today.[2]

Because the undermining of competitive bidding in government contracts undermines the efficiency and morality of capitalism, it is abundantly clear that international business requires sound regulatory oversight in this regard. This soundness requires a fair degree of objectivity, and should (ideally) not be highly politicized. No-bid, insider contracts (and contracts approved by public authorities on the basis of private politics or outright bribery) create conflicts of interest that undermine such sound oversight. Such practices produce a weakened version of capitalism in which competition is throttled, externalities are left unchecked, subsidies are rampant, taxes are not collected, and in which insufficient funds are available to create the needed public goods to support a well-regulated, competitive marketplace.

As we see below, many MNCs have believed that non-market practices and elaborate tax evasion strategies are justified by the mandate to deliver maximum shareholder value. But the value of free markets without good public governance is dubious; the existence of viable property laws,[3] contract rights enforcement, and peaceful, objective resolution of disputes in accordance with the rule of law[4] are public goods that are necessary for viable business transactions. The political and legal system in which a business operates matters to the success of that business, as managers of U.S. MNCs discover in host countries where they are met by the outstretched hand of "public servants," chaotic or non-existent systems of property rights, and byzantine (or opaque) regulations.

Wherever MNCs suffocate local governments in the developing world by depriving them of oxygen (tax revenues), they also deprive those systems of the much-needed enforcement and supervision of antitrust and anti-bribery laws, banking and securities regulation, enforcement of property and contract rights, and the securing and maintaining of such public goods as highways, bridges, ports, air traffic controls, weather information, parks, education, and defense. The problem here is the classic "free rider": if my company shirks taxes and lets others pay, my shareholders are better off. But wherever such strategic non-participation becomes widespread, it defeats the chance of creating a system of good public governance.

A landmark study by Raymond Baker (an avowed and successful capitalist) demonstrates how MNCs engage in multifarious methods of tax avoidance, using transfer pricing and accounting tricks to avoid taxation by the U.S. and E.U. countries. As Baker describes it, the

> ...combination of mispricing, transfer pricing, tax havens, dummy corporations, shielded foundations, secrecy jurisdictions, flee clauses, the whole gamut of techniques and structures that supports dirty money, affords a quasi-legal veneer over a system that revels in its ability to walk on the edge and get away with subterfuge.[5]

Baker also notes that, while low tax rates are good for economic growth, tax evasion is not, because it undermines the rule of law and the ethical notion of "transparency" that is vital to healthy organizations and societies: "For every dollar owed but not collected by the IRS, either taxes must rise or budget deficits must widen, sending interest rates higher and placing a heavy burden on our children to pay down the debt."[6] Baker argues that falsified pricing, tax havens, secrecy structures, and the illicit movement of "trillions of dollars out of developing nations and transitional economies break the social contract, however defined, that Adam Smith incorporated into the core of the free-market system."[7]

Thanks in large part to the tax lawyers, accountants, and bankers who facilitate this system, corporate taxes as a percentage of total U.S. tax revenues have gone down significantly since the early 1990s. Baker also notes the sobering reality that many MNCs are using the same offshore facilities as drug lords, the mafia, and terrorists, and concludes that all these "free riders" on the global capitalist system represent a threat to sustainable free markets, and that these threats are clearly located in the world's tax havens, where both money laundering and MNC transfer pricing take place.

Yet, when it comes to tax avoidance, many shareholders would the practice cheer as long as it is not against the law. It seems like "good business" if it's (1) not illegal, and (2) saves shareholders money. So why not do it? The best answer is that we all have a stake in the success of capitalism, that is, in helping nation-states work within the international community to secure human rights, create social capital, and protect the natural environment. Those ends cannot be met by a system in which every corporation pursues its short-term, narrow self-interest regardless of the economic, social, and environmental consequences to others. The evidence for this is found in the familiar post-Cold War

parade of horribles: rogue and failing states, severe environmental degradation, liquidity and credit crises that threaten systemic financial breakdown,
starvation and disease, Al Qaeda, persistent slavery, and genocide.

These facts alone should be sufficient to persuade all governments, corporations, citizens, and institutions of civil society that they have a stake in seeing
that the capitalist system is both well-understood and correctly regulated to enhance values of choice, merit, transparency, competition, and efficiency, both
in developed and developing countries. If business embraces those values, it
can be a global force for human rights, sustainability, and social equity. As
Raymond Baker puts it in his final chapter, "Renewing Capitalism:"

> Western corporations can enjoy a competitive advantage in lawful op-
> erations. They cannot be as successful as others in lawless operations.
> Responsible business interests should understand that they have much
> more to gain from supporting and extending rather than from sub-
> verting and weakening legal structures...Illicit, disguised, and hidden
> financial flows create a high-risk environment for criminals and thugs.
> When we pervert the proper functioning of our chosen system, we
> lose the soft power it has to project values across the globe. Capitalism
> itself then runs a reputational risk...Our own security and prosperity
> are in part dependent on others having a solid stake in the legitimate
> free market system.[8]

Accordingly, if we believe in "good business"—where private enterprise is
part of creating and maintaining a good society—we must recognize that business ethics must be consistent with the basic principles of a legitimate free
market system. Thus, we must recognize that it is simply free-ridership—and
not principled capitalism—when a company creates complex offshore transactions that deprive elected governments of revenues required to fund an adequate level of public goods.

The same ethical critique applies to market manipulations, anti-competitive
practices that are legally proscribed such as price-fixing, market divisions, and
the exercise of monopoly power to suppress competition. Even when not illegal, such practices are manifestations of a drive to profit unfairly beyond
the moral boundaries of competitive capitalism. Similarly, the use of political
power to gain private profit from public law—whether to secure subsidies,
special favors, or no-bid contracts that could easily be placed on a more competitive basis—amounts to non-market, or political, manipulation. All such
attempts to "rig the system" in favor of those with access, money, and power
undermine the ethics of capitalism. In sum, if we believe in the benefits of a robust system of competitive capitalism, there is no ethical room for companies
to undermine effective public governance through tax evasion, suppressing
competition, using bribes to gain business, or engaging in political angling that
amounts to favoritism over fair competition.

MNCs and Human Rights

While "human rights" is a an amorphous concept, there are a number of notable international treaties, conventions, and court decisions that signal where businesses should take special notice of the rights of their employees and the people in the communities in which they operate. For example, all members of the United Nations have ratified a number of important international human rights agreements ("conventions"), including the Universal Declaration on Human Rights (1948), the International Covenant on Economic, Social and Cultural Rights (1966), the International Covenant on Civil and Political Rights (1966), The International Convention on the Elimination of All Forms of Racial Discrimination (1965), and the Convention on the Rights of the Child (1989). In addition, many companies have agreed to voluntary codes of conduct with regard to human rights, such as the Equator Principles and the European Parliament's Code of Conduct for European enterprises operating in developing countries.

Even if such conventions and guidelines didn't exist, businesses would find that respecting human rights is necessary to protect their overseas investments. For example, Talisman Energy Inc., a Canadian oil company, sought to expand internationally in the 1990s and cast its eyes toward the relatively new oilfields of Sudan, acquiring the African holdings of Arakis Energy. Because oil production in Sudan consistently exceeded expectations, Talisman quickly became Canada's top producing oil and gas company. However, Talisman's stock price did not reflect this success; it declined 11 percent in the first weeks after the company entered Sudan, and was unsteady throughout March 2003, when it sold its share in the country's oilfields.

The disconnect between the success of Talisman's Sudan oil operations and its rapid exit from the country lay in its failure to recognize the need for a "social license" to operate in the developing world. While Talisman had a legal license from the government to operate, it ignored the needs and concerns of the Sudanese people in the oil concession areas. Talisman needed some of those people to be moved from their homelands in order to drill. The Sudanese government used this as an opportunity to increase its efforts to displace the non-Muslim population in the country's South, many of whom were killed or maimed as the government burned everything to ensure that the Christians and Animists would not return to the area. Most southern Sudanese drew a connection between this displacement and Talisman's access to the oilfields.

In addition to the displacement, revenues from the oilfield benefitted the Muslim population in northern Sudan rather than the local population, and the Sudanese government used a large part of those revenues to beef up its military, purchasing several helicopter gunships that were then used to attack villages and drive people out of the oil concession area. The government never took seriously the proposals to have the company's oil revenue placed in a trust fund to be administered by non-governmental institutions on behalf of the people.

As part of its operations, Talisman constructed roads into the oil concession area, and built an airstrip (used primarily for helicopters). As the government's actions against the population in the area increased, it began to use the infrastructure built by Talisman for its military operations. The roads facilitated military access to southern Sudan, resulting in more violence over a larger expanse of the country. The government also used Talisman's airstrip to launch helicopter attacks on villages in the south. That Talisman appeared to have sanctioned all of the above—whether true or not—made the company appear complicit in the government's human rights abuses, and led many southern Sudanese to view Talisman's operations as legitimate targets for physical attack.

Talisman also was attacked legally, sued by an NGO for aiding and abetting Sudan's alleged genocide in Southern Sudan. The lawsuit was ultimately dismissed, but the time and expense involved in litigating, coupled with the subsequent negative publicity, damaged both Talisman's reputation and its bottom line. Here's the lesson: Today, a MNC cannot rely on the traditional model of foreign direct investment in which local governments take whatever political or legal actions they see fit in their own territory, while companies "mind their business."

Moreover, not all MNCs escape legal liability for human rights violations. Under the U.S. Alien Tort Statute (ATS), corporate complicity with nation-states who violate "the law of nations" is actionable in U.S. courts by non-U.S. citizens. For example, in 1992, the French oil company, Total, S.A., entered into a production-sharing agreement with the Burmese government in the Yadana natural gas field, located in the Gulf of Martaban off the coast of southern Burma. The Yadana pipeline was designed to collect offshore gas and deliver it to markets in Thailand, with the intent of gas becoming Burma's single largest source of hard currency. Unocal, a U.S. corporation based in California, agreed to join the project as a joint venturer. The Burmese government—a military junta originally known as the State Law and Order Restoration Council, or SLORC—agreed to provide access to, and security in, the pipeline construction areas, and to guarantee the safety of Total and Unocal employees.

Almost as soon as the project began, allegations of human rights violations by the Burmese government's security forces began to surface. "The right to life," established by Article 3 of the Universal Declaration of Human Rights, allegedly was violated repeatedly by summary executions of rebels in the area, of workers who tried to escape, and of employees who failed to carry their work loads. Widespread acts of torture and brutality also were alleged, all in violation of Article 5 of the Universal Declaration. The military allegedly and repeatedly confiscated personal property and food from villagers living in the path of the pipeline, and prohibited people from using ancestral fishing areas where pipeline equipment was being stored. The leveling of entire villages in the path of the pipeline and forced relocations were allegedly common. Because of its collaboration with SLORC, Unocal became the target of protests and, eventually, legal action. After years of legal wrangling, a lawsuit filed in the United States (based on the ATS) was settled in December of 2004, for an undisclosed amount. Unocal, for its part, maintained throughout the proceedings that it did not authorize the actions of the military, and did not condone human rights violations.

Increasing protests and the threat of global boycotts have affected both the reputations and profits of corporations in recent years. This is partly due to the expanded role and increased powers of social NGOs. That NGOs exert more influence than ever is both a result, and a cause, of changing social expectations about the role of business. Initially, NGOs sought to expand their reach where they saw governments failing in their responsibilities to their citizens, becoming advocates for those ignored or abused by their own leaders. Noting the effects of the increasing power of the private sector over the public sphere, NGOs began to turn their focus to business, an early example of which was the South Africa divestment movement of the 1980s, when social activists pressured investors to divest from companies doing business in apartheid South Africa.

NGOs also played a significant role in Talisman's decision to sell its Sudan operations, pressuring institutional investors such as TIAA-CREF and CALPERS to sell their stock in the company. Although it is difficult to quantify the exact effect such movements have on stock prices, there is little disagreement that a well-organized divestment campaign will have at least some negative impact. Clearly, such campaigns can result in negative publicity for a corporation. In 2001, Talisman's CEO aptly summed up the situation for MNCs by noting that "[c]orporations...are increasingly being asked to step into roles that were once the domain of governments or international bodies such as the United Nations." This is certainly true in the area of human rights, where corporations are likely to be held increasingly accountable for their actions.

MNCs and Environmental Integrity

There are only a few binding international environmental treaties. Instead, most environmental standards and regulations vary considerably from nation to nation; and for "the global commons," regulatory standards are rare. The Montreal Protocol, which effectively limits emissions of chlorofluorocarbons (CFCs) into the stratosphere, is a notable exception. Thus, corporations are tempted to take advantage of lenient standards, or lack of enforcement, in host countries, with the result that companies often put "profit above planet."

It is evident that existing laws, national and international, have not adequately addressed the entire range of environmental problems that plague the planet. Corporations thus may profit by: overfishing the oceans with drag nets, trading in endangered species or taking them for "scientific research" (killing of whales by Japanese and Norwegian crews), using the black market to trade in CFCs, engaging in bio-piracy, creating and selling products spawned by new technologies onto the market before an adequate risk/benefit assessment has been accomplished, depending on heavy use of fossil fuels (and opposing any limits to those activities), using chemicals or industrial processes in developing countries in ways that would be forbidden in developed nations, and destroying tropical forests for highly marketable wood (teak, mahogany).

MNCs are able to engage in such activities because there is no strong regulatory oversight. When such activities are challenged in courts, companies often work overtime to defend their actions. For example, a U.S.-based oil company that pollutes large areas of land in another country may be subject to tort litigation, either on the basis of negligence (breach of a general duty of care) or intentional tort (nuisance or trespass). That has been the case with Texaco's oil drilling activities in Ecuador, which allegedly spilled 16.8 million gallons of oil directly into the environment, and left behind 600 open waste pits. If the allegations are true, such spills amount to some six million gallons more than the amount of oil spilled by the Exxon Valdez in Alaska in 1989. In 1993, a group of Ecuadorian citizens in the Oriente region filed a class action lawsuit in U.S. federal court against Texaco and, in 1994, Peruvian citizens living downstream from the Oriente region also filed such a suit. Both complaints alleged that, between 1964 and 1992, Texaco's oil operations polluted the rainforests and rivers in Ecuador and Peru, resulting in environmental damage and damage to the health of those who live in the region. Both lawsuits were dismissed by a U.S federal court in 2002 on *forum non conveniens* grounds (meaning that the U.S. court found that Ecuador was a more appropriate venue for litigating the claims). In achieving this dismissal, Texaco argued that the Ecaudorian courts were "available and adequate" to hear the case and, in 2003, the trial was moved to a ramshackle court in Lago Agrio, a "nondescript, dusty town near Colombia's lawless frontier."[9]

The Ecuadorian litigation was in the form of a class action suit brought against Chevron, which had aquired Texaco. Judicial inspections by a court-appointed scientific team of the contaminated sites began in August 2004. In early 2008, a purportedly independent expert recommended to the court that Chevron pay $7 to 16 billion in compensation for the pollution. In 2008, Chevron reportedly lobbied the U.S. Government to end trade preferences with Ecuador over the lawsuit. In 2009, Chevron accused the Ecuadorian judge of bias, claiming that he had been bribed, and offering secretly videotaped footage as evidence. Even as the judge offered to recuse himself, Chevron made application for arbitration of the dispute under the rules of a U.S.-Ecuador investment treaty.

For their part, Chevron's website brings up a number of reasons why it is not legally, morally or financially responsible. By contrast, the documentary film "Crude," released in fall of 2009, claims that Texaco spent three decades systematically contaminating one of the most bio-diverse regions on Earth, poisoning the water, air, and land—effectively creating a "death zone" area the size of Rhode Island. Increased rates of cancer, leukemia, birth defects, and a multiplicity of other health ailments have devastated the indigenous population and "irrevocably impacted their traditional way of life."

While there may be legal arguments in Chevron's favor, the company does not claim to have been a careful steward of the Ecuadorian environment; instead, it blames the damage on the State oil company, Petroecuador, which still drills in the area. Chevron also argues that the legal-political system in Ecuador is now tilted to the left since the election of Rafael Correa, a U.S.-educated economist who has called the devastation a "crime against humanity," and who supports the plaintiffs in the case. But in gaining dismissal in U.S. court under the doctrine of *forum non conveniens* in 2003, the company took the position that Ecuadorian courts provided an "adequate and available" judicial forum that would best serve both private and public interests. However, once the Ecuadorian court seemed headed toward a multi-billion dollar judgment, Chevron switched grounds and argued that Ecuadorian courts were inadequate. The company also has tried to enlist U.S. diplomatic pressure, challenged the presiding judge's fairness, and requested arbitration in Europe to avoid a judgment from the Ecaudorian court.

In a similar situation, U.S. fruit and chemical companies argued repeatedly throughout the 1990s that Central American courts were adequate to deal with claims from banana workers made sterile by DBCP (a pesticide banned in the U.S. but used in Honduras, Nicaragua, and elsewhere). When U.S. courts ruled that worker plaintiffs could just as well sue in their home countries, the fruit and chemical companies did not expect that Nicaragua's legal system then would take the cases of Nicaraguan plaintiffs, allow class actions, and actually impose substantial penalties. When it did, the companies convinced the U.S. Department of State to exert pressure to undo what the Nicaraguan legislature and courts had done, and have resisted enforcement of Nicaruaguan judgments in the United States.

In short, multinational companies are prone to use "political influence" and "legal compliance" as strategies to modify their moral responsibilities, whether those relate to the environment, human rights, or the health of workers abroad. For environmental issues in particular, it is undoubtedly tempting for firms to seek short-term economic benefits by damaging the natural environment when they can do so legally. But here again, such a strategy ignores the social license aspect of doing business abroad, affects company reputation in negative (if hard to measure) ways, and risks large damage awards in foreign courts. An eventual judgment against Chevron from the courts of Ecuador in the billions of dollars would be a non-trivial sum in anyone's accounting. In contrast, there are often market advantages that accrue to those MNCs who infuse their strategies with a realistic understanding of the environmental problems their operations create. That's good business.

MNCs and Social Equity

Social equity means that the populace in a developing country has a fair opportunity to earn a living wage, receive an appropriate education, and have access to other resources and rights vital to human well-being. Lack of social equity (social injustice) occurs when oppressive regimes deny full political rights and participation—although social injustice can exist in democratic regimes, as well. The concept of social equity is that each society has a stock of "social capital," that, when invested properly, can create the possibility of human thriving, not just merely surviving. The concept of social equity is not normally on the radar of MNCs seeking profitable new markets in developing nations. Historically, such issues have been regarded as purely governmental responsibilities.

In fact, too many developing nations suffer from inadequate education, health resources, and poor physical infrastructures. Hence, when corporations invest in developing nations, they often find that local expectations are raised that they will provide needed roads, hospitals, schools, bridges, and clean water—the list can be endless. Because MNCs cannot expect a clear division of responsibilities between the public and private spheres in developing nations, they face increased expectations with regard to questions of social equity. When governments cannot, or will not, take care of these basic needs, the local populace sees the provision of such public goods as part of the company's mandate.

Even when companies are not forced to make infrastructure investments in hospitals, schools, and roads, there are numerous other areas in which they will be seen as having social responsibilities. For example, a U.S. company may be expected to: follow higher worker safety standards than the host country allows; refuse to hire children even when it is legal to so; hire women or members of a discriminated against race or ethnicity; and, refuse to use local contractors whose practices are unethical or unsafe. Even freedom of speech issues may be seen as involving social equity: when a company like Google or Yahoo enters the Internet service market in China, and submits to government controls and turns over the IP address of an anonymous blogger protesting political or social injustices, it affects the social order by agreeing to web censorship, and thus limits free speech and political participation.

Dealing with social equity issues isn't easy, and we offer no simple answers. Nor is it clear that a company generally risks a significant loss of profit, or reputation, in "doing as the Romans do" with regard to social equity issues involving labor practices or freedom of speech. But there are notable exceptions where such costs have been incurred: Unocal lost reputational capital in using forced labor in Burma, and several firms suffered moral condemnation for doing business in South Africa while complying with the racially discriminatory practices of the apartheid regime. On the positive side, there may be unexpected benefits for an MNC that looks closely at a host country's cultural, political, and legal environment—and then discerns what practices and policies are consistent with the company's core principles, the need for sustainable profit, and widely accepted social standards. For example, Arvin Meritor, a parts supplier to the global auto industry, found that worldwide monitoring of the safety of their workers improved employee morale and productivity, and also lowered operating costs.[10] And MNCs who work toward ISO certifications are saying, implicitly, that certain standards will not be compromised, regardless of the location of their operations. In sum, the art of international business ethics is for MNCs to find a middle way between unthinking and unblinking acceptance of "local norms," on the one hand, and the different, and often higher, standards of their own home countries, on the other.

---

[1] Charles Hampden Turner and Alfons Trompenaars, *The Seven Cultures of Capitalism: Value Systems for Creating Wealth in the United States, Japan, Germany, France, Britain, Sweden and the Netherlands* (New York: Doubleday, 1993).

[2] Frontline (PBS). (2009). The Business of Bribes: An Investigation into International Bribery, available at http://www.pbs.org/frontlineworld/stories/bribe/

[3] Hernando DeSoto, *The Mystery of Capital: Why Capitalism Triumphs in the West and Fails Everywhere Else* (New York: Basic Books, 2000).

[4] Cass Sunstein, *Free Markets and Social Justice* (New York: Oxford University Press, 1997).

[5] Raymond, Baker, *Capitalism's Achilles Heel: Dirty Money and How to Renew the Free-Market System* (Hoboken, NJ: Wiley & Sons2005), p. 136.

[6] Robert Kuttner, "How Corporate Tax Evaders Get Away with Billions," *Business Week,* June 23, 2003, at 24.

[7] Baker, note 5, p. 138.

[8] Baker, note 5, p. 369.

[9] Juan Forero, "Rain Forest Residents, Texaco Face Off in Ecuador." National Public Radio, Morning Edition, April 30, 2009. Available at http://www.npr.org/templates/story/story.php?storyId=103233560

[10] ChipMcClure, CEO of Arvin Meritor, speech on "Business Ethics" at Oakland University, School of Business Administration, Rochester Michigan, April 2006.

CHAPTER 14

The Multinational's Dilemma: Cultures in Conflict

by Doug Allen

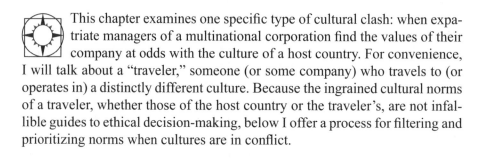 This chapter examines one specific type of cultural clash: when expatriate managers of a multinational corporation find the values of their company at odds with the culture of a host country. For convenience, I will talk about a "traveler," someone (or some company) who travels to (or operates in) a distinctly different culture. Because the ingrained cultural norms of a traveler, whether those of the host country or the traveler's, are not infallible guides to ethical decision-making, below I offer a process for filtering and prioritizing norms when cultures are in conflict.

The Complexity of Culture

In 1884, anthropologist E.B. Tylor defined culture as "...that complex whole which includes knowledge, belief, art, morals, law, custom and any other capabilities and habits acquired by man as a member of society."[1] In the years since Tylor, studies of culture have focused mainly on discrete societies: nations, tribes, and subcultures—such as regions, religions, and even business organizations. This chapter is primarily focused on national cultures.

Without question, values embedded in a culture are important moral guides to its members. Culture—influenced by tradition, religion, and other sources of moral perspective—historically served as a powerful moral compass in traditional societies. As societies became more complex, particularly with the emergence of the nation-state, the values of each society were codified and institutionalized as sets of laws. In many cases, groups of nation-states will have similar values deriving from membership in a particular "civilization," and vexing value conflicts will arise from the value differences that distinguish various civilizations.[2] The role and treatment of women in many parts of the Middle East, for example, can prove problematic for travelers from the United States and many parts of Europe.

If values were universal there would be little conflict when cultures interact. However, cultural values are often context-specific and, thus, unreliable as moral guides outside their home culture. As our hypothetical traveler engages in cross-cultural interactions, here are some things he or she might usefully keep in mind: culture deserves respect; there is often more than one right solution to cultural conflicts related to ethical choices; ethical differences often are a matter of prioritizing values; culture should not be used as an excuse for unethical behavior; cultures are dynamic; and host-country nationals are not always reliable guides to local culture.

Cultures Deserve Respect

In situations where conflicts arise, mutual respect for cultural practices is essential. A manager locating in a foreign country should make an effort to understand the basis for cultural differences he or she discovers in the local context. The traveler must remain respectful of local culture even when significant differences arise. Respect, however, does not require that local cultural values be unquestioningly embraced: While local laws must be obeyed, companies have the choice to refuse to do business where the laws of the host nation offend the ethical values of the company. For example, many Western companies refused to do business in South Africa during the apartheid era when the laws of that country violated Western values of equality. This is not to say those companies refused to honor local cultural norms, because there is no necessary relationship between a nation's cultural values and its current laws. At any given time, a nation's laws may or may not reflect its implicit social contract or the values of its citizens.

Yet, laws often do reflect cultural norms, and respect for local norms is generally warranted, for the many cultures of the world represent the societal equivalent of a biological gene pool, representing a wealth of perspectives achieved over thousands of years.[3] Each culture embodies many generations worth of collective wisdom, spiritual values, and practical approaches to social, physical, and technical problems encountered in the local context. Thus, travelers and hosts alike can benefit from a mutual and respectful sharing of perspectives; every cross-cultural encounter is an opportunity to learn and to teach.

More Than One Right Answer

There is often more than one right answer to the culturally-based ethical challenges the traveler faces. Some challenges are not really ethical, but more accurately, matters of etiquette. Some cultural collisions may just represent differences of taste (chopsticks versus silverware) while, in other cases, they may involve basic differences in moral priorities (personal freedom versus social stability). In many cases, differences across cultures do not result from the acceptance or rejection of universal (core) values; instead, they reflect a different prioritization of *multiple* shared values. For example, when Asians give priority to the family (or the group) over the individual, it does not mean that they place no value on the individual.

Not All Answers Are Right

Some cultural practices and habits, for example murder and bribery, should simply be judged as wrong. While bribery is widely practiced in many parts of the world, it is seldom, if ever, *valued* as a positive cultural practice. Instead, people may resign themselves to accepting it as a necessary evil, one so widely practiced that there appears to be no alternative but to participate in it. But this does not confirm bribery as a cultural *norm*. Widespread bribery also can be a serious deviation from long-accepted cultural values. In many societies, the values of truthfulness, honesty, and trustworthiness have eroded in the business arena to the point that many people come to view cheating and lying as acceptable, in at least some circumstances. Thus, "respecting" the local practice of bribery is not so much respect for a core value as it is a perpetuation of (or a *de facto* endorsement of) an erosion of cultural values that actually are in need of restoration.

At the same time, what appears to be bribery—the giving of some value in anticipation of a reward or favor—may very well not be, depending on the local context. In the United States, for instance, giving a gift to a professor is often viewed as a bribe for a favorable grade whereas, in other parts of the world, the same gift would be viewed as a sign of respect. In many cases, understanding the cultural context of a given behavior is critical to establishing whether it is right or wrong.

Culture Should Not Be Used as an Excuse

A common criticism of the philosophy of cultural relativism ("When in Rome, do as the Romans do") is that it avoids making value judgments about local behaviors; perhaps worse, it offers a license to engage in what would be considered unacceptable practices "back home." If we accept the fact that our own culture is not an infallible compass, then it also follows that no other culture should be viewed as such. Too often, local cultural practice has been used as an excuse to conduct business in a way that deviates dramatically from the core values of Western travelers. But respecting local culture should not mean putting moral blinders on, whether one is a traveler or a host.

Host Country Locals Are Not Always Reliable Sources

It is tempting for the traveler to accept local wisdom at face value. At the extreme, the traveler casts all critical thinking to the wind and simply relies upon one, or a few, local informants to learn about values and practices of the host culture. However, critical examination of the credibility of an informant is essential for three reasons:

- The culture itself is likely to be changing, and different members of society will have been exposed to these changes in uneven ways. As a result, some may be very aware of, and able to describe clearly, the changes under way; while others will have been sheltered from the change, missed it altogether, or dismissed it as trivial.

- Not all members of a culture have a single and clear understanding and perspective on its values. For instance, male executives in a host country may be less enthusiastic about changes in equal promotional opportunities for women than recent female MBA graduates would be.

- Local informants may have an interest in misleading the traveler. Employees may assure a newly arrived manager that it is an accepted cultural practice to rest between two to four in the afternoon. Before operating on that advice, it may well be worth checking with other locals and seasoned visitors to determine whether it is true, and whether it is such a strong value that serious attention should be given to its accommodation.

In brief, each local informant should be viewed as one source among many. Because so much individual variation occurs, the traveler must view what she is learning from locals as hypotheses to be accepted, or modified, as the traveler acquires additional knowledge and perspective.

Mapping and Prioritizing Cultural Dilemmas

Not all cultural collisions are created equal. Both traveler and host will have varying stakes in the clashes that inevitably arise. It is useful to assess these stakes early on. Many clashes of culture involve fairly superficial issues of taste or preference. While not exactly trivial, these clashes often deserve less attention, although it is important to determine the level of commitment to what may be trivial to one party and vital to another. For example, a choice whether or not to eat meat is a matter of taste or preference for many people, while for others the choice involves deeply held religious or personal values. In cases where neither party is deeply invested in the issue, it can be comfortably and legitimately demoted from an issue of value to an issue of taste, thus allowing greater flexibility.

When Cultural Values Collide

Cultural collisions can be mapped on a two-by-two matrix (*Exhibit 1*). A collision occurs when different values, norms, expectations, or tastes bump up against each other. When such a collision occurs, a decision must be made to accommodate, impose, or seek some kind of hybrid solution that satisfies the needs of both parties. The latter may entail pioneering new territory not suggested directly by either culture. As suggested by the matrix, a significant number of cultural clashes can be dispatched toward the default position with little energy invested.

Exhibit 1: Cultural Collisions

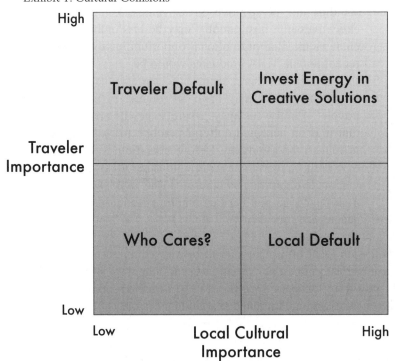

In clashes where the stakes are of low importance for both parties (lower left quadrant), the resolution can be tilted toward either culture with low risk of concern or offense to either. In fact, where a spirit of true collaboration exists, both parties may actually prefer to respect the cultural preference of the other in these low-stakes situations. If there is a tilt, or default in this quadrant, it should probably be toward local practices unless the host chooses to show courtesy by defaulting toward the traveler's preferences. When a traveler from China visits the United States, for instance, a low-stakes cultural difference might involve food preference. My own practice when hosting such a traveler is to extend a choice out of courtesy: would the traveler prefer to dine at a Chinese restaurant, or try local cuisine? Some travelers will desire to take advantage of an opportunity to experience local cooking, while others may have had more than their fill of local food, and would appreciate the opportunity to get a taste of home. A similar low-stakes situation might involve questions of schedule, which probably can be accommodated without objection by either party.

In the upper left and lower right quadrants, the nature of the culture clash suggests a relatively straightforward course of action. Where the issue is of importance to the host and not to the traveler, it should not be hard for the host to make his case quickly and carry the day, and vice versa when the issue is of cultural importance to the traveler, yet insignificant to the host. For example, if a company is giving training sessions in the United States to Chinese travelers, following the usual Chinese protocol of allowing a two-hour break at lunch would be thoughtful and appreciated, unless for some reason the operational requirements for the U.S. host make it impractical to do so.

Finally, culture clashes representing high-stakes situations for both parties (upper right quadrant) deserve the most attention, energy, and creativity. Such situations are likely to involve strong feelings on both sides and less willingness to compromise. There is no obvious default move that will satisfy both parties. A novel approach thus must be sought, perhaps involving substantial effort to find a creative resolution that might satisfy both traveler and host.

When Operational Needs Collide with Cultural Norms

Some culture clashes juxtapose operational needs and cultural practice. A two-by-two matrix (*Exhibit 2*) helps identify which of these situations is worthy of the most attention. Where cultural and operational stakes are low, the outcome really does not matter; the decisions probably should default toward local preference. Where a clash involves a significant stake for operations only (top left), the operational need probably takes precedence. In the opposite situation, where the culture has a significant stake in the outcome and there is little operational consequence, it is preferable to accommodate the cultural preference. What appears to one party to be a trivial issue (culturally or operationally), may not be viewed as such by the other party. Location on the matrix is determined by the feelings of each, not by a prescriptive assumption of importance driven by lack of cultural understanding toward either party (similarly, some individuals' preferences may deviate from the norms of their own culture).

Some culture/operations clashes involve relatively high stakes on both sides. For instance, a new manufacturing plant may require an on-time start at 7:00 a.m. in a culture that does not define punctuality in such precise terms. Local employees might tend to arrive any time between 6:30 a.m. and 10 a.m. without apology. Should the manager respect the local cultural approach to punctuality and adjust expectations for the plant, or insist that employees be ready to work at seven? In this example, an operational need clashes with a local cultural practice, yet there is no obvious *moral* dilemma involved. When confronted with this problem, one American manager decided that the plant start-time could not be compromised, so he decided to make it attractive to the employees to arrive on time: he offered a breakfast of bread and jam every workday just before the plant's starting time, providing an effective incentive for punctuality.

Exhibit 2: Collisions between Culture and Operations

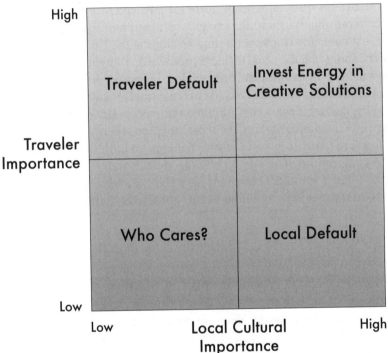

Collisions As Opportunities For Creativity

Cross-cultural collisions are often regarded as events to be avoided. However, anthropologists point out that it is only through such clashes that learning takes place. An encounter between different perspectives may well result in new ideas and approaches; the dynamism creates a fertile ground for innovation. For instance, in the early 1980s, a Japanese automobile company established a manufacturing plant in the United States and experienced an extremely high absentee rate among its American workers. As the company explored the problem, they were told American automobile companies experienced the same rate of absenteeism and had to put up with it, as well.

Rather than respecting what might *appear* to be a cultural norm, the Japanese company held that the situation was not acceptable. They were concerned about the impact on quality of a high absentee rate. After a serious examination of options, they implemented an attendance bonus system: if workers were on-time and present every day during a two week period they received a $150 bonus. A second bonus was offered to employees who had a perfect attendance record for a year. This combination of short- and long-term orientation proved powerful: a decade later, the company was experiencing less than 1 percent absentee rates. This and other innovations introduced by the Japanese transplants were studied closely by American companies. The result was a substantial change in the way they operated. (Some might argue had the U.S. auto industry chosen to adopt more of the exemplary practices introduced by the Japanese transplants, they might have avoided some of the difficulties in which they find themselves today). Hence, it is worth questioning whether the Japanese companies faced an actual "norm" of absenteeism in American society, or a dysfunctionality bred by mismanagement. This underlines the need to examine closely any supposed cultural norms in a host country that seem to create conflicts where, at deeper levels, there may actually by a convergence of values.

Corporate Remote Control: Fostering a Bias for Success

All cross-cultural circumstances cannot be anticipated before a manager is sent abroad, or before a company makes a direct investment in a foreign country. It would be ideal to suppose that the traveling manager will go abroad with all the answers, but this is not realistic. Rather, the best a company can expect is that its employees go abroad armed with the perspectives necessary to exercise good judgment in the field.

One way to inculcate such perspective is to place heavy training emphasis on a limited number of general principles the traveler can apply in a wide range of situations. Here are three such principles for managing "values in tension:" "(1) respect for core human values, which determine the absolute moral threshold for all business activities; (2) respect for local traditions; and (3) the belief that context matters when deciding what is right and what is wrong."[4] Starting with such foundational principles, companies can develop their own codes of conduct to reinforce them, the application of which can be tailored to each company's unique character. Such a code should provide clear guidelines, while offering flexibility for dealing with local contexts and circumstances.

Companies can use such principles as the basis for training and preparation for employees before sending them overseas (in fact, *all* employees could benefit from such training and preparation, as it is not only overseas travelers who are faced with such dilemmas). To illustrate these principles in action, companies can identify a number of frequently encountered field situations where the core principles of the company may be challenged. Employees then can be trained to apply the general principles in the unique circumstances they will encounter in the workplace.

Certain types of cross-cultural issues can be expected, and possible responses thus rehearsed. For instance, how to respond to a request (or offer) of what appears to be a bribe. Rehearsing for such eventualities builds confidence, and allows the traveler to approach potentially difficult situations with a sense of familiarity, whereas starting from scratch in real-time may yield hasty and poorly thought-out results. Having thought through a variety of scenarios in advance, the traveler will come prepared with a repertoire of possible responses from which she can draw.

According to recent estimates, only about half of companies provide employees (and even less frequently their families) with cross-cultural training before departure. Training in "mini-anthropologist" skills, combined with specific cultural preparation for the area being visited, offers the traveler an invaluable set of tools that can be used in assessing and understanding the context in which a dilemma has arisen. Armed with this knowledge, a traveler will be able to more confidently seek creative ways in which to re-solve high-stake cultural dilemmas. However, no matter how thorough the training, much will remain to be learned on the ground.

A spirit of learning is key to the continuous improvement in a company's approach to cross-cultural challenges. A system should be established to debrief returning executives and representatives who are stationed in the field. In each case, the goal should be to document challenging cross-cultural circumstances that were encountered, and how these were handled, along with an assessment of the outcomes. These experiences then can be processed and shared throughout the organization, in some cases adding to the "stories" on which future travelers can rely for guidance.

Example Through Action and Accountability

The actions, decisions and words of leaders set the tone for the behavior of all employees of an organization. Accountability for adherence to principle sets a powerful example, as well. Laxity in the enforcement of expected behavior can quickly send an organization-wide message that immediacy matters more than core principles. When principles are known to have been violated, quick developmental and other corrective action must be taken to ensure that the violator, and observers alike, know that such action is unacceptable and not tolerated. For example, suppose a U.S. firm operating a delivery business in an Asian country requires its employees to wear safety helmets when they deliver goods by motor scooter. However, a "macho" strain in the local culture creates resistance to the requirement, even among some managers. In this instance, where operational needs have a high priority, it would be important for the company to take disciplinary action so as not to send the wrong message to employees.

On the other hand, cultural resistance may create a situation where management must reconsider its rules, lest general employee morale suffer. For many years, United Parcel Service told its employees in the United States that dogs could not accompany drivers on deliveries. This operational judgment created resistance among employees in the United Kingdom, where UPS drivers greatly valued the companionship of canine friends. UPS was forced to reconsider its rule, just as Disney had to reluctantly reconsider its rule against facial hair at Disney Paris. When well-entrenched cultural norms are in opposition to operational requirements, management must reconsider how essential those operational requirements are.

Corporate Culture As Guide

A strong corporate culture serves as a powerful behavioral guide for employees. Reinforced and reflected through the actions, traditions, and values of the organization, corporate culture builds the habits that can help employees default to appropriate and principled behavior when on their own. In particular, stories that illustrate the company's culture serve as a memorable and powerful means for reinforcing good judgment in the field. For instance, stories about a founder (or other prominent figure) whose actions are noteworthy, consistent with company values, and (hopefully) colorful enough to capture the imagination, can systematically familiarize employees with company values—particularly when the individual took exemplary actions when faced with moral dilemmas or cultural collisions. When faced with a moral dilemma, it is particulary helpful when an employee can ask, "What would my leader do in this situation?" At Hewlett-Packard, stories about company founders Bill Hewlett and Dave Packard served a generation of HP employees who asked, "What would Bill or Dave have done?"[5]

Know Your Own Culture; Know The Local Culture

Culture is a prime source of perspective. Greater awareness of one's home culture leads to an enhanced ability to make behavioral choices consciously when abroad, rather than simply defaulting out of habit to one's home cultural practices. Obviously, familiarity with the host culture is extremely valuable for the traveler. Knowing where a host may stand on a given issue is invaluable in finding the middle ground. A detailed understanding of local culture can also help the traveler distinguish between values that are genuinely embedded in the local culture and those that are simply a personal preference of the host. Ample study before arrival, as well as some strategies for quick familiarization with the local culture, will be key.

In this mode of inquiry, the traveler should ask many questions, and then triangulate the information she receives from other sources. As noted, the biases and agendas of local informants are likely to affect the accuracy of any information received. The more familiar the traveler is, both with her own culture and that of the host country, the more she will be empowered to seek and find solutions that are acceptable to all parties concerned.

Utilize Sources of Local, Home and Global Perspectives

Since a universal set of human values is, at best, emergent, it is valuable to think ahead about what sources of perspective, or guidance may be available to the traveler as she moves from place to place. A few candidates are briefly discussed below:

> *Local law* in the host country serves as a primary source of guidance. The traveler will need to make a fundamental choice: can she abide by the local laws? If the answer is "no," most likely, she shouldn't be working in the host country. Obedience to local laws in almost every case is a requirement enforced by most host countries and accepted by most travelers, whether or not the local law is more stringent than the standards of one's home country. In many cases, adherence to local law may be a necessary, but not sufficient, standard for acceptable behavior.

> *Home country law* can provide valuable perspective, even though it may be inapplicable in a host country. In cases where home country law is more stringent, the traveler likely will want to consider local law as the *minimum standard*, and then use good judgment to determine when the home country standard should apply, even if it is not binding. Safety and environmental laws frequently fall in this category.

> *International law* represents a growing body of rules and guidelines arrived at through agreements between countries. These laws and principles, often promulgated through international agencies, address relationships between countries and, at times, the relationship between host countries and travelers operating within their borders.

> *U.N. treaties* such as the Universal Declaration of Human Rights, the Convention on the Elimination of All Forms of Discrimination against Women, and other globally agreed upon documents provide valuable perspective as well—in many cases representing a global position on issues of values. In many cases, the vast majority of the world's countries have signed on to these agreements or, at least, affirmed support for their goals and principles. It is quite possible the values of travelers and hosts alike can find support in these (somewhat) universally accepted documents.

Core human values: Many ethicists argue that a set of core human values should inform all decisions and behavior. While there may be some legitimate debate about the precise list of these values, it certainly would include: "respect for human dignity, respect for basic rights, and good citizenship."[6] These values can be used as a constant guide in varying cultures, their application is more tricky than might be assumed. As noted, the *context* of behavior must be assessed before a value judgment can be made.

Anticipate Personal Non-Negotiables

Every traveler can think ahead usefully about what behaviors and values are not subject to local assessment because of her religious beliefs, personal morals, or preferences. For instance, a vegetarian might think ahead about how situations where meat is served should be handled. Individuals whose religions prohibit the consumption of alcohol may want to plan ahead for situations in which liquor is served. Such non-negotiables will vary by person and, ideally, can be respected by all parties concerned. However, a traveler should consider the unlikely scenario that the non-negotiable will not be respected. In such a case, is the non-negotiable really non-negotiable? If so, the traveler must be prepared to stick to her position, even if it means resisting pressure to do otherwise.

The traveler should limit the list of non-negotiables to the smallest number possible and be conscious of the fact that each non-negotiable, even if perfectly understandable to one's host, could at some point result in an impression of inflexibility. To compensate, the traveler is well advised to demonstrate a spirit of flexibility and camaraderie whenever the situation allows. Having refused an alcoholic toast, the traveler may regain credibility and rapport by partaking in some of the other culinary delights offered—even if that might include live scorpions (as has occurred on more than one occasion in the author's experience!).

Travelers can be picky in the wrong places; a wise traveler will exercise good judgment in prioritizing which elements of a local culture she chooses to acquiesce to, and which elements she chooses to challenge. The matrix above offers a built-in opportunity to diagnose cultural issues in order to choose the most fruitful battles. In order to build the social capital needed to engage hosts in creative solutions to high-stakes collisions, the traveler will want to challenge the local culture only where it is vital for her to do so, either because of moral or operational imperatives.

Assess Results and Learn

Much cross-cultural interaction begins as a trial-and-error process, some efforts being more successful than others. The traveler can hone her repertoire of responses by evalua ing the success of a given interaction. Which behaviors cause offense, which were innocuous, and which resonated particularly well with one's hosts? If the reaction was different than expected, what changes in behavior might be useful moving forward? Where possible, seeking a cross-cultural "debrief" from a trusted local could help build understanding about what transpired. Every opportunity to work across cultures represents an opportunity to learn and to continue to build one's tool kit.

Unity in Diversity!

In this age of globalization, a majority of business people will be travelers at one time or another. Each and every cultural interchange they engage in represents an opportunity for learning and teaching. It also represents a substantial challenge. On one hand, travelers must relentlessly, and without apology, hold true to their basic values and principles as they move around the world. Of course, sound judgment must be exercised in the application of these values when abroad, always incorporating respect and courtesy for local cultures.

As the matrixes above demonstrate, not all cultural collisions require the same amount of attention. The greatest effort to resolve cross-cultural conflicts should be reserved for potentially high-stakes collisions for both parties. By respecting local practices when there is no moral or operational imperative to do otherwise, the traveler strengthens the ability to exercise leadership, seeking creative solutions when thorny cross-cultural issues arise. The traveler will have set the stage for a respectful interaction that may yield a morally and operationally sound approach to even the most challenging cultural issues.

---

[1] E.B. Tylor as quoted in Gusfield, Joseph R. (2006) "Culture," *Contexts*, Vol 5:1, Winter p43

[2] Huntington, Samuel P. (1996), *The Clash of Civilizations and the Remaking of World Order*

[3] Bahá'í International Community (1995) *The Prosperity of Humankind*, New York, NY

[4] Donaldson, Thomas (1996) "Values in Tension," *Harvard Business Review*, September-October

[5] Peters, Thomas J. and Waterman, Robert H. Jr. (1982) *In Search of Excellence: Lessons from America's Best-Run Companies*, 245-46.

[6] Donaldson, Thomas (1996) "Values in Tension," *Harvard Business Review*, September-October

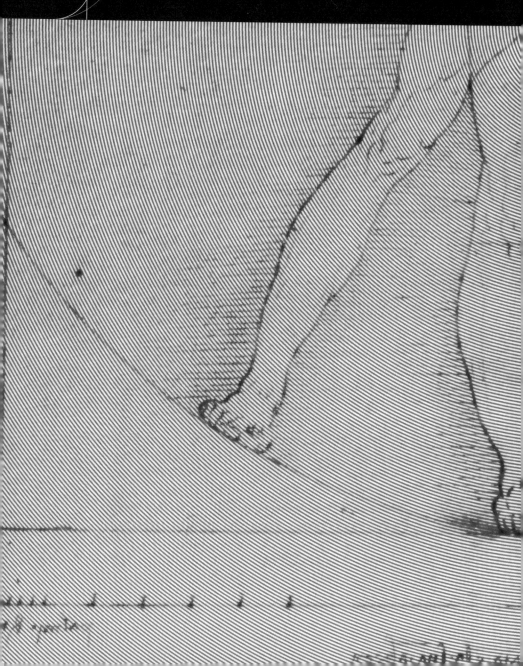

PART IV

A View from the Top

by Bob Vanourek

The leader of the future...will be one who creates a culture, or a values system, centered on principles.
—Stephen R. Covey

Every few years, an egregious ethical scandal plagues American business. The 2008-09 global financial crisis is the latest, preceded earlier this decade by the "hall of shame" of Enron, Tyco, Adelphia, World-Com, and others.

The Sarbanes-Oxley Act was passed in 2002 to address such ethical transgressions but, nonetheless, here we are again. Good regulations, properly enforced, are essential to encourage ethical behavior, as are punishments for lawbreakers. But these remedies alone are insufficient. So how can we instill more ethical behavior in business?

Ethical lapses occur in business not just because a few people are crooks. Unethical behavior in business is a failure of *leadership*. Too few executives have fully grasped that corporate leadership must be based on a foundation of ethics. Business schools, the media, corporate boards, and executives focus too much on the personal traits and characteristics of leaders, the situations to which they respond, their uses of power, their charismatic persuasiveness, and their relationships with followers—all of which, indeed, have a place in the study of leadership. But these approaches alone, even coupled with more regulations, will not give us the ethical corporate leadership we desire. Above all, a different type of leadership is required to instill ethical behavior: *values-based leadership*.

This essay outlines why ethical lapses occur, what values-based leadership is, and how it can instill ethical behavior by creating a values-based culture.

Ethical Challenges in Business

My experience has been forged in high-pressure turnarounds. As a turnaround CEO brought into "fix" broken companies, I have had to clean-up after such ethical lapses as:

- shipments of products past quarterly cutoffs in order to pad revenue

- lies to customers overstating product functionality

- financial conflicts of interest

- sexual misconduct

- misstatements of asset values, and much more

Such unethical behavior was inevitably devastating, causing shareholders to lose hundreds of millions of dollars, employees to lose jobs, managerial reputations to be ruined, and legal penalties to be paid.

Fortunately, I also have observed countless examples of behavior that meets the highest ethical standards. In my thirty-plus years in business, my colleagues and I have had award-winning successes in transforming ethically challenged organizations. Over this period, I slowly discovered values-based leadership. I didn't know what it was called at the time but, in retrospect, I see that the reintroduction of ethical behavior during our successful turnarounds was, in fact, a collective act of values-based leadership.

Sometimes our work involved simple things like removing sexually offensive pictures from tool-room walls; sometimes it involved bigger things, like telling an important prospective client the truth he did not want to hear, and thereby losing a big order. Most importantly, it involved creating a new culture. In some cases, the new culture continued for years; in others, it died because subsequent management reverted to an old paradigm of leadership. Once, my insistence on doing things a new way took too much time to produce the quarterly earnings demanded by an impatient board, and that cost me my job. What I learned from these experiences is that implementing values-based leadership is challenging, and it can be risky. Still, scars and all, I would not do it any other way.

Why Is There Unethical Leadership?

Ethical failures typically occur for several reasons: erroneously thinking that, "if it is legal, it is ethical," intense performance pressure, addictions, toxic leaders, and overblown egos.

Thinking Legal is Ethical: Often, managers rationalize that if an action is legal, it is okay. But, legal is merely the initial test of ethical behavior, and regulations can never anticipate all the ethical nuances found in a dynamic marketplace. Regulations invariably can be circumvented by the creative human mind and some managers gamble that there is a low probability of their being caught in an illegal act.

Intense Pressure: Unethical behavior often starts with small steps taken by good people under intense pressure. "Make your numbers! Understand? Just make your numbers," says the driven VP. "Yes, the software will do that," says the desperate salesperson. "Have you heard that this product causes pacemakers to malfunction?" says the unscrupulous short-seller spreading an unsubstantiated rumor. I have heard all these comments and worse, along with such rationalizations as: "Everyone's doing it," "We have to keep up," and "We can't change the whole industry."

At one company I led, we had an entrenched board that included one member from a firm that was doing millions of dollars of business with us each year. He was in a position to influence whether or not we did that business, and which firm should receive it. I knew this was a conflict of interest and asked that he resign from the board. I incurred intense pressure to withdraw this request from other board members who were his friends. Finally, I stated an ultimatum: Either he resigns, or I do. It was a tense situation, but he resigned.

Addictions: The desire for power is a common motive for leadership. Some leaders are addicted to "the game" and get a buzz from winning. Many of the white-collar felons marched off to jail in recent years were addicted to the power game and all its trappings. They did not need the money. Rather, their persona became wrapped-up in financial success, defining their identity and fueling their sense of self-worth. Without their title, perks, and perceived successes, they would feel empty. If they had to cut corners to succeed, they easily rationalized their behavior.

Another motivation to lead is to achieve something for oneself. I certainly fell into that trap as a young B-school graduate. My goal was simple: I wanted to run something. Note the *I* (it was all about me). Note the *run* (to be in control of, to be in charge). Note the *something* (it didn't really matter what, as long as I was running it). Once, after returning from yet another week-long business trip, before going into the office (again) on Saturday, my wife said, "Why are you working such long hours?" "Why, it's for us, honey, for you and the kids," I replied. She looked me dead in the eye and said, "Baloney, it's for you." She was right; I was addicted to the game.

I finally listened to her and to my inner voice, realizing the work I was doing didn't feel right. At the time we were integrating acquisitions, closing plants, and terminating the former owners. My inner voice was telling me that there must be a better way to run a business. So, I quit and embarked on an odyssey of many years to find that better way.

Toxic Leaders: In some cases leaders are just plain toxic. Some leaders are bullies, others are narcissists, and some are intimidators; some are all three! They lack integrity and arrogantly deny reality. They preside rather than lead, exploiting fears, stifling criticism, and exploiting scapegoats. Sometimes, greed blinds these toxic leaders to the ramifications of their behavior. I have encountered a few such leaders in my career.

Excessive Ego: The biggest ethical leadership trap is excessive ego. The most egregious example I ever saw was "Chainsaw Al" Dunlop, the self-proclaimed genius who publicly announced that his turnaround of Sunbeam was complete after only eighteen months. In reality, he had instilled a culture of fear and was fraudulently managing earnings.

Leaders certainly need confidence to lead in tough times and to cope with the inevitable criticism that comes with the job. But, as with other virtues, confidence becomes a vice when carried to excess. Suddenly the leader's sense of self, fueled by success, takes on a presumed superiority that is full of conceit and exaggerated self-importance. Furthermore, there are always a few sycophants around willing to murmur in the leader's ear, telling him how wonderful he is, and encouraging him to breathe his own vapor. "Your ego is not your amigo," as my friend Chuck Wachendorfer rightly reminds us.

The best antidotes for excessive ego are empathy, belief in relationships, and the humility found in recognizing one's own fallibility. These understandings don't come easily or naturally; for most of us, they are born in the crucibles of tough times that whack us in the gut. The antithesis of ego is a sincere belief in the incredible capabilities inherent in other people, which instills in a leader the desire to work with others to achieve something of value for everyone in an organization.

The best way I have found to overcome these four drivers of unethical behavior is through values-based leadership.

Elements of Values-Based Leadership

In the leadership crises of today, people often ask, "Where are the great leaders we need?" Unfortunately, framing the question this way undermines our search for great leaders because a search for heroes is doomed to fail. It is a quest for larger-than-life people whom we put on a pedestal, enticing their egos to run amok. Playwright Bertoldt Brecht once said, "It is unhappy the land that needs to search for heroes." We need and value heroes, of course, but not to run our organizations.

There are hundreds of definitions of leaders and leadership. For example, Peter Drucker tells us a leader is someone who has followers. A popular definition these days is *leadership is an influence relationship.* I do not find such definitions very useful. Just how does a leader gather followers? My barber has an influence relationship with me; does that make her a leader?

I believe leadership should be described by what it does and I want to focus here on *great* leadership, the kind that instills ethical behavior and creates a high performance organization. I believe great leadership achieves positive, substantive, and sustainable results through people. Let us deconstruct this statement carefully:

- Great leadership achieves the desired results (not just change, as many leadership authors advocate)

- The results are positive for all the organization's stakeholders (Hitler doesn't make the cut)

- The results are substantive because leadership is about achieving something important (not just superficial deck chair rearrangements)

- The results are sustainable (because even bad leaders can get temporary results)

Even this definition does not encompass ethical leadership fully because it doesn't indicate *how* results are to be achieved, which is the essence of ethical leadership. So, we need to add one more element: values. Whose values? The values of the highest authority? No. Values-based leadership is based on the shared values of the group.

Ethical behavior is instilled by values-based leadership. By my definition, therefore, *ethical leadership achieves positive, substantive, sustainable results based on shared values.* This shift to leadership based on shared values moves the center of gravity from an individual to the group. I submit that great leadership—values-based leadership—is a group activity and not centered in a single person. Great leadership is an organizational phenomenon, a dynamic interaction among people. "Leadership, like democracy, is a process," James O'Toole, the leading proponent of values-based leadership, tells us. Furthermore, it is a process among and between people. As Ken Blanchard notes, "In a company that manages by its values, there is only one boss—the values."

In my experience, there are three practices necessary to create values-based leadership in a company: synthesizing a shared future, moving flexibly between the hard and soft edges of leadership, and encouraging plural leadership.

Synthesizing a Shared Future: The shared future of an organization consists of shared values, purpose, and vision. Values are the deep, sacrosanct beliefs held collectively by people in an organization. Such values form the behavioral and moral compass of an organization and are the glue that binds people together. Shared values constitute the long-lasting essence of how a group aspires to behave both externally and internally. Shared values are the explicit articulation of the intrinsic desires shared by all members of a group.

Shared values can be transformational, taking people out of their personal concerns and giving them a larger focus.

Shared values address *how* results should be achieved. This is ethically critical because toxic leaders can get results; the problem is that their ends do not justify their means. Results matter for leaders, of course, but *how* the results are achieved matters just as much.

Shared values might be a set of single words, or they might be some guiding principles. Here are the stated values of several excellent companies:

- **Disney***:* Trust, Quality, Optimism, Self-Expression, Creativity, Storytelling, Imagination, Entertainment

- **Procter & Gamble***:* Leadership, Ownership, Integrity, Passion for Winning, Trust

- **Trinity Health Care***:* Respect for Human Dignity, Social Justice, Compassion, Care for the Poor and Underserved, Excellence

- **IBM***:* Dedication to every client's success; Innovation that matters, for our company and for the world; Trust and personal responsibility in all relationships

Shared values are not the personal values of a leader imposed on the group. They are truly "shared" in that they are drafted, carefully discussed, revised, and synthesized until a consensus of the group emerges. The dialogue itself—the involvement of people in the determination of their shared values—is more important than the specific words chosen; the work is in the conversations.

Values-based leaders also synthesize an inspiring shared purpose for the organization. An organization's core purpose addresses the reason it exists. I prefer "purpose" to "mission," because a mission can change, while purpose implies something long-lasting. People hunger to know that their organization's reason for being is worthwhile and that it connects them to something larger than themselves. In this way, organizational purpose gives meaning to their work. The ideal statement of purpose is short, memorable, inspiring, and enduring. For example, at 3M: *To solve unsolved problems innovatively*. For Disney: *To make people happy*.

Finally, a shared future involves a vision—a common, collective, shared view of a better future. The responsibility of leaders is to awaken people to their dreams. By synthesizing a vision of the future, leaders create a compelling call to action. When Thomas Paine and Martin Luther King, Jr. described their visions for America, they gave a moving voice to the longings of the people they served. The visions were inherent, but dormant, in the people, and Paine and King gave them the inspiring words needed to breathe life into their hopes and dreams. The leader weaves the followers' implicit desires together in new and inspiring ways so that all can see clearly where they want to go in the future. As with shared values, the leader does not impose his personal vision on the organization. Since leaders come and go in organizations, visions that change with every new leader create more confusion than meaningful direction.

Value-based leaders weave shared values together with purpose and vision to create a climate in which their companies can flourish. I learned this lesson at Monarch Marking Systems (a Pitney Bowes subsidiary) at a 5 a.m. third-shift employee meeting in the company cafeteria. A brave young manager challenged the obtuse purpose and vision statements I had drafted for the company which started with an uninspiring, "Our purpose is to maximize our shareholders' return on their invested capital…" and droned on from there with lots of B-school jargon. No one else had summoned the courage to voice objections. But when that brave manager spoke up, I listened and began to change my leadership approach. From that point forward, we engaged in a collaborative discussion throughout the company that led to truly shared purpose, values, and vision. Our final version began, "Our purpose is to create value for people—our customers, employees, partners, the community, and our owners."

Within eighteen months, we launched a revolutionary new product, the Pathfinder, which was the world's first hand-held bar code printer. The team that developed the Pathfinder was a direct outgrowth of our new collaborative approach to leadership. This team operated with unprecedented authority, guided by clear goals and our shared values. Thanks to this empowered team, Pathfinder became one of the most successful products in Monarch's history.

Moving Between the Hard and Soft Edges of Leadership: Leadership is an immensely complex, multi-faceted subject. Values-based leadership acknowledges a fundamental duality in leadership that all successful leaders must learn to live with. The yin and the yang of Chinese philosophy is an apt metaphor for this duality. The *yin* is the decisive side, or hard edge, of leadership where authority and power must be exercised. This is the side that requires the confidence to know when, and when not, to make a decision. The yin involves execution through the organizational hierarchy to get results, using positional authority to drive implementation and alignment. This leader-centric behavior can be lonely. Tough decisions often are required, including which casualties must be incurred in order to move forward. Sometimes, the casualties are innocent people who, through no fault of their own, must be laid-off to protect the enterprise. Other times, the casualties are obstructers who threaten the healthy culture of the organization and who refuse to change.

This unilateral aspect of leadership comes into play when the focus is on doing something now and one person must make the call. I had to make frequent executive decisions in this manner in my turnaround work, but I found that this hard edge of leadership has inherent risks. Excessive ego tends to creep in and the leader can start to believe that he is, indeed, "the savior" and ignore wise input and counsel from others.

The *yang* is the softer edge of leadership in which serving and achieving for the group are paramount. Here the leader shows humility and focuses on building and maintaining a positive culture while involving and empowering other leaders. The leader patiently seeks collaboration and alignment, listening to and connecting people throughout the organization by way of shared purpose, values, and vision. Diversity in talent, thought, and approaches are celebrated to unleash innovation. The yang side is leadership-centric, not leader-centric.

My most important work in rebuilding companies was accomplished by using this softer edge of leadership but it, too, contains inherent risks. It can be viewed as "touchy-feely," indecisive, and insufficiently macho. Because it must be slow-brewed and role modeled, rather than mandated from above, it is sometimes hard to implement when there is need for crisp execution.

In Chinese philosophy, the yin and yang are synthesized, thus unifying, complementing, and completing one another. The whole is incomplete without both elements. So it is in values-based leadership: the successful leader has the versatility and judgment to be able to assess when to operate closer to the yin or closer to the yang, flexibly flowing back and forth between them as appropriate, but probably spending most of the time on the soft edge. Critically, though, the values-based leader always relies on the organization's shared values as his or her compass. Shared values are the common core of both the yin and the yang, the inviolate soul of leadership.

Encouraging Plural Leadership: The final element for instilling values-based leadership involves a powerful and challenging phenomenon I call "plural leadership." Values-based leadership recognizes that no single person can, or should, be the leader at all times. Of course, every organization has a formal hierarchy, but leadership in a high-performance organization should ebb and flow among various individuals depending on the situation, the expertise, passion, and organizational responsibility of the managers involved. That leadership, again, should be based on shared values. To allow leadership to flow, hierarchical authorities must recognize the wonderful capabilities latent within those they lead. The successes I have experienced in business were not due to brilliance on my part; instead, they resulted from the wonderful creativity and commitment of the many leaders who emerged in our organizations.

Similarly, the great successes of history were frequently the result of groups of people, rather than a single person. We need only recall the many Founders of our nation, including Washington, Adams, Jefferson, Franklin, Hamilton, and Madison.

Sometimes plural leaders are individuals without authority, liberated to act by shared values and an encouraging corporate culture. I'm reminded of the young engineer at Sensormatic, when I was the CEO there, who emerged from a brown-bag group lunch as the designated leader of a rapid action team formed to implement an idea she had proposed. I had been thinking of the same idea but kept quiet when she voiced her thoughts, encouraging her to describe them further. Her idea was a roaring success and it encouraged other managers to take the initiative to create additional action teams to implement other promising projects. Such plural leadership based on shared values ultimately led to a successful turnaround at Sensormatic.

Values-based leadership can be developed by synthesizing a shared future, moving flexibly between the hard and soft edges inherent in leadership, and encouraging plural leadership. Why go to all this trouble? Why not just put a great person at the top to drive the organization? Because values-based leadership is also the key to creating a powerful, high-performance culture.

Why Values-Based Leadership Is Powerful

Values-based leadership is powerful for at least four reasons: it engenders self-empowerment, it drives ethical decisions, it avoids the trap of the heroic leader, and it creates a healthy, ethical culture.

Engenders Self-Empowerment: Policies and processes are important in well-run organizations, but moments of decision often require employees to make on-the-spot judgments when they do not have the opportunity to consult a policy book or ask a supervisor for permission. By recalling the organization's shared values, employees can intuitively sort out what to do and, thus, assume the role of plural leaders themselves. Shared values engender this self-empowerment. When individual managers empower people to act, it can be paternalistic. In contrast, when shared values empower people to act, it is liberating because the people can act with the assurance they are doing the right thing.

Also, since no leader is immune to mistakes, shared values empower people to speak up and hold the leader—and each other—accountable to the organization's values. A painful example from my experience at Sensormatic illustrates this point. Sensormatic had experienced rapid growth in electronic security systems to over $1 billion in revenue. Just as I was recruited to join the company as COO, soon to become the CEO, it was discovered that the company had been improperly recording revenue for years. A scandal emerged, followed by class-action lawsuits and an investigation by the Securities and Exchange Commission. Predictably, employee morale faltered and customers were aghast.

In my judgment, it was essential to reestablish integrity through a values-based leadership approach. So, collaboratively, we crafted our values, posted them everywhere, and talked about them often:

- Leadership (detailed in a "Star Leader" model we developed),

- Integrity (to reestablish ethical behavior),

- Teamwork (to bridge warring, finger-pointing factions), and

- Excellence (in our dealings with each other and our stakeholders).

Then, at one stressful Saturday morning staff meeting in the early days of our turnaround, I lost my temper at a VP who was late on an essential project. After the meeting, a courageous colleague, empowered by our Star Leader model, called my attention to my poor behavior, holding me accountable to the values we had developed. I was stunned and embarrassed. I reconvened the meeting and apologized to the VP and the staff, asking for their forgiveness.

This incident turned out to be one of the catalyzing moments in bringing our values to life. After parting company with a few toxic individuals, the leadership team then embraced values-based leadership and the company excelled, reversing a negative flow of $100 million per year to a positive cash flow of $100 million within four years. We settled all lawsuits and won breakthrough new business. All along, we upheld our shared values and the Star Leader model.

Helps Drive Ethical Decision-Making: Values-based leadership helps people avoid the pitfalls that drive unethical behavior. Shared values supplement laws and regulatory guidelines, helping people make better decisions under stress. With the organization's values acting as a moral compass, people are engaged in a social contract that helps them to resist pressures to cut ethical corners. Shared values help people resist both the addiction of winning their "game" and the siren calls of ego. They reinforce that inner voice warning against taking the tempting, easy course. They empower others to call attention to questionable, unethical, and ego-driven behaviors.

Avoids the Trap of the Heroic Leader: When values-based leadership is deeply instilled, it transcends the individual authority figures who come and go. Shared values are powerful because, when people hold each other accountable, they help the organization overcome a cult of personality based on the myth of the heroic leader. By recognizing that it is their shared values that actually lead, that the authority at the top may be wrong, and that action is encouraged based on those values, people will learn to step up, speak up, and act with confidence. Cynicism thus dies out, the muttering stops, and creative minds that used to shut down remain open and engaged. It is then that the tipping point is surpassed, creating a powerful and aligned group of people engaged in a common endeavor. It is here that the values-based, high performance organization emerges.

Creates a Healthy, Ethical Culture: Fundamentally, the culture of a corporation is how work gets done within the organization. Culture influences the way people think and behave, setting norms for acceptable behavior, and creating the conditions for what happens when the authorities are not present. Values-based leadership involves creating a positive, healthy, ethical culture.

In essence, culture is the legacy of leadership. Unethical leaders who don't behave in accordance with shared values instill a toxic culture where people engage in a conspiracy of justifications and rationalizations. In contrast, an ethical culture is the legacy of values-based leadership in which all people, including the authorities, are held accountable to shared values.

Developing a Values-Based Culture

Three forces within business organizations create culture: the board, the CEO, and the leadership team. These people are, in effect, the "trustees" for the shared values, culture, and leadership mode of the organization.

Board of Trustees: Having served on or advised dozens of boards, I can testify that most boards don't "get" culture, or the importance of values-based leadership. They don't see shaping culture or values as their responsibilities. They leave that soft stuff to the CEO or the VP of Human Resources; but they couldn't be more mistaken. If a board is not committed to creating a healthy culture, then even an outstanding CEO will be hard-pressed to establish one. Indeed, I use the term *trustees* here, rather than *directors*, to underscore the fiduciary trust that board members should have for the shared values and culture of a firm.

Board trustees influence culture and values by their own deportment— the tone at the top—and by the quantitative goals they set for the CEO. For example, when they set unrealistic goals to satisfy Wall Street speculators, they create pressures that can lead to unethical behavior. Boards most directly influence corporate culture through the selection, support, and coaching of the CEO. When most boards select a new CEO, the criteria are usually past economic performance, pedigree, reputation, and chemistry with board members. Important considerations, surely, but all too often the candidate's values orientation, leadership philosophy, and interest in building a sustainable, high-performance culture are not even on the board's radar screen.

Fortunately, there are positive examples of extraordinary board attention to culture and values. For example, Jack Krol, the lead outside director at Tyco, and Ed Breen, Tyco's CEO, recruited a whole new board in 2002 after an ethical meltdown occurred under the company's former CEO. In recruiting new board members, they placed a premium not only on expertise and diversity, but also on the candidates' track records with regard to culture, values, and ethical behavior.

CEO: To build a values-based, high-performance culture, one does not need a hero at the top. An ordinary mortal must, of course, suffice. Peter Drucker noted, "No institution can possibly survive if it needs geniuses or supermen to manage it. It must be organized in such a way as to be able to get along under a leadership composed of average human beings." So, boards should avoid the trap of seeking a celebrity hero and, instead, focus on find-ing someone who understands the duality—the hard and soft edges—of great leadership and who has developed a healthy personal core in body, mind, emo-tional intelligence, and a heart with a moral compass. These characteristics may be insufficient, because performance pressures on even ethically strong leaders are great in today's business climate. That is why leaders also need the organization's shared values, reinforced by colleagues and board trustees, in order to remain ethically strong.

I have worked in turnarounds where the boards, unfortunately, did not care about anything but the stock price. Once I engaged an attorney to investigate an outside agent we suspected of dirty practices against our company. I felt great pressure to do so at the time, and I didn't ask how the attorney would gather the information. I guess I really didn't want to know. The attorney never found anything, but I now regret that action as a personal ethical lapse. Having a board that reinforced values-based, ethical management at all times might have changed my behavior.

Values-based CEOs do not seek to be *the* great leader because that would stifle the emergence of a healthy culture. Instead, a values-based CEO suc-ceeds by enabling great leadership to emerge from the group and to cascade throughout the organization—becoming what James O' Toole calls a "leader of leaders."

Leadership Team: The behavior of leadership teams is also critical to the creation of a healthy culture. A leadership team must understand and embrace the concepts of values-based leadership, ensuring that their own behavior rein-forces the work of the CEO and board. Just as for the CEO, the ideal members of a leadership team have healthy personal cores, understand both the hard and soft edges of leadership, and buy in to the shared values as their means to operate. They carefully select who will join the organization, and put the goals of the group ahead of their own individual needs. As a result, they have faith, confidence, and trust in each other.

Values-based leadership is about trust and trusteeship and balancing author-ity with the willingness to let others, even those without authority, become leaders throughout the organization. The vertical authority of the CEO may be necessary to ensure that the leadership team champions the development of a healthy culture. If team members are working at cross purposes to that culture, confusion will reign supreme if the CEO espouses a values-based approach but condones actions by others that undermine those values. Thus, officers who operate outside the shared values must change their behavior or be carefully redirected elsewhere.

When the board, the CEO, and the leadership team are operating in sync on shared values, then a positive, healthy, high-performance culture will emerge. Such a culture is a powerful force for producing extraordinary results.

Summary

Values-Based Leadership

What values-based leadership does	Achieves positive, substantive, sustained results through people based on shared values
What it is not	An individual person
What it creates	A group dynamic of leadership in a culture of ethical, high performance
How it is developed	Synthesizing a shared future of values, purpose, & vision Moving between the hard and soft edges of leadership Encouraging plural leadership
What it needs	A supportive board of trustees A supportive CEO A supportive leadership team

Instilling ethical behavior—while achieving positive, substantive, and sustained results—is the primary challenge of leadership today. Values-based leadership is simply the best way to meet that challenge. Unfortunately, such leadership is not yet the accepted leadership model; not everyone understands or embraces it. Nevertheless, my experience has shown that values-based leadership is a powerful approach for creating an ethical, high-performance culture in which people can achieve remarkable things together.

The world is desperately searching for leadership that is both ethical and effective. That leadership is values-based. I don't know about you, but I am tired of being taken advantage of by unethical leaders who are really in it just for themselves. As John Bogle says in the title to his latest book, *Enough.* It is time for all of us to embrace a superior leadership model; it is time for values-based leadership.

Epilogue:
At Daniels, Ethics is a Contact Sport

by Buie Seawell

Unlike other subjects, business ethics is about pedagogy (the how) as much as it is about content (the what). In reality, the two cannot be separated; both are inextricably connected. At the Daniels College of Business, where business ethics has been taught as a required course for more than twenty years, we have a saying: "Ethics is a contact sport." The engagement with the daunting task of teaching business ethics is no mere intellectual pastime at the College, rather, it is personal and communal. Business ethics is not the domain of the department bearing the name *Business Ethics and Legal Studies*; instead, ethics is taught through every human contact and interaction. To the extent the College has succeeded in teaching business ethics, we have made the subject nothing less than the defining element of the Daniels culture.

As is commonly acknowledged among scholars, every serious ethicist has a slightly different definition of ethics: "There are as many definitions for the word ethics as there are ethicists."[1] At its core, ethics is about values and meaning—about the meaning of our lives, the value of our careers, and the responsibilities we assume within the enterprises in which we invest our energy. At Daniels, business ethics is about the value and meaning of the life, the profession, and the enterprise of business. It is what we teach, it is who we are, and it is why we exist. In essence, we exist to bring *meaning* to the vocation of business.

In 2005, in a survey of corporate recruiters, *The Wall Street Journal* named Daniels' graduates the third most "ethically sensitive" business recruits in the world. An amazing sense of pride permeated every program and department of the College when we learned of that distinction. Pride not in ourselves, but in all the men and women whom we have counseled, mentored, instructed, and learned with over the years. In the end, it is not about what you have taught, but about whom you have touched, the contact as much as the content.

When I came to Daniels in 1995, there were two required business ethics courses: Values I and Values II. Values I covered the personal and professional dimensions of business ethics, and Values II centered on corporate responsibility. As a new recruit to the College, I was paired with my friend Bruce Hutton, the former Dean who had pioneered the new MBA curriculum (which included a major focus on business ethics). Late in the fall quarter, just prior to Christmas break, Bruce and I were team teaching a class of some thirty MBA students. Bruce had an amazing set of those old transparent overheads and was lecturing away, describing and visualizing the interrelationships of society, environment, and the corporation, when out of nowhere he shifted gears, and clicking off the projector, said:

> You know, it's really simply about this...like what Charles Dickens wrote in *A Christmas Carol*...Scrooge is all upset that the dead vision of his former business partner, Jacob Marley, is one of an old man in chains and money boxes. And Scrooge protests, "But Marley you were always such a good business man." And Marley answers, "Business? Business? Mankind was my business."

All the Venn diagrams in the world could not do what that singular metaphor did. I instantly understood what the Daniels College of Business was all about.

There are many who refuse to believe that ethics can be taught. We often hear even informed and thoughtful business executives questioning the need for such devotion in business education. They do not mean the various approaches to ethical analysis (the disciplines of ethics as a branch of philosophy) cannot be taught, because it has been for two millennia. Rather, they mean no amount of formal education can significantly change the basic moral character of a person. We at Daniels dare to disagree.

Business ethics is a branch of applied ethics (as opposed to theoretical ethics). Hence, at Daniels, we believe the most significant learning of ethics occurs in practice. As students grapple with applied ethics, they achieve real personal growth. In *The Fifth Discipline*, Peter Senge bemoans the lack of "practice fields" for the development of a business professional's competence. Daniels is actively doing something about that deficit: we have literally taken the teaching of business ethics into the hills, fields, streams and oceans of the planet, engaging not just with ideas, but with each other and with the real challenges facing individuals and society in the 21st century.

Applied or experiential learning takes place almost every day and in every classroom of the Daniels College. Experiential learning is pervasive in learning teams, business case challenges, simulated in-classroom exercises, community projects, dilemma deliberations, public policy issue debates, business plans, and real estate construction projects. Here are some examples of how Daniels is a place for active learning and applied ethical engagement:

The Edge/10ᵗʰ Mountain Division Experience

On one of those crystal clear Sunday mornings for which Colorado is known, Bruce Hutton opened up the local newspaper to find a story about the renowned 10ᵗʰ Mountain Division. The 10ᵗʰ was world-famous, created out of the critical need during World War II for a fighting force capable of waging war in ferocious winter conditions: in mountain snow on skis. It was the largest volunteer unit in the armed services, with more than 14,000 men trained at Camp Hale, Colorado. But the newspaper article was not about war. It was about innovation and creativity. The 10ᵗʰ Mountain Division established more than a dozen patents (predecessors to the snow cat and snowmobile, medical evacuation techniques, aluminum carabineers, to name a few) as it sought ways to gain competitive advantage in rough, mountainous winter terrains. As Bruce investigated the 10ᵗʰ Mountain Division's experiences further, he uncovered a story about an organization that embraced values, creativity, teamwork, servant leadership, self-awareness, and high performance.

At that moment, the Daniels College was working on the redesign of its MBA curriculum to address a variety of interdisciplinary educational needs, such as creativity and entrepreneurial spirit, globalization, ethics, and sustainability. It appeared to Bruce that the 10ᵗʰ was a perfect metaphor for the kind of personal and organizational results the college was seeking in its MBA program. The one remaining question was whether the values and ethics that guided the members of the 10ᵗʰ were unique, or were they transferable to other organizations? The answer emerged in the postwar accomplishments of the members of the 10ᵗʰ, the amazing record of such leaders as Bill Bowerman, University of Oregon track coach and cofounder of Nike, David Brower, first executive director of the Sierra Club, Paul Petzoldt, founder of the National Outdoor Leadership School (NOLS), and Bob Dole, Senator and Presidential candidate. The life achievements of those remarkable men stood as proof of the transferability of the 10ᵗʰ Mountain's values and skills to every sector of society—public, private, and civil.

Bill Daniels' own service experience during the war made him a believer in boot camps; for almost 20 years, the college has incorporated some kind of experiential component that resembles such an experience. The current, and most rigorous, of these programs, based on the boot camp practices of the 10ᵗʰ Mountain Division, is called Leading at the Edge. It is a three-day, intensive, outdoor experience that was first delivered at Camp Hale, and now is based at The Nature Place, an outdoor leadership camp created by Sandy Sanborn, a 10ᵗʰ Mountain veteran.

At The Nature Place, our students are divided into teams and, for the first two days, undergo intensive outdoor exercises (orienteering, high ropes courses, leadership, and team building) with each team led by a trained facilitator and faculty member. The third day, student teams are exposed to six different scenarios in which they have to accomplish multiple tasks using the skills developed over the previous two days. They are given a map and have to orienteer to different locations where they engage in such activities as climbing and rappelling, creating a bridge to cross a stream, dealing with a disaster scenario involving non-English speaking victims, and solving ethical dilemmas framed around physical activities. While these experiences have caused some to cry, and some to push themselves beyond what they felt were their limits, the students rate the value of this three-day experience as the high point of the MBA program.

The Sail-training Program

On a snowy winter night in 1997, I had dinner with Sarah Cavanagh (world-class sailor and former member of the 1995 Americas' Cup All Women's Team) and Paul Stames (then-Director of the Executive MBA program at Daniels) in Beaver Creek, Colorado. Maybe it was the thin air, but they determined that night to do something radically new in business education: teach team building and business ethics aboard off-shore racing sailboats. The metaphor was perfect: *we're all in the same boat!* The strange juxtaposition of a landlocked Colorado school teaching business on the ocean made perfect sense—at least it did after a couple of glasses of wine at 8,000 feet above sea level!

In the years since that crazy winter epiphany, six to seven hundred Daniels Executive MBA students, and over 500 regular MBA students, have taken the "Leadership, Teams, & Values," sailing course. The feedback and evaluations are stunning: "My life will never be the same." "I can't believe how much I learned about myself and what I really want to do with this degree." "This was the most amazing experience I've ever had." Reading the Executive Logs that students keep during the course is akin to hearing testimonials at a religious revival; reading the Integrative Reports they turn in for their grades is both an academic and literary pleasure.

Many of the skippers of the boats used in the course are Sarah Cavanagh's former team members from the 1995 Americas' Cup Challenge. They are aided by faculty members from all departments of the College. The course has been taught in Montenegro, Greece, San Diego, Miami, Vancouver, and Tortola. Under the pressure of learning something radically new (sailing), and with their natural inclination to compete, business students are forced to reflect on how they behave and perform under truly intense conditions. Their learning and change curves could not be steeper.

The Oxford Readings

In 2007, the Daniels College did a truly unusual thing: it fixed something that was not broken. Despite the success that had been achieved by its ethics curriculum over the years, the College nonetheless introduced a variety of substantial curriculum and pedagogical revisions. A subtle, but powerful, one is called *The Oxford Readings*. Drawing on the ancient teaching traditions of Oxford University, a portal course (The Essence of Enterprise) was developed which requires entering MBA students to read, discuss, and synthesize a large number of both classic and contemporary articles about business organizations, professionalism, and sustainability, in order to gain familiarity with the seminal writings in the field of business.

Then, in the five person learning teams formed during the 10th Mountain Experience, students meet with faculty members to discuss the readings. The intimacy of these "tutorials" is powerful. MBA students not only get to know each other as scholars, but the faculty become directly and personally engaged in the careers and lives of our students. We thus have replaced the lonely, traditional approach of reading, lecturing, and testing with a rich environment of shared learning and deliberation, a true learning community in which intellectual seeds sown will be harvested in the succeeding two years of the MBA program.

The Community Capital Project and Service Learning

As Bruce Hutton notes in his Prologue, in the mid-1990s, the Daniels College was a leader among business schools in terms of integrating content across various disciplines, and using team teaching as the primary mode of delivering this integrated curriculum. Experimentation flourished during this period. For example, a course that integrated ethics, public policy, and law included a service-learning requirement. Students were required to engage in one day of community service during the quarter, write a reflective paper on the experience, and share their reflections on the last day of class. Student reactions to the experience were strong and consistently positive in terms of increasing their sensitivity to community issues, and to the personal satisfaction of contributing to community needs.

In 2007, with the advent of a new MBA curriculum and its focus on team building, ethics, and sustainability, the scope of the service project was increased substantially. Now, teams remain together for the first two quarters of the program, during which time they identify a need, or "gap," in the community, engage major stakeholders involved in the issue, and develop a set of possible options to address the gap in community capital. A major highlight of this initiative has been the Community Capital Fair at the end of the first quarter, an event held at the College to which community members are invited. To wander through the maze of 50-to-60 teams has been a moving experience for faculty and students alike. All teams make presentations about their projects during a two-hour session in which they share their ideas using computers and poster boards. These projects have included a wide range of ideas for improving the Denver community: increasing financial literacy among low-income groups, placing quality day care programs in vacant public schools, improving access to health care for the uninsured, fostering intergenerational learning and understanding, and reducing teen drug use.

During the second quarter, student teams probe further into these issues and explore possible solutions. Rather than taking an abstract, removed perspective on the problem, the teams interview key community stakeholders. This makes them listen, engage, and understand the people behind the issues. From these engagements, the student teams summarize their interactions and outline a set of possible solutions. Community capital projects allow students to develop their team building skills, as well as skills related to planning and organizing team efforts around a common purpose. Moreover, students learn to appreciate the complexity of community issues, the systems in which the problems are located, and the divergent needs of different groups.

Voices of Experience/Grand Rounds
Beginning in 2004, the Daniels College has hosted a series of lectures by successful business leaders, including such notables as Jack Welch, Norman Augustine, Jamie Dimon and Charles Knight. Their message: ethics is the foundation of successful business leadership. While the program was initially intended for Daniels MBA students, today the majority of attendees come from the business community, as does financial support for the program. After paying for the events, sponsors have also contributed over $10,000 to student scholarships, and provided monetary support for the sailing program described above.

Race & Case
In 2003, the Daniels Graduate Business Student Association created the *Race & Case* competition to bring national recognition to the College's distinctive ethics curriculum by capitalizing on its winter setting in the Colorado's Rocky Mountains. Teams of MBA students come to Denver to participate in a business ethics case competition, which is followed by a downhill ski race in Vail, Colorado.

Over the last seven years, such leading business schools as Harvard, Yale, George Washington University, and Boston College, have sent teams to Colorado to compete to take home the "Daniels Cup." Future plans include opening the competition to international teams. More than 725 Daniels students have taken part in this experience as competitors, organizers, and volunteers.

International Internships
The capstone course in the new Daniels MBA program is Enterprise Solutions, a consultancy based experiential course in which students work on real

projects/challenges faced by "client" organizations. Approximately 40 percent of the students travel to a location outside the United States, which allows them not only to apply their technical and strategic skills, but also to increase their intercultural competence and knowledge about sustainable development. For example, students have partnered with Newmont Mining to work on environmental issues in Ghana and Peru, the Peace House Foundation to work on secondary Education and Entrepreneurship in Tanzania, and The Thousand Hills Venture Fund to evaluate capital projects in Rwanda. The long run intention is to have all full-time Daniels MBA students participate in an international project.

Conclusion

When *The Wall Street Journal* ranked Daniels among the top three or four best business colleges in the world for "the ethical sensitivity of its graduates," the honor did not come simply as the result of the School's curriculum, programs, or pedagogy. It is a reflection on who our students are, and what their lives are about.

A business enterprise does not become ethical just because its Board of Directors is composed of good and upstanding people, or because its CEO is personally committed to CSR, or because its mission statement is posted on bulletin boards throughout all its offices, or because it offers ethics seminars to its employees, or because its legal department makes sure its employees comply with Sarbanes-Oxley requirements.

All these are important, but we should recall the Enron Corporation had one of most distinguished Boards of Directors imaginable, one of the finest mission statements on corporate social responsibility ever written, extensive training programs for employees on responsible business practices, and ethics officers throughout the company. Yet in practice, none of that added up to an ethical culture at Enron.

In fact, business ethics is about *meaning*: it is about creating a culture that gives to its participants a sense that they are valued, that their lives make a difference, and that their work for the enterprise amounts to more than just making a living or turning a profit. Human beings need to feel valued in order to create value, and that is why increasing numbers of business executives are beginning to understand that building an ethical culture is not optional. Rather, it is the foundational underpinning of corporate profitability and sustainability.

That is why at the Daniels College of Business—unlike so many business schools around the world—ethics is *not* an elective. We believe ethical development occurs through human engagement; that is, how we exercise our values with respect to one another. The Daniels College attempts to be the practice field, the place of cognitive disequilibrium where serious students can achieve serious ethical development. As our colleague James O'Toole points out in his book *Leading Change: the Case for Values-Based Leadership,* "The values-based leader begins by changing himself." We at Daniels seek to create a safe and challenging place where business students can take fundamental steps in their ethical development. Steps that will prepare them to create organizational cultures that are ethical, effective, and sustainable.

---

[1] Preface to Tom L. Beauchamp & Norman E. Bowie, *Ethical Theory and Business,* 2000

Contributors

Doug Allen is Associate Professor and Director of Global Business Programs at the Daniels College of Business. He is co-author of *Formula 2+2: The Simple Solution for Successful Coaching*.

Sam Cassidy is a former Lieutenant Governor of Colorado and CEO of the State Chamber of Commerce. He has taught at the Daniels College of Business as a Clinical Professor for 10 years.

Dave Cox is Assistant Dean, Full-time MBA Programs for the Daniels College of Business, and a Senior Lecturer at the College's Reiman School of Finance. He teaches corporate finance, international finance, and sustainable development.

Cynthia Fukami is Professor of Management at the Daniels College. She teaches organizational behavior and human resource management, and is co-editor of *Handbook of Managerial Learning, Education and Development*.

John Holcomb is Professor of Business Ethics and Legal Studies at the Daniels College. He is former Executive Director of the Foundation for Public Affairs, and has written on corporate political strategy, crisis management, global corporate governance, and campaign finance.

Bruce Hutton is Dean Emeritus and Piccinati Professor in Teaching Innovation at the Daniels College. A Professor of Marketing, his current teaching, research and writing focus on interdisciplinary themes of sustainable development and corporate social responsibility.

Ruth Jebe is Senior Lecturer in the Department of Business Ethics and Legal Studies at the Daniels College of Business, where she has taught for the past five years.

Stephen Martin is Executive Director of the Institute for Enterprise Ethics and Clinical Professor at the Daniels College. He has served as a federal prosecutor, and corporate in-house counsel responsible for compliance and government investigations.

Don Mayer is Professor in Residence at the Daniels College of Business. He is co-author of *International Business Law: Cases and Materials* (2009), and has authored numerous articles in business ethics journals and law reviews.

Kevin O'Brien is Associate Professor, Louis B. Beaumont Professor, and Chair of the Daniels College Business Ethics and Legal Studies Department. He actively blogs for *Race to the Bottom*.

Paul Olk is Professor of Management at the Daniels College of Business and co-author of *Entrepreneurial Alliances* (2009).

James O'Toole is the Daniels Distinguished Professor of Business Ethics. He is author or editor of some seventeen books, including *The Executive's Compass, Leading Change*, and *Transparency*.

Stephen Pepper is Professor of Law at the University of Denver's Sturm College of Law. He has published numerous articles on ethics, the practice of law, and the nature of professional obligation. Students at Sturm College have selected him as Professor of the Year four times.

Michael Pfarrer is Assistant Professor in the Department of Management at the University of Georgia, and formerly Assistant Professor at the Daniels College of Business.

Buie Seawell came to Daniels College of Business to teach law and ethics after a career in law, government, and politics in Colorado. He has degrees in History, Theology, and Law.

Elizabeth Stapp is Adjunct Professor at the Daniels College. Formerly a federal district court judicial law clerk, she serves as the University of Denver's Mock Trial Team coach.

Bob Vanourek teaches leadership as an Adjunct at the Daniels College of Business. He has been the CEO of Sensormatic Electronics, Recognition Equipment, and several venture-backed companies, and is Chairman Emeritus of the Vail Leadership Institute.

Dennis Wittmer is Professor and Chair of the Management Department in the Daniels College. His publications deal with research on ethical decision making in management contexts.

Acknowledgments

The editors wish to acknowledge the many individuals in the Daniels College of Business who assisted in the preparation of this volume. In particular, Kate Boyd, Marie Pierson, and Julie Lucas all made heroic and essential contributions to the editing process. The cover art and design of the book are the accomplished work of Brandon Russell. The College's Institute for Enterprise Ethics provided financial and administrative support. We speak for all the members of the Daniels faculty when we thank Carl M. Williams for his generous start-up grant to the Institute.

This volume is the brainchild of the inspirational leader of our faculty, Bruce Hutton who, while serving as Interim Dean of the Daniels College, envisioned a practitioner-oriented book to celebrate the College's Centennial and to demonstrate its deep commitment to ethics and values-based leadership. To all our fellow faculty members who labored over multiple drafts in order to capture this unique Daniels approach to business in these chapters, we offer our greatest appreciation. We also wish to recognize the invaluable help of John Holcomb and Buie Seawell who helped create the initial concept for and outline of the book, and to acknowledge the responsive and professional contributions of everyone at Routledge through the good offices of John Szilagyi, Business and Management Publisher at Routledge.

Finally, we acknowledge the important on-going role all the members of the alumni, student body, faculty, and administration of the Daniels College play in manifesting and nurturing the school's commitment to "Good Business."

Index

24.95